First World War

and Army of Occupation

War Diary

France, Belgium and Germany

29 DIVISION
86 Infantry Brigade
Royal Fusiliers (City of London Regiment)
2nd Battalion
25 February 1916 - 1 April 1919

WO95/2301/3

The Naval & Military Press Ltd
www.nmarchive.com
Published in association with The National Archives

Published by

The Naval & Military Press Ltd

Unit 10 Ridgewood Industrial Park,

Uckfield, East Sussex,

TN22 5QE England

Tel: +44 (0) 1825 749494

www.naval-military-press.com

www.nmarchive.com

This diary has been reprinted in facsimile from the original. Any imperfections are inevitably reproduced and the quality may fall short of modern type and cartographic standards.

Contents

Document type	Place/Title	Date From	Date To
Heading	WO95/2301-3 2 Battalion Royal Fusiliers		
Heading	29th Division 86th Infy Bde 2nd Bn Roy. Fusiliers Feb 1916-Mar 1919		
Heading	29th Division. 86th Infantry Brigade. Arrived Marseilles From Egypt 21st March 1916. 2nd Battalion The Royal Fusiliers 25th February to /30th April 1916. Dec 18		
War Diary	Elkutre	25/02/1916	15/03/1916
Miscellaneous	From The Officer Commanding, 2nd Battalion Royal Fusiliers.	18/05/1916	18/05/1916
War Diary	S Salaumia	16/03/1916	05/04/1916
War Diary	Englebelmer	06/04/1916	11/04/1916
War Diary	Mailly Maillet	12/04/1916	30/04/1916
Heading	29th Division 86th Infantry Brigade. 2nd Battalion Royal Fusiliers May 1916		
War Diary	Louvencourt	01/05/1916	08/05/1916
War Diary	Mailly	09/05/1916	27/05/1916
War Diary	Louvencourt	28/05/1916	31/05/1916
Heading	29th Division. 86th Infantry Brigade 2nd Battalion Royal Fusiliers June 1916		
Miscellaneous	From The Officer Commanding, 2nd Battalion Royal Fusiliers.	20/07/1916	20/07/1916
War Diary	Louvencourt	01/06/1916	07/06/1916
War Diary	Mailly	08/06/1916	30/06/1916
War Diary	Trenches	01/07/1916	01/07/1916
Miscellaneous	To 2nd Royal Fusiliers. 1st Lancashire Fus.	28/06/1916	28/06/1916
Heading	29th Division. 86th Infantry Brigade. 2nd Battalion Royal Fusiliers July 1916		
Heading	War Diary of 2nd Bn. Royal Fusiliers for July 1916		
War Diary	Beaumont Hamel	01/07/1916	04/07/1916
War Diary	Mailly.	05/07/1916	05/07/1916
War Diary	Acheux.	06/07/1916	11/07/1916
War Diary	Mcsnil	12/07/1916	23/07/1916
War Diary	Bus	24/07/1916	25/07/1916
War Diary	Beauval	26/07/1916	27/07/1916
War Diary	Wormhoudt	28/07/1916	31/07/1916
Heading	29th Division. 86th Infantry Brigade 2nd Battalion Royal Fusiliers August 1916		
Heading	War Diary of 2nd Bn. Royal Fusiliers From 1st Aug. to 31st Aug 1916 Volume 6		
War Diary	Poperinghe "B" Camp.	01/08/1916	01/08/1916
War Diary	(Brandhoek)	02/08/1916	07/08/1916
War Diary	Ypres	08/08/1916	08/08/1916
War Diary	Trenches	09/08/1916	18/08/1916
War Diary	Ypres	19/08/1916	28/08/1916
War Diary	B Camp	29/08/1916	31/08/1916
Heading	29th Division. 86th Infantry Brigade. 2nd Battalion Royal Fusiliers September 1916 Report on Raid 20th September 1916 attached.		
Heading	War Diary of 2nd Battalion Royal Fusiliers From Sept. 1st 1916 To September 30th, 1916 (Volume 7)		

War Diary	B Camp (Brandhoek)	01/09/1916	08/09/1916
War Diary	Ypres (Prison)	09/09/1916	12/09/1916
War Diary	Trenches Potijze Wood	13/09/1916	14/09/1916
War Diary	Ypres (Prison)	15/09/1916	18/09/1916
War Diary	Trenches	19/09/1916	23/09/1916
War Diary	Ypres	24/09/1916	28/09/1916
War Diary	B Camp	29/09/1916	30/09/1916
War Diary	B Camp (Brandhoek)	01/09/1916	08/09/1916
War Diary	Ypres (Prison)	09/09/1916	12/09/1916
War Diary	Trenches (Potitze Wood)	13/09/1916	14/09/1916
War Diary	Ypres (Prison)	15/09/1916	18/09/1916
War Diary	Trenches	19/09/1916	23/09/1916
War Diary	Ypres	24/09/1916	28/09/1916
War Diary	B Camp	29/09/1916	30/09/1916
Miscellaneous	Ref. Sheet 28 Trench Map House.	17/09/1916	17/09/1916
Miscellaneous	Plan of Raid to be carried out by 2nd Royal Fusiliers on morning of September 20th, 1916.	20/09/1916	20/09/1916
Miscellaneous	My dear Hurle	20/09/1916	20/09/1916
Miscellaneous	General Staff, 29th Division.	20/09/1916	20/09/1916
Miscellaneous	Report on Raid carried out by 2nd Royal Fusiliers.	20/09/1916	20/09/1916
Heading	29th Division. 86th Infantry Brigade. 2nd Battalion Royal Fusiliers October 1916		
Heading	War Diary of 2nd. Bn. Royal Fusiliers. Volume 18		
War Diary	B Camp (Ypres)	01/10/1916	04/10/1916
War Diary	Wormhoudt	05/10/1916	07/10/1916
War Diary	Daours.	08/10/1916	10/10/1916
War Diary	Dernancourt	11/10/1916	13/10/1916
War Diary	Mametz Wood	14/10/1916	19/10/1916
War Diary	Delville Wood	19/10/1916	23/10/1916
War Diary	Trenches	24/10/1916	25/10/1916
War Diary	Switch Trench & Trones Wood	26/10/1916	26/10/1916
War Diary	Bernafay Wood	27/10/1916	30/10/1916
War Diary	Mametz	31/10/1916	31/10/1916
War Diary	B Camp.	01/10/1916	04/10/1916
War Diary	Wormhoudt.	05/10/1916	07/10/1916
War Diary	Daours	08/10/1916	10/10/1916
War Diary	Dernancourt	11/10/1916	13/10/1916
War Diary	Mametz Wood	14/10/1916	19/10/1916
War Diary	Delville Wood	20/10/1916	23/10/1916
War Diary	Trenches	24/10/1916	25/10/1916
War Diary	Switch Trench & Trones Wood	26/10/1916	26/10/1916
War Diary	Bernafay Wood	27/10/1916	31/10/1916
Heading	29th Division. 86th Infantry Brigade. 2nd Battalion Royal Fusiliers. November 1916		
Heading	War Diary of 2nd Battln. Royal. Fusiliers Vol. XX		
Miscellaneous	To Staff Captain 86th Brigade.	02/12/1916	02/12/1916
War Diary	Corbie	01/11/1916	16/11/1916
War Diary	Meaulte	17/11/1916	18/11/1916
War Diary	Briqueterie	19/11/1916	20/11/1916
War Diary	Briqueterie Camp (S).	21/11/1916	22/11/1916
War Diary	Briqueterie Camp (N)	23/11/1916	24/11/1916
War Diary	Les Boeufs (Trenches)	24/11/1916	27/11/1916
War Diary	Briqueterie (Tented)	28/11/1916	28/11/1916
War Diary	Mansel Camp.	29/11/1916	29/11/1916
War Diary	Mansel Camp. XII	30/11/1916	30/11/1916
War Diary	Corbie	01/11/1916	16/11/1916

War Diary	Meaulte	17/11/1916	18/11/1916
War Diary	Briqueterie	19/11/1916	20/11/1916
War Diary	Briqueterie (Camp) (S)	21/11/1916	22/11/1916
War Diary	Briqueterie (Camp) N	23/11/1916	24/11/1916
War Diary	Le Boeufs (Trenches)	25/11/1916	27/11/1916
War Diary	Briqueterie (Tented)	28/11/1916	28/11/1916
War Diary	Mansel Camp XII	29/11/1916	29/11/1916
Heading	29th Division. 86th Infantry Brigade. 2nd Battalion Royal Fusiliers December 1916		
Heading	War Diary of 2nd Battln. Royal Fusiliers From 1st Dec. 1916 To 31st Dec 1916 Vol 21		
Heading	Confidential		
War Diary	Briqueterie Camp.	01/12/1916	02/12/1916
War Diary	Trenches	03/12/1916	06/12/1916
War Diary	Briqueterie Camp.	07/12/1916	07/12/1916
War Diary	Carnoy West No 18.	08/12/1916	10/12/1916
War Diary	Meaulte	11/12/1916	12/12/1916
War Diary	Ailly-Sur-Somme.	13/12/1916	17/12/1916
War Diary	Picquigny	18/12/1916	31/12/1916
War Diary	Briqueterie Camp	01/12/1916	02/12/1916
War Diary	Trenches	03/12/1916	06/12/1916
War Diary	Briqueterie Camp	07/12/1916	09/12/1916
War Diary	Meaulte	10/12/1916	12/12/1916
War Diary	Ailly-Sur Somme	13/12/1916	17/12/1916
War Diary	Picquigny	18/12/1916	31/12/1916
Heading	War Diary 2nd Bn Royal Fusiliers No 23		
War Diary	Picquigny	01/01/1917	08/01/1917
War Diary	Lequesnoy	09/01/1917	09/01/1917
War Diary	Corbie	10/01/1917	10/01/1917
War Diary	Mericourt L'Abbe'	11/01/1917	14/01/1917
War Diary	Carnoy 6 Camp	15/01/1917	16/01/1917
War Diary	Trenches	17/01/1917	18/01/1917
War Diary	Carnoy Camp (No 6)	19/01/1917	21/01/1917
War Diary	Guillemont. R.	22/01/1917	22/01/1917
War Diary	Trenches	23/01/1917	24/01/1917
War Diary	Carnoy Camp (No 6)	25/01/1917	27/01/1917
War Diary	Guillemont R.	28/01/1917	28/01/1917
War Diary	Trenches	29/01/1917	30/01/1917
War Diary	Carnoy Camp (No 6)	31/01/1917	31/01/1917
Heading	War Diary 2nd Bn Royal Fusiliers No. 24. Feby 1917 Vol 12		
War Diary	Carnoy	01/02/1917	03/02/1917
War Diary	Guillemont.	04/02/1917	06/02/1917
War Diary	Carnoy	07/02/1917	08/02/1917
War Diary	Le Neuville	09/02/1917	18/02/1917
War Diary	Meaulte	19/02/1917	19/02/1917
War Diary	Combles	20/02/1917	21/02/1917
War Diary	Sailly Sector	22/02/1917	23/02/1917
War Diary	Fregicourt.	24/02/1917	24/02/1917
War Diary	Bronfay	25/02/1917	26/02/1917
War Diary	Combles.	27/02/1917	27/02/1917
War Diary	Sailly Sector Front Line	28/02/1917	28/02/1917
Miscellaneous	2nd Bn. Royal Fusiliers.	28/02/1917	28/02/1917
Heading	War Diary of 2nd Bn Royal Fusiliers. Vol. 25 March		
War Diary	Front Line Sailly Sector	01/03/1917	01/03/1917
War Diary	Fregicourt	02/03/1917	02/03/1917

War Diary	Bronfay	03/03/1917	03/03/1917
War Diary	Ville	04/03/1917	19/03/1917
War Diary	Airaines	20/03/1917	30/03/1917
War Diary	Berteaucourt.	31/03/1917	31/03/1917
Heading	War Diary April 1917 2nd Bn The Royal Fusiliers Vol 26		
War Diary	Berteaucourt	01/04/1917	01/04/1917
War Diary	Gezaincourt	02/04/1917	02/04/1917
War Diary	Pommera	03/04/1917	05/04/1917
War Diary	Sus St Leger.	06/04/1917	08/04/1917
War Diary	Humbercamp.	09/04/1917	11/04/1917
War Diary	Smencourt	12/04/1917	12/04/1917
War Diary	Arras.	13/04/1917	13/04/1917
War Diary	Trenches	14/04/1917	14/04/1917
War Diary	Chapel Hill	15/04/1917	18/04/1917
War Diary	Monchy	19/04/1917	21/04/1917
War Diary	Arras	22/04/1917	25/04/1917
War Diary	Bernville	26/04/1917	26/04/1917
War Diary	Wanquetin	27/04/1917	27/04/1917
War Diary	Souastre	28/04/1917	30/04/1917
Miscellaneous	Operations-24th April 1917 Left Company ("W' Coy)	24/04/1917	24/04/1917
Map	Pelves		
Map	Map No. 1 Scale Top Section 29th Div. 15.4.17		
Heading	War Diary. of 2nd Battalion Royal Fusiliers Volume 27 May 1917		
War Diary	Souastre	01/05/1917	01/05/1917
War Diary	Gouy	02/05/1917	02/05/1917
War Diary	Arras.	03/05/1917	11/05/1917
War Diary	Bernville	12/05/1917	20/05/1917
War Diary	Monchy Defences	21/05/1917	29/05/1917
War Diary	Brown Line	30/05/1917	30/05/1917
War Diary	Arras.	31/05/1917	31/05/1917
Heading	War Diary 2nd Bn The Royal Fusiliers June 1917 No 28 Vol 16		
War Diary	Arras	01/06/1917	02/06/1917
War Diary	Bernville	03/06/1917	03/06/1917
War Diary	Lanches	04/06/1917	27/06/1917
War Diary	Proven Area	28/06/1917	30/06/1917
Heading	War Diary 2nd Battalion Royal Fusiliers July 1917 Vol 29		
War Diary	Proven Area	01/07/1917	05/07/1917
War Diary	Woesten Area.	06/07/1917	12/07/1917
War Diary	Zwaanhof Sector Trenches	13/07/1917	14/07/1917
War Diary	Zwaanhof Sector	15/07/1917	17/07/1917
War Diary	L. 2. Defences	18/07/1917	19/07/1917
War Diary	Crombeke Area	20/07/1917	23/07/1917
War Diary	Proven Area	24/07/1917	31/07/1917
Heading	War Diary 2nd Bn The. Royal. Fusiliers Vol 30 August 1917		
War Diary	Proven Area	01/08/1917	05/08/1917
War Diary	Forward Area	06/08/1917	06/08/1917
War Diary	Boesinghe Sector	06/08/1917	08/08/1917
War Diary	Boesinghe Sector.	07/08/1917	09/08/1917
War Diary	Woesten Area	10/08/1917	14/08/1917
War Diary	Boesinghe Area	15/08/1917	15/08/1917
War Diary	Boesinghe Sector	15/08/1917	21/08/1917

War Diary	Woesten Area	22/08/1917	29/08/1917
War Diary	Proven Area.	30/08/1917	31/08/1917
Heading	War Diary 2nd Bn The. Royal. Fusiliers Vol. 31 Sept 1917		
War Diary	Proven Area. (Privett Camp)	01/09/1917	07/09/1917
War Diary	Boesinghe Area. (Oxford Camp.)	08/09/1917	10/09/1917
War Diary	Proven Area. (Privett Camp)	11/09/1917	15/09/1917
War Diary	Herzeele	16/09/1917	19/09/1917
War Diary	Proven Area (Privett Camp)	20/09/1917	20/09/1917
War Diary	Elverdinghe Area (Abingley Camp)	21/09/1917	30/09/1917
Heading	War Diary 2nd Bn Royal Fusiliers Vol 32 Oct 1917		
War Diary	Elverdinghe Area (Abingley Camp)	01/10/1917	16/10/1917
War Diary	At Blairville Camp.	17/10/1917	23/10/1917
War Diary	Blairville No 2 Camp	24/10/1917	31/10/1917
Miscellaneous	Report On Action of 9th Oct. 1917. 2nd Battalion, Royal Fusiliers. App A	09/10/1917	09/10/1917
Heading	War Diary November 2nd Bn Royal Fusiliers Vol 21		
War Diary	Blairville Camp	01/11/1917	17/11/1917
War Diary	Haut-Allaines	18/11/1917	18/11/1917
War Diary	Equancourt	19/11/1917	19/11/1917
War Diary	The Attack	20/11/1917	20/11/1917
War Diary	Noyelles	21/11/1917	21/11/1917
War Diary	Marcoing	22/11/1917	22/11/1917
War Diary	Masnieres	23/11/1917	30/11/1917
Heading	War Diary December 1917 2nd Bn Royal Fusiliers 2 RF Vol 22		
War Diary	Les Rues Vertes	01/12/1917	01/12/1917
War Diary	Hindenburgh Support	02/12/1917	02/12/1917
War Diary	Ribecourt	03/12/1917	03/12/1917
War Diary	Havrincourt Wood	04/12/1917	04/12/1917
War Diary	Fins	05/12/1917	05/12/1917
War Diary	Petit Houvin	06/12/1917	06/12/1917
War Diary	Lignereuil	07/12/1917	16/12/1917
War Diary	Canchy	17/12/1917	17/12/1917
War Diary	Wambercourt	18/12/1917	18/12/1917
War Diary	Ergny	19/12/1917	31/12/1917
Heading	War Diary Vol 35 2nd Bn The Royal Fusiliers January 1918		
War Diary	Ergny	01/01/1918	03/01/1918
War Diary	Quelmes	04/01/1918	16/01/1918
War Diary	B Camp (Brandhoek)	17/01/1918	17/01/1918
War Diary	St Jean.	18/01/1918	18/01/1918
War Diary	Front Line	19/01/1918	22/01/1918
War Diary	Bellevue	23/01/1918	24/01/1918
War Diary	California Camp	25/01/1918	26/01/1918
War Diary	B Camp (Brandhoek)	27/01/1918	03/02/1918
War Diary	California Camp.	04/02/1918	11/02/1918
War Diary	Haslar Camp	12/02/1918	19/02/1918
War Diary	Eecke	19/02/1918	28/02/1918
Heading	War Diary. 2nd Battn Royal Fusiliers. March 1918 Vol 37		
War Diary	Eccke	01/03/1918	07/03/1918
War Diary	Brandhoek	08/03/1918	11/03/1918
War Diary	Hasler Camp	12/03/1918	13/03/1918
War Diary	Passchenoix	14/03/1918	15/03/1918
War Diary	Passchendaele Sector	16/03/1918	20/03/1918

War Diary	California Camp	21/03/1918	24/03/1918
War Diary	Passchendaele Area	25/03/1918	30/03/1918
War Diary	Brandhoek	31/03/1918	31/03/1918
Operation(al) Order(s)	2nd Bn Royal Fusiliers Operation Order No 30	29/03/1918	29/03/1918
Operation(al) Order(s)	2nd Bn. Royal Fusiliers Operation Order No. 31.		
Operation(al) Order(s)	86th. Infantry Brigade Operation Order No. 216	01/04/1918	01/04/1918
Miscellaneous	WXYZ		
Operation(al) Order(s)	86th. Infantry Brigade Administrative Order No. 25. (Issued in connection with Brigade Order No. 216)	02/04/1918	02/04/1918
Miscellaneous	2nd Bn. Royal Fusiliers.	02/04/1918	02/04/1918
Heading	86th Brigade. 29th Division. 2nd Battalion Royal Fusiliers April 1918.		
Heading	War Diary April 1918 Vol. 38. 2 R F Vol 26		
Miscellaneous	Cover for Documents. Nature of Enclosures.		
War Diary	Brandhoek	01/04/1918	03/04/1918
War Diary	Hamburg Reserve Area.	04/04/1918	07/04/1918
War Diary	Brandhoek	08/04/1918	09/04/1918
War Diary	Merville Area	10/04/1918	10/04/1918
War Diary	Doulieu & Pradelles Area.	11/04/1918	13/04/1918
War Diary	St Sylvestre Cappel.	14/04/1918	18/04/1918
War Diary	Hondeghem	19/04/1918	30/04/1918
Heading	Vol 39. 2nd Battn Royal Fusiliers War Diary May 1918 Vol 27		
War Diary	Bois Daval	01/05/1918	01/05/1918
War Diary	Papote	02/05/1918	09/05/1918
War Diary	Bois Daval	10/05/1918	14/05/1918
War Diary	Farm Beaulieu	14/05/1918	15/05/1918
War Diary	Bois Daval.	15/05/1918	15/05/1918
War Diary	Papote.	16/05/1918	18/05/1918
War Diary	Papote And Grand Marquette	19/05/1918	19/05/1918
War Diary	Grand Marquette	20/05/1918	26/05/1918
War Diary	Grand Marquette And Swartenbrouch	27/05/1918	27/05/1918
War Diary	Swartenbrouch	28/05/1918	31/05/1918
Operation(al) Order(s)	2nd Bn Royal Fusiliers Operation Order No 37	09/05/1918	09/05/1918
Operation(al) Order(s)	2nd Bn Royal Fusiliers Operation Order No 39	18/05/1918	18/05/1918
Miscellaneous	C Form. Messages And Signals.	18/05/1918	18/05/1918
Operation(al) Order(s)	7th Bn Royal Dublin Fusiliers Operation Order No 28	19/05/1918	19/05/1918
Miscellaneous			
Operation(al) Order(s)	2nd Royal Fusiliers Operation Order No 40	26/05/1918	26/05/1918
Miscellaneous	C Form. Messages And Signals.		
Miscellaneous			
Miscellaneous	C Form. Messages And Signals.		
Miscellaneous	Warning Order		
Miscellaneous	Warning Order.	23/05/1918	23/05/1918
Miscellaneous	86th Inf. Brigade No. G. 2/91	24/05/1918	24/05/1918
Map	La Motte		
Map	Identification Trace for use with Artillery Maps.		
Miscellaneous	O.C. 2nd Royal Fusiliers	30/05/1918	30/05/1918
Heading	War Diary Vol 40 2nd Bn Royal Fusiliers June 1918		
War Diary	Swartenbrouch	01/06/1918	13/06/1918
War Diary	Morbecque	13/06/1918	16/06/1918
War Diary	Bois D'Aval	17/06/1918	18/06/1918
War Diary	Morbecque	19/06/1918	24/06/1918
War Diary	E.7.b.7.7	25/06/1918	27/06/1918
War Diary	Sediment House	27/06/1918	29/06/1918
War Diary	Blaringhem	29/06/1918	29/06/1918

War Diary	La Sablonre	30/06/1918	30/06/1918
Miscellaneous	Bn Will Mons Hold The Line Of frm and E 23a 30.48 to S.		
Operation(al) Order(s)	86th Infantry Brigade Order No. 227.	01/06/1918	01/06/1918
Miscellaneous			
Miscellaneous	Amendment No. 1. to 86th Infantry Brigade Order No. 227.	01/06/1918	01/06/1918
Miscellaneous	Time Table		
Operation(al) Order(s)	Appendix No. 1 to 86th Infantry Brigade Order No. 227.		
Miscellaneous	Operation Orders by Major KCB Tower M.C Comdg 2nd Bn Royal Fusiliers	23/06/1918	23/06/1918
Operation(al) Order(s)	Time Table As Grain In Operation Order No. 42	02/06/1918	02/06/1918
Operation(al) Order(s)	2nd Royal Fusiliers Operation Order No. 44	06/06/1918	06/06/1918
Miscellaneous	C Form. Messages And Signals.		
Miscellaneous			
Miscellaneous	C Form. Messages And Signals.		
Operation(al) Order(s)	2nd Bn Royal Fusiliers Operation Order No 45	11/06/1918	11/06/1918
Miscellaneous	Relief Orders. by Major J.W. O'Reilly	11/06/1918	11/06/1918
Miscellaneous	BM R.4.	12/06/1918	12/06/1918
Miscellaneous	BM R 5.	12/06/1918	12/06/1918
Operation(al) Order(s)	86th Infantry Brigade Order No. 233.	11/06/1918	11/06/1918
Miscellaneous	Relief Table Issued with 86th Inf. Brigade Order No. 233.	11/06/1918	11/06/1918
Operation(al) Order(s)	2nd Bn. Royal Fusiliers. Operation Orders No 46	15/06/1918	15/06/1918
Operation(al) Order(s)	2nd Bn. Royal Fusiliers. Operation Order No 47	17/06/1918	17/06/1918
Operation(al) Order(s)	86th Infantry Brigade Order No. 234.	17/06/1918	17/06/1918
Operation(al) Order(s)	2nd. Bn. Royal Fusiliers Operation Order No 48	25/06/1918	25/06/1918
Miscellaneous	A Form. Messages And Signals.	25/06/1918	25/06/1918
Miscellaneous			
Miscellaneous	C Form. Messages And Signals.		
Operation(al) Order(s)	93rd. Infantry Brigade Order No. 231.	25/06/1918	25/06/1918
Operation(al) Order(s)	Operation Order No 49 2nd Bn Royal Fusiliers	26/06/1918	26/06/1918
Operation(al) Order(s)	2nd Bn Royal Fusiliers Operation Order No 51	29/06/1918	29/06/1918
Miscellaneous	Route to Transport Lieut 2nd Bn Royal Fusiliers		
Operation(al) Order(s)	13th York & Lancaster Rgt Operation Order No 68	27/06/1918	27/06/1918
Operation(al) Order(s)	2nd Bn Royal Fusiliers Operation Order No 52	30/06/1918	30/06/1918
Heading	War Diary of 2nd Bn Royal Fusiliers July 1918 Vol 41		
War Diary	La Sablonniere.	01/07/1918	15/07/1918
War Diary	La Sablonniere.	14/07/1918	21/07/1918
War Diary	Noordpeene.	22/07/1918	31/07/1918
Heading	2nd Battalion. Royal Fusiliers. War Diary-August 1918 Volume 42		
War Diary		01/08/1918	31/08/1918
Miscellaneous	Report on Minor Operations carried out on the 18th August 1918.	18/08/1918	18/08/1918
Heading	2nd Battalion. Royal Fusiliers. War Diary For September 1918 Vol 31		
Heading	War Diary Vol 43		
War Diary	Noote Boom.	01/09/1918	02/09/1918
War Diary	Outersteene	02/09/1918	02/09/1918
War Diary	La Creche.	03/09/1918	05/09/1918
War Diary	Outersteene.	06/09/1918	10/09/1918
War Diary	Hazebrouck	11/09/1918	18/09/1918
War Diary	Dirty Bucket Camp.	19/09/1918	23/09/1918
War Diary	Poperinghe.	24/09/1918	26/09/1918

War Diary	Ypres.	27/09/1918	30/09/1918
War Diary	Gheluwe.	01/10/1918	03/10/1918
War Diary	Ypres	04/10/1918	05/10/1918
War Diary	North of Dadizeele.	06/10/1918	07/10/1918
War Diary	Ledeghem.	08/10/1918	08/10/1918
War Diary	Westhoek.	09/10/1918	10/10/1918
War Diary	Ypres.	11/10/1918	12/10/1918
War Diary	Moorslede.	13/10/1918	13/10/1918
War Diary	Ledeghem	14/10/1918	14/10/1918
War Diary	Barraken.	15/10/1918	16/10/1918
War Diary	Heule.	17/10/1918	20/10/1918
War Diary	Krote.	21/10/1918	21/10/1918
War Diary	Kappaart.	22/10/1918	23/10/1918
War Diary	Cuerne.	24/10/1918	25/10/1918
War Diary	Roncq.	26/10/1918	26/10/1918
War Diary	Bondues.	27/10/1918	31/10/1918
Miscellaneous	2nd Bn. Royal Fusiliers. Narrative of Operations-28th Sept to 2nd Oct 1918	28/09/1918	28/09/1918
Miscellaneous	Narrative of Operations of 2/Royal Fusiliers on 14th October 1918.	14/10/1918	14/10/1918
Miscellaneous	2/Royal Fusiliers. No. 5/27.	20/10/1918	20/10/1918
Map			
Heading	War Diary of 2nd Battalion Royal Fusiliers. For Month Of November. 1918 Vol 33		
War Diary	Bondues	01/11/1918	07/11/1918
War Diary	Luingne.	08/11/1918	09/11/1918
War Diary	Petit Tourcoing.	10/11/1918	10/11/1918
War Diary	Saint Genois.	11/11/1918	11/11/1918
War Diary	Le Quesnoy.	12/11/1918	12/11/1918
War Diary	Arc Ainieres	13/11/1918	13/11/1918
War Diary	Wodecq	14/11/1918	17/11/1918
War Diary	Bassilly.	18/11/1918	20/11/1918
War Diary	Steenkerque.	21/11/1918	22/11/1918
War Diary	Haut Ittre.	23/11/1918	23/11/1918
War Diary	Bousval	24/11/1918	24/11/1918
War Diary	Nil St Vincent.	25/11/1918	26/11/1918
War Diary	Noville Sur Mehaigne. Huy.	27/11/1918	28/11/1918
War Diary	Ouffet.	29/11/1918	29/11/1918
War Diary	Aywaille.		
Heading	2nd Battn Royal Fusiliers War Diary For December 1918. Vol 34		
War Diary	La Reid.	01/12/1918	03/12/1918
War Diary	Malmedy.	04/12/1918	04/12/1918
War Diary	Elsenborn	05/12/1918	05/12/1918
War Diary	Eidersheid.	06/12/1918	06/12/1918
War Diary	Wollersheim.	07/12/1918	07/12/1918
War Diary	Ahrem.	08/12/1918	08/12/1918
War Diary	Sulz.	09/12/1918	12/12/1918
War Diary	Bensberg.	13/12/1918	20/12/1918
War Diary	Berg Gladbach.	21/12/1918	31/12/1918
Heading	Southern (Late 29th) Divn 86th Infy Bde 2nd Bn Royal Fusiliers Jan-Mar 1919		
Heading	2nd Battalion Royal Fusiliers. War Diary. For January. 1919. Vol 47 Jan-Mar 1919		
War Diary	Gladbach.	01/01/1919	12/01/1919
War Diary	Berg Gladbach.	13/01/1919	13/01/1919

War Diary	Forward Zone.	14/01/1919	03/02/1919
War Diary	Gladbach.	04/02/1919	28/02/1919
War Diary	Outpost Zone.	11/03/1919	18/03/1919
War Diary	Gladbach.	19/03/1919	19/03/1919
War Diary	Mulheim.	21/03/1919	26/03/1919
War Diary	Gladbach.	01/03/1919	05/03/1919
War Diary	Outpost Zone.	06/03/1919	11/03/1919
War Diary	Mulheim.	28/03/1919	28/03/1919
War Diary	Dunkerque.	30/03/1919	01/04/1919
Map			

WO95/2301/3

2 Battalion Royal Fusiliers

29TH DIVISION

86TH INFY BDE

2ND BN ROY. FUSILIERS

FEB 1916 - MAR 1919

29th Division.
86th Infantry Brigade.

ARRIVED MARSEILLES FROM EGYPT 21st March 1916.

2nd BATTALION

THE ROYAL FUSILIERS

25th FEBRUARY to /30th APRIL 1916.

1

Rec '18

2nd Bn. Royal Fusiliers.

Instructions regarding War Diaries and Intelligence Summaries are contained in F. S. Regs., Part II. and the Staff Manual respectively. Title Pages will be prepared in manuscript.

WAR DIARY
or
INTELLIGENCE SUMMARY
(Erase heading not required.)

Army Form C. 2118

Place	Date	Hour	Summary of Events and Information	Remarks and references to Appendices
El Kubri	Feb 1916 25th		CO & adjutant visited outposts. All battn employed guards fatigues etc.	
	26th		Very hot day. Same as usual.	
	27th		Draft of 37 men and 3 officers (2/Lts Hood, Sylvester, Thomerson) arrived.	
	28th		Battn off Bde duties, relieved by 8th Bde at 4 pm	
	29th		Struck camp preparatory to move to Railhead. 2/Lt Smith joined battn.	
	March 1st		Moved to Railhead and pitched camp there. One Coy in outpost line at NEW POST 3 miles out.	
	2nd		Worked on defences at Railhead.	
	3rd		Battn moved back to old camp at EL KUBRI and bivouaced there for the night. 2/Lt Wyndham rejoined.	
	4th		Battn moved back to Suez, into old camp.	
	5th		C.O. (Major Cripps) and Quartermaster returned from England. Corps commander Gen. Davies came round to say goodbye before battn left for France. Transport personnel of 36 left for France, also 2 horses.	
	6th		Sunday. Rather bad sandstorm in the afternoon.	
	7th		Draft of 48 men arrived.	
	8th		Hot day. Battn had the range for 4 hours. Training of snipers.	
	9th		Route march to PORT TEWFIK early morning. Brigade night operations, taking a trench.	
	10th		Range all morning. Coys on digging the trench. Remaining two horses & groom departed for France	
	11th		Range all morning and digging. Sandstorm more or less all day.	
	12th		Divisional tactical scheme, attacking a position at BIR SUEZ. Sgt Major Husband rejoined.	
	13th		Sunday. Very hot. Received orders to move next day.	
	14th		Battn embarked at PORT TEWFIK for France, 31 officers & 920 other ranks strong, on SS Alaunia, the ship on which the battn came out to Gallipoli. Sailed in the evening. 2/Lt Wyndham left to attend court of enquiry at Cairo.	
	15th		arrived Port Said and stayed the night. HMS Implacable in harbour at P. SAID. CO. Quartermaster & Warrant officers were aboard	[illegible]

1875 Wt. W593/826 1,000,000 4/15 J.B.C. & A. A.D.S.S./Forms/C. 2118.

11 B.
(5 sheets)

FROM:-

The Officer Commanding,

2nd Battalion Royal Fusiliers,.

TO:- The Officer i/c

A.G's Office at the Base.

Herewith War Diary of 2nd Battalion Royal Fusiliers, for March and April 1916.

Lieut. for Lt-Colonel.

Commanding, 2nd Battalion Royal Fusiliers.

18/5/16.

Vol 142 BEF
from MEF

29

2nd Bn. Royal Fusiliers.

Army Form C. 2118.

WAR DIARY
or
INTELLIGENCE SUMMARY
(Erase heading not required.)

Instructions regarding War Diaries and Intelligence Summaries are contained in F. S. Regs., Part II. and the Staff Manual respectively. Title Pages will be prepared in manuscript.

Place	Date	Hour	Summary of Events and Information	Remarks and references to Appendices
SS Alaunia	May 16th 17th 18th 19th 20th 21st	}	At sea. A very fine crossing. No submarines sighted.	
	22nd		Arrived at Marseilles and entrained 4 pm. Three men evacuated to hospital.	
	23rd		In the train. The men all in trucks. Weather considerably colder all day.	
	24th		Arrived PONT REMY about 8 miles from ABBEVILLE and marched into billets at ~~Eaulons~~ COULONVILLERS, about 10 miles South, arriving at 9 pm. Men all billeted in farmhouses or barns. Officers in cottages. Very comfortable all round.	
	25th		Spent the day settling in billets. Very cold & wet. Casualties: Sick — Rejoined. Officers —. Other ranks 5 — 1.	
	26th		Sunday. Rather finer but cold.	
	27th		Brigade route march, 14 miles. Rather wet & cold day.	
	28th		Batt. route march. Several cases sore feet. Warmer day.	
	29th		Practice move from billets. Marched about 8 miles.	
	30th		Batt. route march, about 6 miles.	
	31st		Moved to BEAUVAL about 15 miles due East.	
	1 June		Settled in billets. All very comfortable. Fine day.	
	2nd		Sunday. Fine day. Casualties: Sick / Rejoined / Seconded. Officers 1. Other ranks 28 / 4 / 1 (Sgt Fitzgibbons, Instructor [illegible])	
	3rd		Practice move, about 3 miles.	
	4th		Moved on to Engelbelmer about 15 miles. Only 2 miles behind the firing line. All very quiet.	
	5th		Settled in billets. 3 mining parties of 20 men all day for work in trenches.	

1875 Wt. W593/826 1,000,000 4/15 J.B.C. & A. A.D.S.S./Forms/C. 2118.

2nd R. Fusiliers

Instructions regarding War Diaries and Intelligence Summaries are contained in F. S. Regs., Part II. and the Staff Manual respectively. Title Pages will be prepared in manuscript.

WAR DIARY
or
INTELLIGENCE SUMMARY
(Erase heading not required.)

Army Form C. 2118

Place	Date	Hour	Summary of Events and Information	Remarks and references to Appendices
Englebelmer	April 6th		Lt Colonel A C Johnson joined battalion & took over command from Major H H Cripps, who took over duties of 2nd i/c. Germans attacked trenches in front of village about 8.30 pm, bombarding for 90 minutes heavily, but did not shell our village at all.	
	7th		Supplied 200 men for digging in redoubts Moulin & Prowse from 6.30 to 10.30	
	8th		Supplied two parties of 4 officers & 200 from 6.30–10.30, & 10.30–2.30 for work on forts and occupied the two forts with a platoon each.	
	9th		Casualties for the week: Officers — Sick nil, Rejoined nil; Other Ranks — Sick 8, Rejoined 7. Forts occupied with 2 platoons.	
	10th		Usual fatigue parties. Very wet. 2 Platoons in Forts.	
	11th		Same fatigues. 2 Platoons & forts.	
Mailly Maillet	12th		Battn moved to Mailly Maillet about 1 mile into billets. Quite comfortable. The town not being shelled up to date. 2 Coy to Auchonvillers rather nearer the line. ~~Mining parties relieved~~	
	13th		1 Coy up to trenches in reserve to R Munster Fus. Remainder of battn on fatigues	
	14th		Battn on fatigues by night in various parts of the fire line & supports. Rest by day	
	15th		2 Coy returned from Auchonvillers. Remainder on night fatigues & day fatigues.	
	16th		All three Coys on night fatigues & small day fatigue. Casualties for the week: Officers —; Sick 8, Rejoined 7	
	17th		Usual fatigues. All by night.	
	18th		Started digging & improving on C. trench 1st avenue with 300 men by night. [illegible] 3rd [illegible]. Y. Coy returned to billets from trenches.	
	19th		Continued digging C. trench at night. Good progress. Very wet.	

1875 Wt. W593/826 1,000,000 4/15 J.B.C. & A. A.D.S.S./Forms/C. 2118.

2nd Bn Royal Fusiliers.

Instructions regarding War Diaries and Intelligence Summaries are contained in F. S. Regs., Part II. and the Staff Manual respectively. Title pages will be prepared in manuscript.

WAR DIARY

or

~~INTELLIGENCE~~ SUMMARY.

(*Erase heading not required.*)

2nd Royal Fusiliers

Army Form C. 2118.

Place	Date	Hour	Summary of Events and Information	Remarks and references to Appendices
Mailly Maillet	April 20		Continued fatigue parties as usual. Very wet weather.	
	21		Continued fatigues by day, but rested at night.	
	22		Very wet weather, pouring all day. Took over trenches from R. Dublin. Fusiliers. Into new H.Qrs, very wet & uncomfortable. W & Z Coys in firing line. X & Y in Auchonvillers in support.	
	23rd		Casualties for week. Officers. Sick — Wounded — Injured —	
			O.R. Sick 16 Wounded 3 Injured 4	
			~~Sta~~ W & Z working in front line as far as possible in the wet. X & Y on dug outs & mining.	
	24th		All employed in pumping water out of trenches	
	25th		No more rain trenches in many places clear of rain	
	26th		Commenced deepening footway to 3' below fire step	
	27th		Worked on improving trenches	
	28th		Divisional commander on going round our trenches expressed his approval of the work done.	
			During the night relieved by the Border regiment marched back to LOUVENCOURT	
	29th		arriving about 3 30 A.M.	
			During our tour in the trenches we only had one man slightly wounded by a shell splinter	
	30th		Spent the day cleaning up & kit inspections. LOUVENCOURT is a fairly large farming village. The Bn are in quite comfortable billets	

29th Division

86th Infantry Brigade.

2nd BATTALION

ROYAL FUSILIERS

M A Y 1 9 1 6

2nd Bn Royal Fusiliers

2 Royal Fus
Vol 3

29

Instructions regarding War Diaries and Intelligence Summaries are contained in F. S. Regs., Part II. and the Staff Manual respectively. Title pages will be prepared in manuscript.

WAR DIARY
or
INTELLIGENCE SUMMARY.
(Erase heading not required.)

Army Form C. 2118.

Place	Date	Hour	Summary of Events and Information	Remarks and references to Appendices
	May		Strength Officers 33 OR 940 | Casualties for last week OR 1 Wounded, 22 Sick, 13 Rejoined	
LOUVENCOURT	1		While in Corps reserve the following programme is to be carried out. 50 men trained as bombers under Brigade Bombing Officer. A Raiding party of 2 officers & 40 OR trained. One NCO & one man from each platoon trained in erecting wire entanglements & revetting under an R.E. NCO. Every morning ½ hour physical drill for all. Every other day 450 men on Outside Fatigues. Every other day a route march. Lectures to NCO's in map reading. ½ hours close order drill every day when not on fatigue. 2Lt Whitlock, Meredith & Westaway joined	
	2.		Fine weather a shower in the afternoon. Lt PEARSON sick to hospital Lt NICKOLLS took on duties as acting adjutant	
			A draft of 100 men joined from 15th Bn	
	3.		In the evening the Battalion occupied the brown line for practice returning to billets about 11-30 pm	
	4		Brigade route march about 8 miles. 2Lt Hyett joined	
	5		The whole battalion marched to Mailly Maillet, 7 miles distant, dug for four hours & returned	
	6		2 Lt DERNFORD joined. Battalion on Fatigue	
			Strength Officers 33 OR 949 Casualties Officers 1 OR 17 Sick	

12.B. (3 sheets)

T2134. Wt. W708-776. 500000. 4/15. Sir J. C. & S.

Instructions regarding War Diaries and Intelligence Summaries are contained in F. S. Regs., Part II. and the Staff Manual respectively. Title pages will be prepared in manuscript.

WAR DIARY 2nd Bn Royal Fusiliers.
or
~~INTELLIGENCE SUMMARY.~~
(Erase heading not required.)

Army Form C. 2118.

Place	Date	Hour	Summary of Events and Information	Remarks and references to Appendices
	May			
LOUVENCOURT	7		Sunday, observed as such, no work, Church Parade.	
	8		The Brigade moved into the line in the evening. 2 Bn in trenches 2 in reserved.	
	0		We moved to MAILLY-MAILLET about 3000x behind front line	
MAILLY	9		Whole Bn on fatigue mostly mining deep dug outs in support trenches	
	10		2 Lt LEANING joined. The whole battalion on fatigue digging a new support trench all night. 2nd Lt J S LEANING joined	
	11		Worked all night on new trench	HMR
	12		Worked all night, 2nd Lt J R B white ~~joined~~ 2 Lts CHESTER RUSSELL	
	13		Rained hard no work at night. Effective strength officers 43 OR 936	Casualties week ending 13th OR 18 sick
	14		Sunday, church Parade worked at night on new trench.	
	15		~~We~~ Worked on new trench. 2 Lt C.F.FOX & MAJ G.S. GUYON joined (13th)	
	16		a warm sunny day work on new trench continued	
	17		Worked on new trench.	
	18		No work during day – took over trenches from 1st R.D.F on night of 18th/19th 2 Coys in front line, 1 Coy in support, 1 Coy in AUCHONVILLERS.	
	19		Slight activity by our artillery and enemy's machine guns, Rifle fire [illegible] Nil. Work done strengthening wire and improving fire and communication trenches.	
	20		Work done same as 19th inst.	

1577 Wt. W10791/1773 500,000 1/15 D. D. & L. A.D.S.S./Forms/C. 2118.

Instructions regarding War Diaries and Intelligence Summaries are contained in F. S. Regs., Part II. and the Staff Manual respectively. Title pages will be prepared in manuscript.

WAR DIARY
or
INTELLIGENCE SUMMARY.
(Erase heading not required.)

Army Form C. 2118.

Place	Date	Hour	Summary of Events and Information	Remarks and references to Appendices
Mailly	May 21		Sunday observed as such. Work started at stand down – improving fire trench.	
	22		Ordinary Trench Routine and Work.	
	23			
	24			
	25		Ordinary Trench Routine and Work.	
	26			
	27			
LOUVENCOURT	28		Handed over trenches to 1st Essex. Proceeded to LOUVENCOURT	
	29		Troops employed by cleaning up. Kit inspections etc. Officers & N.C.Os exercised in signalling with aircraft.	
	30		Ceremonial – Kit inspections etc.	
	31		Battalion on duty for the Brigade, numerous working parties found. Guards etc. Weather fine and warm.	[illegible]

29th Division.

86th Infantry Brigade

2nd BATTALION

ROYAL FUSILIERS

J U N E 1 9 1 6

13.B.
(4 sheets)

20/7/16.

From:- The Officer Commanding,
2nd Battalion Royal Fusiliers.

To:- Officer i/c D.A.G's Office
Base, B. E. F.

Herewith War Diary of 2nd Battalion Royal Fusiliers, for the month of June 1916.

Percy Boult[?] for Captain,
Commanding, 2nd Battalion Royal Fusilers.

29

Instructions regarding War Diaries and Intelligence Summaries are contained in F. S. Regs., Part II. and the Staff Manual respectively. Title pages will be prepared in manuscript.

WAR DIARY
~~or~~
~~INTELLIGENCE SUMMARY.~~
(Erase heading not required.)

Army Form C. 2118.

Place	Date	Hour	Summary of Events and Information	Remarks and references to Appendices
	June			
LOUVENCOURT	1		Battalion on duty for the Brigade, numerous working parties found. Guards etc. Weather fine and warm.	
	2		Bathing Parades for whole Battalion, with a few exceptions.	
	3		Officers and N.C.Os taken by the C.O. to view enemy positions, marked out on training area.	
	4		Battalion exercises the attack on training area	
	5		do do do	
	6		do do do	
	7		Move to MAILLY MAILLET	
MAILLY	8		Work on ESSEX St under Company arrangements. Find further working parties for the Brigade.	
	9		do do do	
	10		do do do	
	11		Move to Huts in MAILLY WOOD. Weather very bad.	
	12		Working parties interfered with by heavy rain. All work cancelled at night.	[initials]

T2134. Wt. W708-776. 500000. 4/15. Sir J. C. & S.

Instructions regarding War Diaries and Intelligence Summaries are contained in F. S. Regs., Part II. and the Staff Manual respectively. Title pages will be prepared in manuscript.

WAR DIARY

~~or~~

~~INTELLIGENCE SUMMARY.~~

(Erase heading not required.)

Army Form C. 2118.

Place	Date	Hour	Summary of Events and Information	Remarks and references to Appendices
	June			
MAILLY	13		Parties continue to work inspite of weather, which is very wet and cold.	
	14		Every available man taken for working parties by day and night.	
	15		Move into the Trenches Take over from 1st R.D.F	
	16		Ordinary trench routine and work.	
	17		2/Lieuts BARRETT & HUMPHERUS rejoin.	
	18		Ordinary trench routine and work.	
	19		Relieved by the 1st R.D.F. – return to MAILLY WOOD	
	20		Coy training. Lecture by C.O. to the whole battalion. Find 180 men for working parties by night.	
	21		Two Coys proceeded to ACHEUX WOOD and encamped. (X and Y)	
	22		Above Coys took part in Div^l Field Day at LOUVENCOURT, returning MAILLY WOOD in the evening.	
	23		W. Coy and 10% of Battalion Take over Trenches from 1st R.D.F. (under Major Guyon)	JWR

Instructions regarding War Diaries and Intelligence Summaries are contained in F. S. Regs., Part II. and the Staff Manual respectively. Title pages will be prepared in manuscript.

WAR DIARY
or
~~INTELLIGENCE SUMMARY~~.
(Erase heading not required.)

Army Form C. 2118.

Place	Date	Hour	Summary of Events and Information	Remarks and references to Appendices
	June		Major Guyon takes over command of the 16th W Yorkshire Regt	
MAILLY	24		Start of Bombardment. Suffer 3 casualties in the line.	
	25		Bombardment continues. Troops bivouac out on field to the West of MAILLY WOOD during night	
	26		Bombardment continues. Casualties slight.	
	27		Major H A Cripps rejoins and takes over second in Command. 2/Lieut Hule and 15 men attempt raid on German trenches. Unsuccessful. Casualties. 1 Wounded 1 Missing only.	
	28		Bombardment continues. A few enemy shells (HE) burst near camp during night. No casualties. Capt. Barff (wnd)	
	29		Troops bivouac on field to the West of MAILLY WOOD. 2/Lieut C.J. FOX killed by shell fire up in the line	
	30		The Batt 10% occupied front line until relieved by remainder of Batt. at 11.30 PM in this formation :- X.Y.Z Companies in front line with W in support. Very few casualties. 2/l BARRETT – K. J. Wounded.	
TRENCHES	July 1		Bombardment very fierce until 7.25 AM, when Batt attacked	P.S.B

T2134. Wt. W708–776. 500000. 4/15. Sir J. C. & S.

S E C R E T.

To

2ND ROYAL FUSILIERS.
1ST LANCASHIRE FUS.
****

The G.O.C., General de Lisle, has himself given the following verbal message over the 'phone:-

"Please tell 2nd Royal Fusiliers and 1st Lancashire Fusiliers that I intended to come and wish them good luck before they enter this most important battle in which British troops have ever fought.

I was more anxious to see them today, as it is the anniversary of our fight at Gully Ravine last year, where these two battalions did so well and reached their final objective.

I am completely confident that the men of these battalions will do as successfully tomorrow, and I send them my best wishes and good luck."

Ian Grant

Captain,

28/June/1916. Brigade Major, 86th Infy.Bde.

29th Division.
86th Infantry Brigade.
--6-------

2nd BATTALION

ROYAL FUSILIERS

JULY 1916

86/29

War Diary

of

2nd. Bn. Royal Fusiliers

for

July 1916

H.B. (Bn 1st)

Instructions regarding War Diaries and Intelligence Summaries are contained in F. S. Regs., Part II. and the Staff Manual respectively. Title pages will be prepared in manuscript.

86/29

WAR DIARY

or

~~INTELLIGENCE SUMMARY~~.

(Erase heading not required.) 2nd Bn Royal Fusiliers.

Army Form C. 2118.

Vol 5

Place	Date	Hour	Summary of Events and Information	Remarks and references to Appendices
Beaumont Hamel	1/7/16		From early dawn until 0720, bombardment was very fierce. The big mine opposite HAWTHORNE REDOUBT was then exploded and "Z" Company rushed forward to occupy crater, but were immediately met by heavy machine gun fire and artillery barrage. 5 minutes after this (Zero time) the general attack along the whole front was launched. Very few of our men reached as far as the enemy barbed wire. Owing to our artillery persistently shelling the 2nd and 3rd line of the enemy's first system, the Germans were enabled to fully use their own front line, and therefore resisted all attacks upon it. This continued to about 12 mid-day, when the few remaining men in "no mans land" were forced to retire.	App. I
		1 P.M.	Major H H Cripps was ordered to Brigade Headquarters to take over the duties of Brigade Major, but was seri[illegible] wounded within two hours. Lt Colonel A.V. Johnson was [illegible] in the front line trench by one of our own High Expl[illegible]	P.T.O.

1577 Wt. W10791/1773 500,000 1/15 D. D. & L. A.D.S.S./Forms/C. 2118.

Army Form C. 2118.

Instructions regarding War Diaries and Intelligence Summaries are contained in F. S. Regs., Part II. and the Staff Manual respectively. Title pages will be prepared in manuscript.

WAR DIARY
or
~~INTELLIGENCE SUMMARY~~.

(*Erase heading not required.*)

Place	Date	Hour	Summary of Events and Information	Remarks and references to Appendices
Beaumont Hamel.	1/7/16		and severely shaken. Major G. S. Guyon was killed leading the 16th Bn. West Yorkshire Regt. Casualties were:- Officers, Killed 3 Wounded 12 Wounded & Missing 1 Missing 4 missing believed killed 1 Other Ranks, Killed 54 Wounded 276 Missing 140.	
	2/7/16		Enemy artillery and our own very active, our front line and support receiving especial attention. Salvage of dead and wounded still remaining in our own trenches actively carried on, also repairing of trenches. Lt Colonel R.V. Johnson wounded (shell shock). Captain F. W. Swift assuming command with Captain G. V. Goodliffe as 2nd in Command and Lieut. D.T.O. Boult as Adjutant.	P.T.O.
	3/7/16		Relieved 1st Bn Lancashire Fusiliers, having Battalion Headquarters in TENDERLOIN. Dispositions:- "W" Company in front line, "X" Company in support, and "Y" & "Z" Companies in reserve. A small patrol on SUNKEN ROAD.	

1577 Wt. W10791/1773 500,000 1/15 D. D. & L. A.D.S.S./Forms/C. 2118.

Army Form C. 2118.

Instructions regarding War Diaries and Intelligence Summaries are contained in F. S. Regs., Part II. and the Staff Manual respectively. Title pages will be prepared in manuscript.

WAR DIARY
or
~~INTELLIGENCE SUMMARY.~~

(Erase heading not required.)

Place	Date	Hour	Summary of Events and Information	Remarks and references to Appendices
Beaumont Hamel	4/7/16		Relieved by two Battalions of the 4th Division. ie. 1st Bn Royal Irish Fusiliers (left-sector) 1st Bn Royal Warwicks (right-sector). Casualties all ranks. 5 Killed 1 wounded. Returned to MAILLY wood about midnight. Very wet.	
MAILLY	5/7/16		Moved from MAILLY wood to canvas huts in ACHEAUX wood.	
ACHEUX	6/7/16		Kit inspection and practice for night digging, and re-organizing Battalion. Draft of 90 men arrived	
	7/7/16		-ditto- Draft of 65 men arrived. Very wet.	
	8/7/16		Battalion moved to MESNIL in the afternoon with "Y" Company at HAMEL. Practically no accommodation for troops except a few disused artillery dug-outs.	R.T.O.S.
	9/7/16		Two small working parties with an officer each, to JACOBS LADDER. Found better accommodation for the troops.	
	10/7/16		Two working parties for JACOBS LADDER	
	11/7/16		Ditto.	

1577 Wt. W10791/1773 500,000 1/15 D. D. & L. A.D.S.S./Forms/C. 2118.

Army Form C. 2118

WAR DIARY
or
~~INTELLIGENCE SUMMARY~~.
(Erase heading not required.)

Instructions regarding War Diaries and Intelligence Summaries are contained in F. S. Regs., Part II. and the Staff Manual respectively. Title pages will be prepared in manuscript.

Place	Date	Hour	Summary of Events and Information	Remarks and references to Appendices
MESNIL	12/7/16		Same working parties plus 160 men for carrying gas cylinders	
	13/7/16		Found two small working parties in addition.	
	14/7/16		2/Lt R. G. Pape rejoined. Most of the Battalion on working parties.	
	15/7/16		2/Lt R. E. Cameis killed at 12-30 A.M. (Shell) Relieved the 1st Battn Lancashire Fusiliers by 8 p.m., with "Z" and "X" Companies in front line, "Y" Company in support at HAMEL, and "W" Company in reserve at MESNIL.	
	16/7/16		All the Battalion on detailed work. 2 officers and 160 men for carrying gas. Half of this party was caught in a bombardment of gas shells.	P.T.08
	17/7/16		Quiet along our sector. New fire trench dug by the Monmouthshire Regt: and known as the (New Support Trench). Rain most of the day.	
	18/7/16		Quiet along the line. Raiding Party of the 1st Battalion Worcestershire Regt: started from our front line at 0240.	
	19/7/16		2/Lt D. B. Bell joined. Another trench dug during the night	

Instructions regarding War Diaries and Intelligence Summaries are contained in F. S. Regs., Part II. and the Staff Manual respectively. Title pages will be prepared in manuscript.

WAR DIARY
or
~~INTELLIGENCE SUMMARY.~~
(Erase heading not required.)

Army Form C. 2118.

Place	Date	Hour	Summary of Events and Information	Remarks and references to Appendices
	19/7/16		in front of new Support Trench and known as (New Fire Trench) Weather fair.	
	20/7/16		Most of Battalion on detailed work. Major G.A. Stevens. D.S.O assumed command of Battalion.	
	21/7/16		2/Lt C.F. Jackson joined. The General thanked the following men for specially fine scouting round the MILL. No. 13603 Cpl. H. Floyd, 18022 Pte T.W. Pratt, 14181 Pte F.A. Spires, and 12765 Pte G.L. Ashby. New Fire Trench Garrisoned by 1 Officer, 50 men, and Lewis Gun.	
	22/7/16		Enemy quiet all day, but at 2320 started an intense bombardment lasting for one and a half hours. We were unable to get artillery support for over three quarters of an hour. 2/Lt D.B. Bell wounded. Following officers joined:- Lt C.E.C. Penny, 2/Lts T.M. Edgar, R.S. Page-Green, E.F. Banks, J.K. Cowie, W.L. A-G. Reade, G.F.B. Daniell, H.L. Bentley, A.K. Sutcliffe, W.E. Bird, C.L. Barlow, D.L. Lewis. 2/Lt E.H. Humphreys rejoined.	P.T.O.

1577 Wt. W10791/1773 500,000 1/15 D. D. & L. A.D.S.S./Forms/C. 2118.

Army Form C. 2118.

Instructions regarding War Diaries and Intelligence Summaries are contained in F. S. Regs., Part II. and the Staff Manual respectively. Title pages will be prepared in manuscript.

WAR DIARY

or

~~INTELLIGENCE SUMMARY.~~

(Erase heading not required.)

Place	Date	Hour	Summary of Events and Information	Remarks and references to Appendices
	23/7/16		Relieved by 1st Battn Wiltshire Regt. and Battn bivouacked in Bus wood.	
BUS	24/7/16		Battalion marched to BEAUVAL, starting at 0930 and arriving at 1500	
BEAUVAL	25/7/16		Routine work. Inspections and baths.	
	26/7/16		Company arrangements in the morning. 2/Lts. H. H. Daniel and W. A. Sayer joined.	
	27/7/16		At 1134 the Battalion entrained for WORMHOUDT arriving at 1630	
WORMHOUDT	28/7/16		Training of bombers etc	
	29/7/16		- do - Brigadier inspected draft.	
	30/7/16		Officers and Mens' shooting match.	
	31/7/16		At 0730 the Battalion entrained for POPERINGHE and then marched to camp at Square G.6D. 6.3. Sheet 28 N.W. Belgium. 2/Lt A. J. Edwards joined.	P.O.B.

A. R. Stone Major
Cmdg. 2nd Roy. Fus.

1577 Wt. W10791/1773 500,000 1/15 D. D. & L. A.D.S.S./Forms/C. 2118.

29th Division.
86th Infantry Brigade

2nd BATTALION

ROYAL FUSILIERS

AUGUST 1 9 1 6

15.B.
(50 sheets)

Vol 6

CONFIDENTIAL

WAR DIARY

of

2ND BN. ROYAL FUSILIERS

From 1st Aug. to 31st Aug

1916

(VOLUME ~~XVI~~)

Instructions regarding War Diaries and Intelligence Summaries are contained in F. S. Regs., Part II. and the Staff Manual respectively. Title pages will be prepared in manuscript.

WAR DIARY
or
~~INTELLIGENCE SUMMARY.~~
(Erase heading not required.)

Army Form C. 2118.

Place	Date	Hour	Summary of Events and Information	Remarks and references to Appendices
	AUG 1916			
"POPERINGHE" "B" Camp. (BRANDHOEK)	1.		Cleaning up camp and settling down. Specialists courses started	
	2.		Brigade Route march 0700–0900.	
	3.		Ordinary Parades. Capt. F.W. Swifte. left as an instructor at ROUEN.	
	4.		" " . LT. C.E.C. PENNY took over command of W Coy.	
	5.		Route march.	
	6.		Church Parade.	
	7.		Brigade Sports. 2LT. A. D. HUME joined.	
YPRES	8.		Relieved the 1st K.O.S.B. at the prison YPRES. at 10-30 P.M. the Germans gassed our front, and even we in support in the "PRISON" slightly felt the gas – NO casualties from the gas.	
TRENCHES	9.		Took over Right of the left half of Divnl Sector from 1st INNISKILLINGS FUSILIERS. no casualties during relief but 1 man killed and 2 wounded in the afternoon when Prison was slightly shelled. Relief took place by night.	
	10		Very quiet in trenches. 'Spitlocked' a trench (for filling sand-	P.T.C.B. 9th ...

1577 Wt. W10791/1773 500,000 1/15 D. D. & L. A.D.S.S./Forms/C. 2118.

Army Form C. 2118.

Instructions regarding War Diaries and Intelligence Summaries are contained in F. S. Regs., Part II. and the Staff Manual respectively. Title pages will be prepared in manuscript.

WAR DIARY

or

~~INTELLIGENCE SUMMARY~~

(Erase heading not required.)

Place	Date	Hour	Summary of Events and Information	Remarks and references to Appendices
	AUG			
TRENCHES			bags) 18 ~~feet~~ yds behind front line.	
	11.		Very quiet, except for a certain activity on behalf of enemy snipers. Large working parties putting out more wire + strengthening parapets also building parados.	
	12.		Corps Commander visited trenches. Working at night on wire.	
	13.		Enemies snipers much quieter than when we first took over.	
	14		Two front line Companies W & Y were relieved by two support companies, namely X & Z. Very quiet all day.	
	15.		Enemy peppered our trenches a little (slight damage) with "MINNIES".	
	16		Same as 15th inst.	
	17.		2Lts. M.F. Willis; E.H. HUMPHERUS; A.D. HUME were sent to 4th Battalion R.F. Front very quiet. 2Lt G.C. PEARSON. R joined.	
	18.		All Battalion working at night on front line + new wire.	
YPRES	19		Heavy RAIN: Relieved by 1st K.O.S.B's. + took over reserve area occupied by Worcesters:- Y coy at Ecole. X in RAMPARTS. Z in HORNWAIK. W in	P.T.O. [illegible]

1577 Wt. W10791/1773 500,000 1/15 D. D. & L. A.D.S.S./Forms/C. 2118.

Instructions regarding War Diaries and Intelligence Summaries are contained in F. S. Regs., Part II. and the Staff Manual respectively. Title pages will be prepared in manuscript.

WAR DIARY
or
~~INTELLIGENCE SUMMARY.~~
(Erase heading not required.)

Army Form C. 2118.

Place	Date	Hour	Summary of Events and Information	Remarks and references to Appendices
YPRES.	19.		RAMPARTS.	
	20		ALL Battalion working on (night) - HAYMARKET, DUCK WALK, & CAMBRIDGE COMMUNICATION TRENCH.	
	21.		Do Do Do	
	22		Weather bad Do Do.	
	23.		Weather fine. Do Do.	
	24.		Do Do Do.	
	25.		Enemy aeroplanes rather active. Same night work.	
	26		At night, all Battalion out wiring and completed 400x.	
	27.		Three parties of 72 O.R. under an offr carried down gas cylinders	
	28.		Two " Do Do , Do Rained hard.	
"B" CAMP	29.		Relieved by 1st Lancashire Fusiliers. and returned to "B" Camp.	
	30.		Rained hard. Cleaning up camp. 2Lt. A.V. EVANS joined.	
	31.		Specialists parades. Lt. H.W. PERSSE rejoined and took over W Coy.	P.T.O. [illegible]

1577 Wt. W10791/1773 500,000 1/15 D. D. & L. A.D.S.S./Forms/C. 2118.

29th Division.
86th Infantry Brigade.

2nd BATTALION

ROYAL FUSILIERS

SEPTEMBER 1 9 1 6

Report on Raid 20th September 1916 attached.

86/29

CONFIDENTIAL

Vol 7

War Diary

of

2nd Battalion Royal Fusiliers

FROM September 1st, 1916 TO September 30th, 1916.

(Volumn XVII)

1972
8B

16 B.
(5 sheets)

Army Form C. 2118.

Instructions regarding War Diaries and Intelligence Summaries are contained in F. S. Regs., Part II. and the Staff Manual respectively. Title pages will be prepared in manuscript.

WAR DIARY

or

~~INTELLIGENCE SUMMARY.~~

(Erase heading not required.)

Place	Date	Hour	Summary of Events and Information	Remarks and references to Appendices
	SEPTEMBER.			
"B" CAMP	1		Party of 9 officers and 400 O.R. digging cable trench near YPRES	
(BRANDHOEK)	2.		Busy preparing camps for winter. 80 more men for completion of cable trench.	
"	3.		Corps Commander attended our Church Parade – with Divisional Band.	
"	4.		Battn supplied with new Small box respirator. Battn training specialists	
"	5.		Rained hard all day.	
"	6.		Weather fine. D.A.D.M.S. inspected all huts of Battn. "X" Coy proved best [illegible] for inter-Battalion Sniping (Bgde) contest.	
"	7.		Weather good. Usual Coy training.	
"	8.		" Do . Relieved 1st K.O.S.B at Prison Ypres. Travelled by 8.PM train from Camp.	
YPRES (PRISON)	9.		Relieved 1st Inniskilling Fusiliers at Potyze Wood.	
"	10.		2/Lt C.E.C. PENNY evacuated sick. Line very quiet.	
"	11.		Weather fine. Enemy quiet. Capt J. F. DEARDEN went on a Senior Officer's Course at Corps. 2/Lt W.J HOOD temporarily took over charge of "X" Coy	
	12		Rained hard. Difficulty in obtaining R.E. stores.	

1577 Wt. W10791/1773 500,000 1/15 D. D. & L. A.D.S.S./Forms/C. 2118.

194

Instructions regarding War Diaries and Intelligence Summaries are contained in F. S. Regs., Part II. and the Staff Manual respectively. Title pages will be prepared in manuscript.

WAR DIARY

~~or INTELLIGENCE SUMMARY.~~

(Erase heading not required.)

Army Form C. 2118.

Place	Date	Hour	Summary of Events and Information	Remarks and references to Appendices
	SEPTEMBER			
TRENCHES. (Potijze Wood)	13.		Weather fine. Hard at work clearing mud from trenches.	
	14.		Enemy very quiet. Relieved by 1st Lancashire Fusiliers, + returned to PRISON	
YPRES (PRISON)	15.		Four officers and 250 working for R.E. at night. Were forced to cease work owing to enemy liveliness. 2Lt R.S. PAGE-GREEN admitted to Hospital.	
"	16.		Same working parties. 2Lt HURLE on patrol with party	REF: Sep. A
"	17.		150 men on work "MONMOUTH TRENCH". 2Lts THOMERSON, BIRD, + MEREDITH, patrolled no mans land,	
"	18.		Relieved 4th Worcesters at RAILWAY WOOD) having Battalion HQ in F11. Later the original Bn HQ in F13 was re-occupied.	
TRENCHES	19		Raining. At 5.45 AM. the enemy tried to blow-in our galleries just beyond 2A crater. no damage.	
	20		2/Lt HURLE + party. Raided enemy trenches at 2 AM) see	REF. Sep. B.
	21.		Weather fine. Adjutant reported at Brigade to receive instructions for expected move of Battalion.	

1577 Wt. W10791/1773 500,000 1/15 D. D. & L. A.D.S.S./Forms/C. 2118.

Instructions regarding War Diaries and Intelligence Summaries are contained in F. S. Regs., Part II. and the Staff Manual respectively. Title pages will be prepared in manuscript.

WAR DIARY
or
~~INTELLIGENCE SUMMARY~~.
(Erase heading not required.)

Army Form C. 2118.

Place	Date	Hour	Summary of Events and Information	Remarks and references to Appendices
SEPTEMBER.				
TRENCHES.	22		Very quiet.	
"	23.		Corps Commander (Sir. AYLMER HUNTER-WESTON. KCB: DSO) inspected	
"			trenches. [Relieved by 1st Lancs Fusiliers.)	
YPRES.	24		Companies distributed as follows. W Coy in Ecole, X in HORNWALK.	
"			Y & Z in RAMPARTS.	
"	25.		Two hundred men working nightly for R.E.s	
"	26		" Do " Do.	
"	27.		a draft of 80 men (nearly all Derby men). Two hundred yds of wire	
"			put up by Y & X Coy in support lines of Sector occupied by Lancs Fus.	
"	28.		Relieved by 1st Lancs & returned to "B" camp by 10.30PM train.	
"B" Camp	29		Kit inspections & general cleaning up.	
"	30		All men marched to POPERINGHE for Baths.	

S. A. Stevens Lt. Col.
Cmdg: 2nd Roy: Fus:
28/9/16

T2134. Wt. W708—776. 500000. 4/15. Sir J. C. & S.

2 K [illegible]

Army Form C. 2118.

Instructions regarding War Diaries and Intelligence Summaries are contained in F. S. Regs., Part II. and the Staff Manual respectively. Title pages will be prepared in manuscript.

WAR DIARY
or
INTELLIGENCE SUMMARY.

(Erase heading not required.)

1916

Place	Date	Hour	Summary of Events and Information	Remarks and references to Appendices
	SEPTEMBER			
B Camp (BRANDHOEK)	1.		Party of 9 officers and 400 O.R. digging cable trench near YPRES	
	2.		Busy preparing camp for winter. 80 more men for completion of Cable trench.	
	3		Corps Commander attended our Church Parade – with Divisional Band	
	4.		Bn supplied with new small box respirator. Battn. training [illegible]	
	5.		Rained hard all day.	
	6.		Weather fine. DADMS inspected all huts of Bn. 'X' Coy proved best Coy for [illegible]. Battalion Sniping (Bgde) contest.	
	7		Weather good. Usual Coy training.	
	8		" " Relieved 1st K.O.S.B. at Prison YPRES travelled by 8. P.M. train from Camp.	
YPRES (Prison)	9		Relieved 1st Inniskilling Fusiliers at Potijze Wood.	
	10		Lt C.E.C. TANNY evacuated sick. Line very quiet.	
	11		Weather fine. Enemy quiet. Capt T.F. DEARDEN went on a Senior Officers course at Corps. Capt. W.T. HOOD temporarily took over charge of 'X' Coy.	
	12		Rained hard all day. Difficulty in obtaining R.E. Stores.	

A5834 Wt. W4973/M687 750,000 8/16 D. D. & L. Ltd. Forms/C.2118/13.

Instructions regarding War Diaries and Intelligence Summaries are contained in F. S. Regs., Part II. and the Staff Manual respectively. Title pages will be prepared in manuscript.

Army Form C. 2118.

WAR DIARY
or
INTELLIGENCE SUMMARY.
(Erase heading not required.)

Place	Date	Hour	Summary of Events and Information	Remarks and references to Appendices
	SEPTEMBER			
TRENCHES.	13		Weather fine. Hard at work clearing mud from trenches	
(POTIJZE WOOD)	14.		Enemy very quiet. Relieved by 1st Lancs Fusiliers and returned to Prison	
YPRES (PRISON)	15		Four Officers and 250 O.R. working for RE's at night were forced to cease work owing to enemy liveliness. 2nd Lt R.S. PAGE GREEN, admitted to hospital.	
	16.		Same working parties. 2nd Lt. H S HURLE on patrol with party.	
	17		130 Men working on MONMOUTH TRENCH. 2nd Lt. F.L. THOMERSON, W.E. BIRD and H.T. MERIDITH. patrolled No Mans land.	REF: Sept A.
	18		Relieved 4th Worcesters at RAILWAY WOOD, having Bn HQ in F11 Later the original Bn HQs in F.B. were re occupied.	
TRENCHES	19.		Raining at 5.45 A.M. The enemy tried hard to blow in our galleries just beyond 2A Crater.	
	20.		2nd Lt H S HURLE and party raided enemy trenches at 2 A.M. (See	REF. Sept B.
	21.		Weather fine. Adjutant reported at Brigade to receive instructions for expected move of Battalion	

A5834 Wt. W3973/M687 750,000 8/16 D. D. & L. Ltd. Forms/C.2118/13.

Instructions regarding War Diaries and Intelligence Summaries are contained in F. S. Regs., Part II. and the Staff Manual respectively. Title pages will be prepared in manuscript.

WAR DIARY
or
INTELLIGENCE SUMMARY.
(Erase heading not required.)

Army Form C. 2118.

Place	Date	Hour	Summary of Events and Information	Remarks and references to Appendices
SEPTEMBER				
TRENCHES.	22		Very quiet.	
	23.		Corps Commander (Sir AYLMER HUNTER-WESTON, K.C.B., D.S.O.) inspected trenches. Relieved by 1st Lancs Fusiliers.	
YPRES	24		Companies distributed as follows:- W Coy in "Ecole", X Coy in "HORNWALK", Y and Z in RAMPARTS.	
	25		Two hundred men working nightly for R.E.	
	26		——— do ——— ——— do ———	
	27		A Draft of 80 men (nearly all Derby recruits of 10 weeks service). Two hundred yards of wire entanglements put up by Y and X Coy in Support line of sector occupied by Lancs Fus.	
	28		Relieved by 1st Lancs Fus returned to "B" Camp by 10.30 P.M. train	
B CAMP	29		Kit inspections and general cleaning up.	
	30		All men marched to POERINGHE for Baths.	

A5834 Wt. W4973/M687 750,000 8/16 D. D. & L. Ltd. Forms/C.2118/13.

Ref. Sheet 28. SECRET. (1)

Trench Map HOOGE.

Plan of Raid to be carried out by 2nd Royal Fusiliers, morning of September 20th 1916.

---

1. Objects to be attained.

(I) Kill as many Germans as possible, & create confusion.

(II) Obtain identifications.

(III) In addition to prisoners bring back portable material.

2. Point selected for Attack

C. 29.c. between 5.1 and 5.4. Point of Entry about 5.2.

3 Time of Raid

2 a.m. 20th September.

4. General Plan

Surprise.

(a) To make two feints by artillery attack at localities on either side of the selected point.

(b) A very short bombardment of the selected area sufficient to make garrison take cover.

A surprise entry.

5. Action of Artillery

(a) Artillery to open fire at 2. a.m on KAISER BILL and THE MOUND, fire to last 30 minutes.

(b) At 2.2 a.m. field guns open fire on the trench system C 29 d 6½. 4 to 6½. 0 & to the E of this line. Fire not to be opened on front line to avoid possibility of interfering with wire cutting parties. Front line will be dealt with by Stokes Guns. Fire to last from 2.2 a.m to 2.7 a.m – At 2.7 a.m fire lifts and forms pocket round selected area.

6. <u>Medium Trench Mortars.</u>
At 2. a.m. attack KAISER BILL + THE MOUND.

7. <u>Stokes Guns.</u>
At 2.5. a.m to 2.7 a.m Stokes Guns attack German front line between C.29.d. 5.4 + 5.0 also ODER HOUSE with rapid fire.

8. <u>Organisation of Raiding Party</u>

	Offs.	Men.
Bangalore Party.	1	4
Raiders – 3 groups of 7 men. (Lieut. MEREDITH)	1	21
Lewis Gun Party		6
Commander + Emergency Men (Lieut HURLE)	1	4
	3	35

In addition a small group of 2nd R.F. N.C.O.s will be in the British trench to insure that none of raiding party are fired at on way back (A different Brigade will be in the line).

9. <u>Detailed Plan of Raid.</u>
Raiding Party assemble in our front line at 1. a.m.
Bangalore Party leaves over front trench at 1.15 a.m, lay Torpedoes in German

wire & fire them as the first guns go off at 2 a.m.
Two torpedoes will be carried for the work & a third taken up to the trenches. 1 spare fuse to each torpedo.
Should this party meet a hostile patrol they will try & avoid detection, in case of necessity they will attack them in determined manner. On completing their duty they will retire to British trench by the ODER HOUSE flank.

Raiding party leave our trench 1.50 a.m., & proceed to the hedge S. of pond & nearest to German wire. Should hostile patrol be encountered, if possible, observation must be avoided, failing this it must be attacked and captured or destroyed.
At 2.7 a.m. the raiding party attacks, led by Lieut. MEREDITH.
1st Group goes up German communication trench towards German support line.
2nd Group to right.
3rd Group to left.
Raid Commander & company men wait at point of entry to deal with unforseen contingencies.
Lewis Gun party remain at hedge near pond at a selected point to cover the operation.

10. <u>Withdrawal</u> On accomplishing

(14)

The [illegible] of the [illegible]

[illegible]

[illegible]

[illegible]

[illegible] of the [illegible]

The [illegible] [illegible] [illegible] [illegible]

[illegible]

[illegible]

the [illegible] [illegible] [illegible] officers.

11. Equipment

[illegible]

[illegible]

[illegible]

[illegible]

[illegible]

[illegible]

[illegible]

12. Reports

To [illegible]

13. After [illegible] the party [illegible]

[illegible]

[illegible]

[illegible]

14. Details

Care [illegible]

[illegible]

[illegible]

to [illegible] lines.

In the absence of [illegible] officer.

(5)

in the sector during the night of the raid, the raid will not take place.

15. Practice

Practice will take place at a point near 2nd R. F. Transport lines between 9 a.m. & 1 p.m. & 9 p.m. & 10.30 p.m. on 18th Sept. Word will be left of exact site at Transport Lines.

(sgd) G. A. Stevens LT. Col.
Comdg. 2nd Roy. Fus.

17-9-16.

S E C R E T.

Plan of Raid to be carried out by
2nd Royal Fusiliers on
morning of September 20th, 1916.

Reference:-
Sheet 28.
Trench Map HOOGE.

1. OBJECTS TO BE ATTAINED.

(i) Kill as many Germans as possible to create confusion.

(ii) Obtain identifications.

(iii) In addition to prisoners, bring back portable material.

2. POINT SELECTED FOR THE ATTACK.

C.29.d. between 5.1 and 5.4.
Point of entry about 5.2.

3. TIME OF RAID.

2 a.m. 20th September.

4. GENERAL PLAN.
Surprise:-

(a) To make two feints by Artillery, and attack at localities on either side of the selected point.

(b) A very short bombardment of the selected area; sufficient to make garrison take cover.
A surprise entry.

5. ACTION OF ARTILLERY.

(a) Artillery to open fire at 2 a.m. on KAISER BILL and the MOUND. Fire to last 30 minutes.

(b) At 2-2 a.m. Field Guns open fire on the trench system C.29.d.6½.4. to 6½.0., and to the East of this line.
Fire not to be opened on front line to avoid possibility of interfering with wire cutting party.
Front line will dealt with by Stokes Guns.
Fire to last from 2-2 a.m. to 2-7 a.m.
At 2-7 a.m. fire lifts and forms "pocket" round selected area.

6. MEDIUM TRENCH MORTARS.

At 2-0 a.m. attack KAISER BILL and the MOUND.

7. STOKES GUNS.

At 2-5 a.m. to 2-7 a.m. Stokes Guns attack German front line between C.29.d.5.4. and 5.0, also ODER HOUSE with rapid fire.

8. ORGANISATION OF RAIDING PARTY.

	Officers.	Men.
Bangalore party (Lieut. BIRD.)	1	4
Raiders. 3 groups of 7 men. (Lieut. MEREDITH.)	1	21
Lewis Gun party.		6
Commander and emergency men. (Lieut.HURLE)	1	4
	3	35

Eos

In addition a small group of the 2nd Royal Fusiliers N.C.O's will be in the British trench to ensure that none of the raiding party are fired at on the way back. (A different Brigade will be in the line.)

9. DETAILED PLAN OF RAID.

Raiding party assemble in our front line at 1-0 a.m.

Bangalore party leaves our front trench at 1-15 a.m., lay torpedoes in the German wire and fire them as the first guns go off at 2-0 a.m.
Two torpedoes will be carried for the work, and a third taken up to the trenches. One spare fuze to each torpedoe. Should this party meet a hostile patrol, they will try and avoid detection, and in case of necessity they will attack them in am determined manner.
On completion of their duty they will retire to British trench, by the ODER HOUSE flank.

The raiding party will leave our trench at 1-50 a.m., and proceed to the edge South of the POND, and nearest to the German wire. Should a hostile party be encountered, observation must be avoided if possible. Failing this, it must be attacked and captured or destroyed.

At 2-7 a.m. the raiding party attacks, led by Lieut.MEREDITH.

1st group goes up German communication trench towards German support line.

2nd group to Right.

3rd group to Left.

The raid Commander, Lieut.HURLE, and emergency men wait at point of entry to deal with unforseen contingencies.

Lewis Gun party remain at hedge near the POND at a selected point to cover the operation.

10. WITHDRAWAL.

On accomplishing the object of the raid the party will withdraw on a signal given by the raid Commander(not yet settled), two other members of the raid will be authorised to give the signal in event of casualties to the leaders. On withdrawal the men will make their own way back to the British lines.
Lewis Guns not to retire until they receive the order from an Officer.

11. REPORTS.

To Battalion Headquarters at POTIJZE WOOD.

12. EQUIPMENT.

In each group of seven men :-
3 men Revolvers and bludgeons.
2 " Rifles and Bayonets.
2 " Bayonets.
Each man will carry ten bombs.
In each group there will be 4 P bombs to make a smoke barrage before retirement.

h28

13. After the raid the party will return to the prison at YPRES, and during the day, to Camp.
Hot drinks will be ready for them

14. DETAILS.

Care will be taken that no identification marks or documents are on the raiders.

Tape will be taken to mark the route back to the British lines.

In the event of a hostile Gas attack in the sector, during the night of the raid, the raid will not take place.

15. PRACTICE.

Practice will take place at a point near the 2nd Royal Fusiliers Transport lines, between 9 a.m. and 1 p.m., and 9 p.m. and 10-30 p.m., on the 18th September.
Word will be left of exact side at Transport lines.

Lt.Colonel,
18/9/16. Commanding 2nd Royal Fusiliers.

30th Sept: 1916.

My dear Hurle,

I just want to put in writing my admiration for what you and Meredith & Bird and the men with you did this morning in that raid.

I don't suppose war would be war if one won every time & one must just take the knocks it is bound to give with a good face.

Now I don't want any of you to get your tails down over the show, or to think that what you did was in vain.

Remember this little enterprise of ours has its little niche in the great battle now going on. There were something like 15 raids taking place last night, the main object is to so worry Fritz that he __must__ keep strong forces all along his line & prevent the blighter sending up reinforcements to where the decisive struggle is going on.

If we took entrench a business

defence Fritz could safely leave the defence of his trenches to a few sentry groups or even his dear old "frontier guards." These raids prevent the blighter from doing that & makes him hold his line strongly as was undoubtedly proved last night by the way he showed his hand against you — he is afraid.

At first I thought the fates were against you last night but after carefully thinking it over I have come to the opposite conclusion. The Germans are holding their trenches so strongly & they are evidently so alert that even had you got in to his trench I doubt if you would have got out without very heavy loss.

It would of course have been nicer to have brought back a few dozen prisoners but even so I hold you quite accomplished your task in worrying him the way you did

& helping to force the bride
to keep more troops here than
we wants to.
Let the men know what I
think about this & tell them
"Frenchies" never let their
tails down

Yr Son

L. C. Stevens.

General Staff,

29th Division.

Herewith report on the raid carried out by the 2nd Bn.Royal Fusiliers, on the 20th September.

Brigadier-General,

20/9/16. Commanding 86th Infantry Brigade.

S E C R E T.

Report on Raid
carried out by
2nd Royal Fusiliers.

Reference,
Trench Map,
St.JULIEN,
28 N.W.

1. In accordance with your instructions a detachment of this Battalion carried out a raid on the German trenches at 2 a.m. on the 20th September.
I regret to report that the raid was not successful.

2. The original plan submitted on the 17th September was adhered to with the exception that from reconaissance a gap through the two lines of the German wire was proved to exist, and two officers and a N.C.O. had actually passed through the gap on to the German parapet. In consequence of this it was determined to attempt a surprise by passing through the gap without attempting to widen it. As a precaution a bangalore torpedoe party went a short distance ahead to destroy hostile wire if necessary.

3. The raiding party left our trenches in accordance with the plan laid down. The bangalore party followed by about 12 of the raiding party actually passed through the gap in the first line of the German wire. Whilst going through the wire a hostile patrol (about 3 or 4 men) was reported to the North, but disappeared in the darkness. About the same time footsteps of a large number of men were heard in the German trench. These were believed to be, either a relief in progress, or else a working party. Up to this time the raid was apparently unperceived.

4. After passing through the gap in the first line of wire, the gap in the second ~~in the second~~ line could not at once be located; it was either just missed, or probably been closed by two knife rests which were observed and which had certainly not been there when the previous ~~was~~ reconaissance was m ade. Without delay the officer in charge of the wire destroying party placed his torpedoe through the wire, and ignited the fuze, the whole party lying down. The fuze detonated all right, but the torpedoe failed to explode, just blowing the wooden stopper out and giving out a lot of smoke.(the fuze had been firmly secured by wire). Almost immediately bombs were thrown from the hostile trench, and rifle shots fired.

5. Lieut.BIRD then got hold of the reserve bangalore torpedoe and placed it in position (this of course took a little time), meanwhile a strong German patrol came up from the South, between the two lines of wire entanglement, and at the same time another party of Germans, estimated at not less than thirty by an officer, came down from the North, between the second line of wire and the German parapet and opened fire. The man setting off the fuze of the second torpedoe was shot, and also wounded by splinters. Lieut.BIRD then tried to ignite the fuze, but before he could do so the torpedoe was drawn away by the enemy.
The raiding party then retired.
Casualties, one man killed, 5 wounded, and two injured (at duty).

I feel confident that Lieut.HURLE (a man of most determined character) and the other officers with him, 2/LT.MEREDITH and 2/Lt.BIRD, did all in their power for success, but that their efforts were defeated by:-

(1) The bangalore torpedoe failed to explode at a critical moment.
(2) The very good state of alertness maintained by the Germans and the large number of men, and the promptness with which they dealt with the situation.

The possibility of missing either, or both of the gaps in the German wire had been forseen, but there was not sufficient time to operate the second torpedoe after the first one had failed.

(Signed) G.A.STEVENS, Lt.-Colonel,

20/9/16. Commanding 2nd Bn.Royal Fusiliers.

208

29th Division.

86th Infantry Brigade.

2nd BATTALION

ROYAL FUSILIERS

OCTOBER 1 9 1 6

17. B.
(5 sheets)

Vol 8

CONFIDENTIAL.

WAR DIARY

of

2ND. BN. ROYAL FUSILIERS.

VOLUME 18

OCTOBER.

Instructions regarding War Diaries and Intelligence Summaries are contained in F. S. Regs., Part II. and the Staff Manual respectively. Title pages will be prepared in manuscript.

WAR DIARY
or
~~INTELLIGENCE SUMMARY.~~
(Erase heading not required.)

Army Form C. 2118.

Place	Date	Hour	Summary of Events and Information	Remarks and references to Appendices
	OCTOBER			
"B" Camp (YPRES.)	1st.		Major General Sir. Aylmer. HUNTER WESTON inspected camp	
	2.		Raining all day. Preparations for move.	
"	3.		Move cancelled. Raining hard. Corps commander	
"	3.		inspected Battalion & presented the military medal to a/CSM. A. Jaylor. 9079 & L/Cpl. F. MARSTON (12964).	
"	4.		Entrained at "Cheese Market" (POPERINGHE) at 3.30 PM. for WORMHOLDT, arriving at 7.30 P.M.	
WORMHOUDT	5.		at WORMHOLDT. Light training	
"	6		Do. Do	
"	7.	10. P.M.	Entrained at WORMHOUDT for HOPOUTRE	
DAOURS.	8.	7. PM	Arrived at AMIENS and marched to DAOURS.	
"	9.		WEATHER heavily.	
	10.	9. AM	Started for DERNANCOURT. arriving about 3.30 PM.	
DERNANCOURT	11.		Raining hard. Companies kit inspections.	
"	12.		Fine day. Short route marches.	
"	13.		Moved to MAMETZ WOOD. S.20.c 9.8.	

1976

T2134. Wt. W708-776. 500000. 4/15. Sir J. C. & S.

OCTOBER

Instructions regarding War Diaries and Intelligence Summaries are contained in F. S. Regs., Part II. and the Staff Manual respectively. Title pages will be prepared in manuscript.

WAR DIARY
or
~~INTELLIGENCE SUMMARY.~~
(Erase heading not required.)

Army Form C. 2118.

Place	Date	Hour	Summary of Events and Information	Remarks and references to Appendices
	OCTOBER			
MAMETZ WOOD	14.		Raining hard, practically no shelter for the men. New teams being trained for Lewis Gun.	
"	15.		Weather fine. 2/Lt. H. S. HURLE took over command of "W" Coy vice T/Capt H. W. PERSSE to England on Senior Officer's Course.	
"	16.		Wet: 1 officer and 100 men temporarily detached for fatigue with R.E.	
"	17		Wet: Parties on draining our camp area.	
"	18.		Weather fine. Men resting.	
"	19		Do. Do	
DELVILLE WOOD	19		Raining hard. Received sudden order to move to line of trenches in front of DELVILLE WOOD. Upon arrival found all trenches blown in and full of water, so were forced to camp out in open, in middle of Wood (S. 12 D. 3.2).	
"	20.		Battalion moved to road South of Wood (S.18 A 3.0 – S18.B.2.0.) and built a few dugouts and lean-to's.	
	21.		Rained all day.	
"	23		Relieved 1st Dublin Fus. on left sector of Bgde area with Batt: H.Q in Sunken Road S. M. 31. B. 9.4 (N. 31. b. 2.1.)	[illegible]

T2134. Wt. W708–776. 500000. 4/15. Sir J. C. & S.

Instructions regarding War Diaries and Intelligence Summaries are contained in F. S. Regs., Part II. and the Staff Manual respectively. Title pages will be prepared in manuscript.

WAR DIARY
or
~~INTELLIGENCE SUMMARY.~~
(Erase heading not required.)

Army Form C. 2118.

Place	Date	Hour	Summary of Events and Information	Remarks and references to Appendices
TRENCHES	24		quiet in the line) 2Lt. A. J. EDWARDS went sick. Casualties:- OR. 2 killed and 5. wounded. Very wet.	
"	25.		Btn HQ rather heavily shelled. OR:- 2 killed. 12 wounded. at 11.30PM relief by "1st Dubs" completed.	
SWITCH TRENCH + TRONES WOOD	26		Heavily shelled and whole Battn (except Z coy) compelled to ~~rest~~ evacuate trench & bivouac in Trones wood (S. 23. B. 9. 2) Casualties. OR - 11 killed: 2. wounded.	
BERNAFAY WOOD	27		moved to BERNAFAY WOOD & took over from 1st Essex Rgt. draft of 8. O.R.	
	28.		Raining. kit inspections & gen routine work.	
"	29		Fine. Light exercises.	
"	30		Started at 8.0 AM. to relieve 3rd Australian Batt. at our old camp at MAMETZ. Pouring with rain.	
MAMETZ.	31		marched to MARECOURT arriving at 4.0PM. Raining hard all day.	

1577 Wt. W10791/1773 500,000 1/15 D. D. & L. A.D.S.S./Forms/C. 2118.

Instructions regarding War Diaries and Intelligence Summaries are contained in F. S. Regs., Part II. and the Staff Manual respectively. Title pages will be prepared in manuscript.

WAR DIARY
or
INTELLIGENCE SUMMARY.
(Erase heading not required.)

Army Form C. 2118.

Place	Date	Hour	Summary of Events and Information	Remarks and references to Appendices
	OCTOBER			
"B" CAMP	1		Major General SIR AYLMER HUNTER-WESTON inspected Camp.	
	2		Raining hard all day. Preparations for move.	
	3		Move cancelled. Raining hard. Corps Commander inspected Battalion and presented the Military [illegible] A/CSM A TAYLOR and L/Cpl F MARSTON.	
	4		Entrained at "Cheese Market" (POPERINGHE) at 3.30 [illegible] WORMHOUDT arriving at 7.30 PM.	
WORMHOUDT	5		At WORMHOUDT. Light training	
	6		do	
	7	11 PM	Entrained at WORMHOUDT for HOPOUTRE	
DAOURS	8	7 PM	Arrived at AMIENS and marched to DAOURS.	
	10		Weather [illegible]	
[illegible]	11		Raining hard. Companies at inspection	
	12		Fine day. Short route marches.	
	13		Moved to MAMETZ WOOD S. 20 C 9.8.	

A5834 Wt. W4973/M687 750,000 8/16 D. D. & L. Ltd. Forms/C.2118/13.

Instructions regarding War Diaries and Intelligence Summaries are contained in F. S. Regs., Part II. and the Staff Manual respectively. Title pages will be prepared in manuscript.

Army Form C. 2118.

WAR DIARY
or
INTELLIGENCE SUMMARY.
(Erase heading not required.)

Place	Date	Hour	Summary of Events and Information	Remarks and references to Appendices
	OCTOBER			
MAMETZ WOOD	14		Raining hard practically no shelters for the men. New teams being trained for Lewis Gun.	
	15.		Weather fine 2nd Lt H S HURLE took over command of "W" Coy vice T/Capt. H W PERSSE. to England on Senior Officers Course.	
	16.		Wet. 1 officer and 100 men temporarily to RE for work.	
	17		Wet. Parties on draining our camp area	
	18.		Weather fine Men resting.	
	19		do	
DELVILLE WOOD	20		Raining hard. Received sudden order to move to line of trenches in front of DELVILLE WOOD. Upon arrival found all trenches blown in and full of water, so were forced to camp out in open in middle of Wood (S.12 D 3.2)	
	21		Battalion moved to road South of Wood (S.18 B 2.0.) and built a few dugouts and lean-tos	
	22.		Rained all day.	
	23		Relieved [illegible] Dublin Fusiliers on left sector of Bde area with Bn. HQ in Sunken Road (M.31. B.4 0.)	

A5834 Wt. W4973/M687 750,000 8/16 D. D. & L. Ltd. Forms/C.2118/13.

Instructions regarding War Diaries and Intelligence Summaries are contained in F. S. Regs., Part II. and the Staff Manual respectively. Title pages will be prepared in manuscript.

Army Form C. 2118.

WAR DIARY
or
INTELLIGENCE SUMMARY.
(Erase heading not required.)

Place	Date	Hour	Summary of Events and Information	Remarks and references to Appendices
	OCTOBER.			
TRENCHES	24		Quiet [illegible] 2nd Lt. A.J. EDWARDS went sick. Casualties – O.R. [illegible] killed 2 wounded. Very wet.	
	25		[illegible] Casualties O.R. – 2 killed 2 wounded [illegible] relieved by 1st Dublin Fusiliers.	
SWITCH TRENCH & TRONES WOOD	26		[illegible] Battalion [illegible] evacuated trenches and [illegible] in TRONES WOOD (S.23.b.[illegible]) Casualties O.R. – 1 killed 2 wounded	
BERNAFAY WOOD	27		Moved to BERNAFAY WOOD and [illegible]	
	28		Cleaning kit inspection after [illegible]	
	29		[illegible]	
	30		Started at 8.0 AM. [illegible] 3rd Australian [illegible] camp at MAMETZ. Pouring with rain.	
	31		Marched to [illegible] arriving at [illegible] p.m. [illegible] all day.	

A5834 Wt. W4973/M687 750,000 8/16 D. D. & L. Ltd. Forms/C.2118/13.

29th Division.

86th Infantry Brigade.

2nd BATTALION

ROYAL FUSILIERS.

NOVEMBER 1 9 1 6

18 B. (Gehalle?)

V319

CONFIDENTIAL

WAR·DIARY

OF

2ND· BATTLN· ROYAL·FUSILIERS

VOL·XX

To. Staff-Captain
86th Brigade

Herewith Volume 20 of War Diary of this Battalion, completed to 30th November.

P. T. W. Bond 2 Lt. a/Adjt.

for O.C. 2nd Bn. Royal Fusiliers

2-XII-16.

NOVEMBER.

Instructions regarding War Diaries and Intelligence Summaries are contained in F. S. Regs., Part II. and the Staff Manual respectively. Title pages will be prepared in manuscript.

WAR DIARY
or
~~INTELLIGENCE SUMMARY.~~
(Erase heading not required.)

Army Form C. 2118.

Place	Date	Hour	Summary of Events and Information	Remarks and references to Appendices
BRIQUETERIE CAMP(S).	21	4.PM	moved to BRIQUETERIE CAMP (NORTH) A 4 b 32. X Coy moved to FLERS LINE -	
	22.		at. " " " .	
BRIQUETERIE CAMP (N)	23		Enemy put a good many shells around camps – no damage.	
"	24		Relieved 2nd Hants. W + Y in front line - SUMMER TRENCH. ZENITH TRENCH.	
LES BOEUFS (TRENCHES)	"		WINDY TRENCH, DEWDROP, THISTLE + FLERS LINE comprising SUPPORT LINE. Casualties. OR 1 Killed, 3 wounded.	
"	25		Raining hard ALL DAY. [Enemy shelled persistently all night (24/25) but very few casualties. All trenches in front line fell in, necessitating their being evacuated except for Lewis gun detachments.	
"	26		Rained hard all day. At 7.20 AM. Two germans were captured by Cpl J. CONNELLY (13908). They were from 133rd (6 Coy) Regt, 24th Divn (Saxons). The suffering of the men in the trenches was appalling.	
"	27		Sudden FROST. Conditions so bad that no man or officer allowed to proceed anywhere alone.	[illegible]
"	27		Relieved by 1st NFLD. Relief very tedious + slow. moved into BRIQUETERIE (TENTED). Total casualties for tour of trenches. OR. 4 killed. 5.W. 1. missing. 57. Evacuated	

1577 Wt. W10791/1773 500,000 1/15 D. D. & L. A.D.S.S./Forms/C. 2118.

Instructions regarding War Diaries and Intelligence Summaries are contained in F. S. Regs., Part II. and the Staff Manual respectively. Title pages will be prepared in manuscript.

WAR DIARY

or

~~INTELLIGENCE~~ SUMMARY.

(Erase heading not required.)

Army Form C. 2118.

Place	Date	Hour	Summary of Events and Information	Remarks and references to Appendices
NOVEMBER.				
BRIQUETERIE (TENTED)	28	2.PM	Moved off for MANSEL CAMP XII. Men very much exhausted.	
MANSEL CAMP. XII.	29		Drying clothes.	
	30		W Coy Relieved Coy of 2nd Hants in FLERS LINE. Rest of Battalion in camp.	

[illegible] Lt Col.
Cmdg 2nd Roy Fus.

1577 Wt. W10791/1773 500,000 1/15 D. D. & L. A.D.S.S./Forms/C. 2118.

Instructions regarding War Diaries and Intelligence Summaries are contained in F. S. Regs., Part II. and the Staff Manual respectively. Title pages will be prepared in manuscript.

WAR DIARY
or
INTELLIGENCE SUMMARY.
(Erase heading not required.)

Army Form C. 2118.

Place	Date	Hour	Summary of Events and Information	Remarks and references to Appendices
	NOVEMBER			
CORBIE	1.		Weather fine. A Conference of Commanding Officers at B.H.Q.	
	2.		Weather fine. Parades as usual	
	3.		" " All companies on Ceremonial Drill	
	4.		" " Bn supplied a guard of honour for H.R.H. DUKE OF CONNAUGHT when he inspected the 1st R[illegible]. The guard was [illegible] complimented by Maj. Gen. H. de B. de Lisle D.S.O.	
	5		Usual Parades	
	6		[illegible] for B.C. [illegible]	
			[illegible]	
	7.		Ceremonial Parades, [illegible]	
			[illegible] Band [illegible]	
			[illegible] Grenadier Guards (Band [illegible])	
			[illegible] to the C.O. of the Royal [illegible]	
			[illegible] the Battalion.	

A5834 Wt. W4973/M687 750,000 8/16 D. D. & L. Ltd. Forms/C.2118/13.

Instructions regarding War Diaries and Intelligence Summaries are contained in F. S. Regs., Part II. and the Staff Manual respectively. Title pages will be prepared in manuscript.

WAR DIARY
or
INTELLIGENCE SUMMARY.
(Erase heading not required.)

Army Form C. 2118.

Place	Date	Hour	Summary of Events and Information	Remarks and references to Appendices
	NOVEMBER			
CORBIE	9.	10.00	Men were in fighting order and looked uncommonly fine. The G.O.C. complimented the C.O. on the smartness of his men particularly upon their "SNAP".	
"	10.		Placed 2 Lewis guns in Tower of church (CORBIE) as anti-aircraft guns.	
	11		No parades. Lt F. G. HAMILTON (Transport Officer) sent to Div Traffic Control	
	12		Church Parades	
	13		Usual Parades. Rev C. MAYNE (Chaplain) transferred to 33rd Div	
	14		— do —	
	15		G.O.C. inspected Transport.	
	16	Noon	Left CORBIE and arrived at MÉAULTE at 5.15 P.M.	
MÉAULTE	17		Very cold	
	18.		Left MEAULTE and arrived at BRIQUETERIE CAMP (TENTED) SOUTH at 12.20. A.7.b.2.9. Rained hard all day.	
BRIQUETERIE	19		W+Y Coy moved to huts at CARNOY CAMP. Bn attached to 8th Bde	
	20		Weather fine and very cold	

A5834 Wt. W4973/M687 750,000 8/16 D. D. & L. Ltd. Forms/C.2118/13.

NOVEMBER.

Instructions regarding War Diaries and Intelligence Summaries are contained in F. S. Regs., Part II. and the Staff Manual respectively. Title pages will be prepared in manuscript.

WAR DIARY
or
~~INTELLIGENCE SUMMARY.~~
(Erase heading not required.)

Army Form C. 2118.

Place	Date	Hour	Summary of Events and Information	Remarks and references to Appendices
CORBIE	1st		Weather fine. A conference of Commanding Officers at B.H.Q.	
"	2nd		" . Parades as usual.	
"	3		" . All Companies on ceremonial drill.	
"	4		" . We supplied a guard of honour for H.R.H. Duke of Connaught, when he inspected the 1st Royal Dublin Fusiliers. Guard was highly complimented by Major Gen. H. de B. de Lisle. C.B. D.S.O.	
"	5		Usual Parades.	
"	6		" . Fatigue party of 100 for A.S.C. Enemy aeroplane bombed CORBIE, but caused no damage.	
"	7		Ceremonial parades.	
"	8		" " . Band of Division used for route march. The Colonel of 2nd DRAGOONS (Royal Scots GREYS) complimented the C.O. of 2nd Royal Fusiliers on the very smart + fine appearance of his Battalion.	
"	9		Major Gen. H. de B. de Lisle: CB. D.S.O. inspected the Battalion	2001

1577 Wt. W10791/1773 500,000 1/15 D. D. & L. A.D.S.S./Forms/C. 2118.

NOVEMBER

Instructions regarding War Diaries and Intelligence Summaries are contained in F. S. Regs., Part II. and the Staff Manual respectively. Title pages will be prepared in manuscript.

WAR DIARY
or
INTELLIGENCE SUMMARY.
(Erase heading not required.)

Army Form C. 2118.

Place	Date	Hour	Summary of Events and Information	Remarks and references to Appendices
NOVEMBER.				
CORBIE	9	1000.	men were in fighting order and looked uncommonly fine. The G.O.C complimented the C.O. on the smartness of his men particularly upon their "SNAP".	
"	10.		Placed two Lewis guns in Tower of CORBIE CHURCH as anti-AIRCRAFT guns.	
"	11		no parades. 2/Lt F.G. HAMILTON (Transport O.) sent to Divn. Traffic control.	
"	12		Church parades	
"	13		Usual parades. Rev. Cyril Mayne (Chaplain) transferred to 33rd Divn.	
"	14		" " .	
"	15.		G.O.C. inspected Transport.	
"	16	NOON	Left CORBIE and arrived at MÉAULTE at 5.15. PM.	
MÉAULTE	17		Very cold.	
"	18.	0900	Left MÉAULTE and arrived at BRIQUETERIE CAMP (TENTED) S[illegible] of 1250 A4.62.8. Rained hard all day.	
BRIQUETERIE	19		W & Y Coys moved to huts at CARNOY CAMP. Battn attached to 8[illegible] Bde	
"	20		Weather fine and very cold. ENEMY artillery normal.	

1577 Wt. W10791/1773 500,000 1/15 D. D. & L. A.D.S.S./Forms/C. 2118.

Instructions regarding War Diaries and Intelligence Summaries are contained in F. S. Regs., Part II. and the Staff Manual respectively. Title pages will be prepared in manuscript.

WAR DIARY
or
INTELLIGENCE SUMMARY.
(Erase heading not required.)

Army Form C. 2118.

Place	Date	Hour	Summary of Events and Information	Remarks and references to Appendices
	NOVEMBER			
BRIQUETERIE (CAMP)(S)	21	4 PM	Moved to BRIQUETERIE CAMP (NORTH) A 4 & 32. X Coy moved to FLERS LINE	
	22		at ——— do ———	
BRIQUETERIE (CAMP) N	23		Enemy put a good many shells around camps – no damage.	
	24		Relieved 2nd Hants. W & Y in front line – SUMMER TRENCH, ZENITH TRENCH, WINDY TRENCH, DEWDROP, THISTLE, and FLERS LINE comprising SUPPORT LINE	
LE BOEUFS (TRENCHES)	25		Casualties OR 1 killed, 3 wounded. Raining hard all day. Enemy shelled persistently all night (24/25) but very few casualties. All trenches in front line fell in necessitating their being evacuated except for [illegible] from detachments	
	26		Raining hard all day. At 7.20 AM two Germans were captured by Cpl T CONNELLY (13988). They were from 133rd (6 Coy) Reg 24th [illegible] (Saxons). The suffering of the men in the trenches was appalling.	
	27		Sudden FROST. Conditions so bad that no man or officer allowed to proceed anywhere alone. Relieved by 1st NFLD. Relief very tedious & slow. Moved into BRIQUETERIE (TENTED). Total casualties for tour of trenches OR 1 killed 5 wounded 1 missing, 57 evacuated	

Army Form C. 2118.

WAR DIARY
or
INTELLIGENCE SUMMARY.
(Erase heading not required.)

Instructions regarding War Diaries and Intelligence Summaries are contained in F. S. Regs., Part II. and the Staff Manual respectively. Title pages will be prepared in manuscript.

Place	Date	Hour	Summary of Events and Information	Remarks and references to Appendices
	NOVEMBER			
BRIQUETERIE (TENTED)	28	2 PM	Moved off for MANSEL CAMP XII Men very much exhausted.	
MANSEL CAMP XII	29		Drying Clothes "W" Coy relieved Coy of 2nd Hants in FLERS LINE. Rest of Battalion in Camp.	

A5834 Wt. W4973/M687 750,000 8/16 D. D. & L. Ltd. Forms/C.2118/13.

29th Division.

86th Infantry Brigade.

2nd BATTALION

ROYAL FUSILIERS

DECEMBER 1 9 1 6

CONFIDENTIAL 19:B. (12 sheets)

WAR DIARY

— OF —

Vol 10

2nd BATTLN. ROYAL FUSILIERS

FROM 1st DEC. 1916 TO 31st DEC 1916

CONFIDENTIAL

Instructions regarding War Diaries and Intelligence Summaries are contained in F. S. Regs., Part II. and the Staff Manual respectively. Title pages will be prepared in manuscript.

WAR DIARY for DECEMBER
or
~~INTELLIGENCE SUMMARY.~~
(*Erase heading not required.*)

Army Form C. 2118.

Place	Date	Hour	Summary of Events and Information	Remarks and references to Appendices
BRIQUETERIE CAMP.	1st		Bn. moved to Briqueterie camp (tented). "Y" continuing to Flers Line. Raining.	
"	2		Small working party for R.E.s. Camp in very bad condition. Frost	
TRENCHES	3.		Relieved 2nd Hampshire Regt by 1945 o'clock. Line quiet. Trenches bad. Slight enemy shelling.	
"	4		Trenches drying up slightly. casualties - O.R. 1. Killed. 1. Wounded.	
"	5.			
"	6.		Div: comdr visited Bn H.Q. Casualties. O.R. 1 Killed. 1 Wounded. Relieved by 1st N.F.L.D	
BRIQUETERIE CAMP	7		at 1100 o'clock BN moved off to CARNOY WEST CAMP (No 18). Raining	
CARNOY. WEST NO 18.	8.		Raining all day. 1 OFF & 55 sent to Divn. labour BN. 12 OFFICERS and 300 men to dig strong points around LES BOEUFS.	
"	9		Raining hard.	
"	10		moved to MEAULTE. weather better. draft of 100 men waiting at Meaulte.	
MEAULTE	11		WET.	
"	12		Transport left for AILLY-SUR-SOMME at 1100. Major Goodliffe took over duties of T. Bgde Major	
AILLY-SUR-SOMME.	13		at 1145 BN moved off to entraining point (Edge Hill) train departing at 1415. arrived at Ailly @ about 2200 after detraining at HANGEST. "Y" Billeted at HANGEST.	
"	14		Cleaning up day. "Y" moved from HANGEST to BREILLY	
	15.		Training started under Bgy arrangements. "Y" moved to Ailly.	P.T.O. Bould. Lt.

A5834 Wt. W4973/M687 750,000 8/16 D. D. & L. Ltd. Forms/C.2118/13.

Instructions regarding War Diaries and Intelligence Summaries are contained in F. S. Regs., Part II. and the Staff Manual respectively. Title pages will be prepared in manuscript.

WAR DIARY for DECEMBER 1916.
~~or INTELLIGENCE SUMMARY.~~

(Erase heading not required.)

Army Form C. 2118.

Place	Date	Hour	Summary of Events and Information	Remarks and references to Appendices
AILLY-SUR-SOMME.	16		Raining hard. Redistribution of Billets.	
"	17		Weather fine. No parades.	
PICQUIGNY	18		Bn moved to Picquigny. Billets fairly good	
"	19		Very busy trying to arrange accomodation for men at Xmas. Weather [illegible]	
"	20		fine. Parades under Coy arrangements	
"	21		Raining. " " " CO. went on leave. Capt Thomson comdg	
"	22		" " " " Bn had baths.	
"	23		Weather better.	
"	24		" Church parade in Cinema Hall.	
"	25		Xmas day. Each Coy had good accomodation for all meals, viz. breakfast, dinner, tea, & supper, with concerts afterwards. Capt Thomson departed on leave. [illegible] comdg	
"	26		No parades. Sgts gave a dinner in the evening.	
"	27		Good weather. Coy parades as usual in afternoon for specialists and ROUTE march in morning to FOURDRINOY	
	28		Coy parades.	
	29		" " especially with regard to open warfare	
	30		Bn inspected in tactical exercise by Brigadier	
	31		Church parade at Cinema.	P. T. [illegible]

A5834 Wt. W4973/M687 750,000 8/16 D. D. & L. Ltd. Forms/C.2118/13.

Army Form C. 2118.

Instructions regarding War Diaries and Intelligence Summaries are contained in F. S. Regs., Part II. and the Staff Manual respectively. Title pages will be prepared in manuscript.

WAR DIARY
or
INTELLIGENCE SUMMARY.

(Erase heading not required.)

Place	Date	Hour	Summary of Events and Information	Remarks and references to Appendices
	DECEMBER			
BRIQUETERIE CAMP	1.		Bn moved to Briqueterie Camp (tented) Y Coy continuing to FLERS LINE. Raining	
"	2.		Small working party for RE' Camp in very bad condition. Frost.	
TRENCHES	3.		Relieved 2nd Hampshire Regt by 19.45 o'clock. Line quiet. Trenches bad.	
	4.		Slight enemy shelling	
	5.		Trenches drying up slightly. Casualties O.R. 1 killed 1 wounded	
	6		Divisional Commander visited Bn HQ Casualties O.R. 1 killed 1 wounded.	
BRIQUETERIE CAMP	7		Relieved by 1st NFLD.	
			at 1100 oc Bn moved off to CARNOY WEST CAMP (No 18) Raining.	
	8		Raining all day. 1 off & 58 sent to Labour Bn.	
			12 officers and 200 men to dig strong points around LEBOEUFS.	
	9		Raining hard.	
MEAULTE	10		Moved to MEAULTE. weather better. draft of 100 men waiting at MEAULTE	
	11		Wet.	
	12.		Transport left for AILLY-SUR-SOMME. at 1100 Major Goodliffe took over duties of Bde Major	
AILLY-SUR SOMME	13		at 11.45 Bn moved off to entraining point (Edgehill) Train departs at 14.15.	
	14		arrived at AILLY about 2200 after detraining at HANGEST. Y Coy billeted at HANGEST	
			Cleaning up day Y Coy moved from HANGEST to BREILY.	
	15.		Training started under Coy arrangements Y Coy moved to AILLY.	

A5834 Wt. W4973/M687 750,000 8/16 D. D & L. Ltd. Forms/C.2118/13.

Instructions regarding War Diaries and Intelligence Summaries are contained in F. S. Regs., Part II. and the Staff Manual respectively. Title pages will be prepared in manuscript.

WAR DIARY
or
INTELLIGENCE SUMMARY.
(Erase heading not required.)

Army Form C. 2118.

Place	Date	Hour	Summary of Events and Information	Remarks and references to Appendices
	DECEMBER			
AILLY-SUR-SOMME	16.		Raining hard. Re distribution of billets	
	17		Weather fine no parades.	
PICQUIGNY	18.		Bn moved to Picquigny. Billets fairly good.	
	19.		Very busy trying to arrange accommodation for men at Xmas Weather dull	
	20.		Fine. Parades under Coy arrangements.	
	21		Raining —— do —— C.O went on leave Capt [illegible]	
	22		" Bn had baths.	
	23		Weather better. Coy parades.	
	24		" " Church Parades in Cinema Hall	
	25		Xmas Day Each Coy had good accommodation for all meals viz: Breakfast, dinner, tea and supper, with concerts afterwards, Capt S Thomson departed on leave Lt Bunell took over command.	
	26		No Parades Sgts gave a dinner in the evening	
	27		Good Weather Coy parades renewed in afternoon for specialists and Route march in morning, to FOURDRINOY	
	28		Coy Parades.	
	29		—— do —— especially with regard to open warfare	
	30		Bn instructed in tactical exercise by Brigadier	
	31		Church parade at Cinema	

A5834 Wt. W4973/M687 750,000 8/16 D. D. & L. Ltd. Forms/C.2118/13.

8a/79

20.B. (6thlndn)

CONFIDENTIAL

Vol XI

WAR DIARY

2ND BN ROYAL FUSILIERS

No 23

Instructions regarding War Diaries and Intelligence Summaries are contained in F. S. Regs., Part II. and the Staff Manual respectively. Title pages will be prepared in manuscript.

WAR DIARY
or
~~INTELLIGENCE~~ SUMMARY.
(*Erase heading not required.*)

Army Form C. 2118.

(1)

Place	Date	Hour	JANUARY 1917 Summary of Events and Information	Remarks and references to Appendices
PICQUIGNY	1st		Brigade cross country run. Cpl PENNEL (2RF) coming in an easy first.	Beautiful Day
"	2nd		Bn under company commanders for training in open warfare	
"	3rd		Bn, including transport, marched to Brigade training ground at CAVILLON for practice of Divn Tactical scheme. (in conjunction with 1st R Dublin Fus).	
"	4th		Lt-Col. Stevens DSO returned from leave.	
"	5		Battalion practised attack at CAVILLON	
"	6		2nd RF and 1st RDF were inspected by G.O.C Divn and afterwards attacked over ground previously prepared. All transport present.	
"	7		No parades - Cinema used for service.	
"	8		Preparations for leaving PICQUIGNY. Borrowed a motor lorry from RFC.	
LEQUESNOY	9		At 1000 Bn moved off to march to LEQUESNOY arriving at 1300. Drizzling during afternoon.	
CORBIE	10		Left LEQUESNOY at 0600, arriving at ARRAINES by 0700. Train did not depart until 0910. Arrived CORBIE NOON and occupied same billets as when last in CORBIE. Transport left PICQUIGNY ~~at~~ at 0700 arriving CORBIE at 1630.	

T2134. Wt. W708–776. 500000. 4/15. Sir J. C. & S.

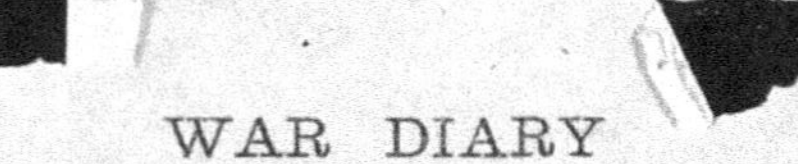

Army Form C. 2118.

(2)

Instructions regarding War Diaries and Intelligence Summaries are contained in F. S. Regs., Part II. and the Staff Manual respectively. Title pages will be prepared in manuscript.

WAR DIARY
or
~~INTELLIGENCE~~ SUMMARY.

(Erase heading not required.)

Place	Date	Hour	JANUARY - 1917. Summary of Events and Information	Remarks and references to Appendices
MÉRICOURT L'ABBÉ	11th		Arrived here at 13.30 from CORBIE, first forming up on Town Square in Quarter Column. Same billets as before. G.O.C Division passed Battalion on march.	
"	12th		C.O inspected new draft arrived just before Xmas. The following 29th Divn wire has been received and is forwarded for your information:-	
		"	To 86th Bde. 11/1/17	
		"	Begins: G.O.C was much pleased with the excellence of the march discipline both as regards troops and transport of your Brigade whom he passed on the march today AAA	
		"	This was especially the case as regards the Royal Fusiliers whose marching was fit for an Inspection Parade AAA ENDS	
			J. S. Goodliffe, Major for Brigade Major 86th Bde.	
"	13		Ceremonial parades; kit inspections etc. Very cold.	
"	14.		Church parade in cinema Hall with Band of IRISH GUARDS.	
CARNOY 6 CAMP	15		Moved off at 1000 for "CARNOY CAMP 6" ($\frac{1}{20,000}$:- A. 8. C. 4. 6. 62. C. N.W.) arriving about 1600:- Sharing same with 1st RDF.	
	16		Moved up to GUILLEMONT CAMP - RIGHT. (T. 19. C. 6. 4. 57. C. S.W)	

T2134. Wt. W708—776. 500000. 4/15. Sir J. C. & S.

Instructions regarding War Diaries and Intelligence Summaries are contained in F. S. Regs., Part II. and the Staff Manual respectively. Title pages will be prepared in manuscript.

WAR DIARY
or
~~INTELLIGENCE SUMMARY.~~
(Erase heading not required.)

Army Form C. 2118.

(3)

Place	Date	Hour	JANUARY 1917 — Summary of Events and Information	Remarks and references to Appendices
TRENCHES	17.		Relieved 1st Lancs Fusiliers in trenches - Right Bn of Right Bde Group - with Bn HQ in Sunken Road leading to MORVAL from HAIE WOOD (see map). SNOW.	
"	18		Very cold - about 20° of frost at night. no communication between companies and H.Q. during day light. G.O.C. Divn visited Bn HQ. 2Lt KIRKPATRICK L.G. joined.	
CARNOY CAMP (NO 6)	19		Relieved by 2nd HANTS by 22.15 oclock. Again intense frost. Cas: O.R. 1 killed. 1 wounded.	
"	20		Weather unchanged. Resting in camp.	
"	21		" " " " Bn commanders conference at 88th Bde H.Q.	
GUILLEMONT R.	22		All in Guillemont Camp by 1630. Weather even colder than usual.	
TRENCHES	23		Same front as before and relieved the Lancs by 21.15. Bitterly Cold.	
"	24		Very quiet in line. Carrying "duck boards" to front line the only possible work - ground too hard for digging. Weather the same.	
CARNOY CAMP (NO 6)	25		Relieved by HANTS by 22.30. Weather very cold. CASUALTIES OR. 1. Wounded: 1. T. feet	
	26		Very strong bitter wind. MEN resting in camp. Inspection of ARMS ETC.	
"	27		" " "	
GUILLEMONT R.	28		Men in G camp by 1730. 16th MIDDLESEX having delayed in camp one hour past time.	
TRENCHES	29		SAME LINE as before (renamed "MORVAL SECTOR" instead of R. Bd. Group) relieved the	

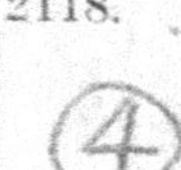

WAR DIARY
or
~~INTELLIGENCE SUMMARY.~~
(*~~Erase heading not required.~~*)

Instructions regarding War Diaries and Intelligence Summaries are contained in F. S. Regs., Part II. and the Staff Manual respectively. Title pages will be prepared in manuscript.

Army Form C. 2118.

(4)

Place	Date	Hour	Summary of Events and Information JANUARY. 1917.	Remarks and references to Appendices
(continued) TRENCHES	29th		1st Lancs by 21.00 in spite of the fact that telephone communications had not been re-established since our last tour of the line. Cold & snow.	
"	30th		Exceptionally quiet. Garrisons in front line slightly reduced so as to increase carrying parties at night.	
CARNOY CAMP (NO 6)	31st		Relieved by 2nd HANTS by 2045. No casualties. Bright moon during relief.	

[illegible] Lieut: Col:
Cmdg: 2nd Roy: Fus:
31/1/17

T2134. Wt. W708–776. 500000. 4/15. Sir J. C. & S.

CONFIDENTIAL

WAR DIARY

2ND BN ROYAL FUSILIERS

No. 24.

FEBY 1917

WAR DIARY
~~or~~
~~INTELLIGENCE SUMMARY.~~

(*Erase heading not required.*)

Instructions regarding War Diaries and Intelligence Summaries are contained in F. S. Regs., Part II. and the Staff Manual respectively. Title pages will be prepared in manuscript.

Army Form C. 2118.

Place	Date	Hour	Summary of Events and Information	Remarks and references to Appendices
			FEBRUARY 1917.	
CARNOY	1st		Companies under Company Commanders. Drums played for first time at Retreat. Slight thaw during the morning.	F.L.T.
"	2nd		War Diary (Vol 23) to 86th Brigade. 2/Lieut. Kirkpatrick left to attend L.G. course at XIVth Corps School – Meaulte.	F.L.T.
"	3rd		Bn. left Carnoy for Guillemont Camp, arriving at about 4.30 p.m. Major Genl. De Lisle left for England. Brig. Genl. Williams took command of Division & Lieut. Col. Beckwith took command of 86th Brigade. (A 5 [illegible])	F.L.T.
GUILLEMONT.	4th		Bn. left Guillemont for line (MORVAL SECTOR) Weather cold. (B 1)	F.L.T.
"	5th		Very Quiet. Cold.	F.L.T.
"	6th		Bn. returned to Carnoy – relieved by 1st Lancs. Fus. CO. attended demonstration attack by French Troops. Cpl. Pepper, L/Cpl. Mepham a/Cpl. Eason left for England. (for commissions.)	F.L.T.
CARNOY	7th		Companies under Company arrangements. Cold	F.L.T.
"	8th		Bn. moved from Carnoy Camp to La Neuville (near Corbie) by Lorries. First Lorry left Carnoy at 11.45 A.M. 'W' & 'H.Q.' Companies arrived at La Neuville at 3.15 p.m. Convoy arrived 4 p.m. Billets:– Officers – Indifferent. Men – Good.	

Instructions regarding War Diaries and Intelligence Summaries are contained in F. S. Regs., Part II. and the Staff Manual respectively. Title pages will be prepared in manuscript.

WAR DIARY

~~or~~

~~INTELLIGENCE SUMMARY.~~

(Erase heading not required.)

Army Form C. 2118.

Place	Date	Hour	Summary of Events and Information	Remarks and references to Appendices
			FEBRUARY 1917.	
Contd.				
CARNOY.	8th	-	2/LIEUTS. E.T. Allen (posted to 'X' Coy.) & A.E. Morris (posted to 'Z' Coy.) joined the Battalion.	H.T.
			2/LIEUTS. Bently & Kirkpatrick rejoined from courses.	
LE NEUVILLE	9th		Company Kit inspections. Weather cold.	H.T.
"	10th		Companies under Company arrangements for training. Major Goodliffe rejoined from Brigade Staff (86th) Capt. Hurle rejoined from course. (Flexicourt.) Lt. Col. Beckwith inspected mens' billets at mid-day. Cold. (A.G. sent.)	H.T.
"	11th		Church Services as usual. Cold & frosty.	H.T.
"	12th		Specialists' classes. Cold.	H.T.
"	13th		Commdg. Officers' Parade:- 9.15 AM. Route March – Corbie & along road to Meaulte to fork road 1½ miles out of Corbie. Practice attack (open warfare.) Drums attended for first time. Bn. arrived back to billets at 12.45pm. Weather:- Bright. Slightly warmer.	H.T.
"	14th		Companies under company arrangements. Major Goodliffe left to take over duties as Brigade Major 86th Brigade. Weather:- Frost, Bright.	H.T.
"	15th		Commdg. Officer's Parade:- 9.15 AM. Bn. marched out 1 mile on the Querrieu Road & practiced Attack. Arrived back to billets at 1 p.m. Letter from of the Hqrs. C.1.	H.T.

T2134. Wt. W708–776. 500000. 4/15. Sir J. C. & S.

Instructions regarding War Diaries and Intelligence Summaries are contained in F. S. Regs., Part II. and the Staff Manual respectively. Title pages will be prepared in manuscript.

WAR DIARY
~~or~~
~~INTELLIGENCE~~ ~~SUMMARY.~~
(Erase heading not required.)

Army Form C. 2118.

Place	Date	Hour	FEBRUARY 1917. Summary of Events and Information	Remarks and references to Appendices
LA NEUVILLE	16th		Companies under Company arrangements. Cold early. Thaw midday.	H.J.
	17th		86th Brigade practice attack. Parade 8.45 A.M. Zero 10.30. Arrived back at billets at 12.45 P.M. Thaw, dull & misty.	H.J.
	18th		Bn. moved to Meaulte. Parade 12 noon. Marched to eastern boundary of Mericourt L'abbe & had dinners. Continued via Treux & Ville to Meaulte. Arrived 5 p.m. Very heavy marching. Billets:- Good. Weather:- Dull.	H.J.
Meaulte.	19th		Bn. marched to Combles by companies. First Company left at 2 p.m. (HQ. W.X.Y.Z.) route:- Mametz, Montauban, Guillemont. Arrived at 6.0 p.m. No billets on arrival. HQrs. 'Y' & 'Z' Companies at Combles Trench. 'W' & 'X' at Haie Wood. All in at 9.0 p.m. QM. Stores at Bronfay Camp No 1. (15a) The Bn. under G.O.C. 50th Brigade. Rain.	H.J.
Combles.	20th		88th Brigade took over from 50th Brigade at noon. Rain.	H.J.
Combles.	21st		Bn. moved to Left subsector Right Brigade. (Sailly sector.) Relieved 1st Border Regt. Companies left Combles at 5 p.m. at 10 minutes intervals. Arrived at the Hebule (Bn. HQrs.) at 6.0 p.m. Guides met at Hebule. Relief complete at 11.0 p.m. Bn. on right Inniskill. Fus. Bn. on Left 1st R. Dub. Fus. Bn. in support 1st Border Regt. Trenches:- 450 yds. Condition:- Very wet. Not revetted or duck boarded. U14 d 95.70 & U14 b 6.6	B.2 C.T. ~~B.1~~

T2134. Wt. W708–776. 500000. 4/15. Sir J. C. & S.

Instructions regarding War Diaries and Intelligence Summaries are contained in F. S. Regs., Part II. and the Staff Manual respectively. Title pages will be prepared in manuscript.

WAR DIARY
~~or~~
~~INTELLIGENCE SUMMARY~~.
(Erase heading not required.)

Army Form C. 2118.

Place	Date	Hour	Summary of Events and Information	Remarks and references to Appendices
			FEBRUARY. 1917	
Continued.	21st		Nature:- FRONTLINE held by posts. Support:- Cane Alley. continuous trench. Reserve: Strong Point. 'W&X' Companies in Front Line. 'Y' Support 'Z' Reserve. Batteries supporting:- 18pdr. - A92. C92. B.92. Howitzer - D92. R.HA - U. Enemy put up a barrage near CHATEAU Wood at 6.pm. Lt. Marsden joined the Bn. posted to 'W' Coy. 2/Lieut Allen left to join Tunnelling Company with 25 men. (Temporarily.) Weather - Bright.	[illegible]
SAILLY. SECTOR.	22nd		Enemy Artillery very active from 3.pm to 6pm. on CANE ALLEY. & CHATEAU WOOD. 2/Lieut BIRD ~~wounded~~ & 3 men wounded. Weather very misty - cleared at midday followed by rain.	[illegible]
"	23rd		Genl. Williams called at Bn. H.Qrs. (Hebules) Enemy Artillery very active at 6.15pm to 6.30pm on Chateau Wood - no damage. Relieved by 2nd Hants Regt. Relief complete at 11.30pm. (Telephone not working) Bn. moved to Fregicourt, less 'Z' Coy to Mouchoir Copse. Dug outs very crowded. Weather dull.	[illegible]
FREGICOURT.	24		Bn. moved to BRONFAY CAMP. No.1 (15A) Companies moved off at 10 minute intervals starting at 10.30Am. marched to TRONES WOOD. Train to PLATEAU 1.0pm. Arrived at Camp 2.15pm. Huts very comfortable. Weather - dull & colder.	[illegible]

Instructions regarding War Diaries and Intelligence Summaries are contained in F. S. Regs., Part II. and the Staff Manual respectively. Title pages will be prepared in manuscript.

WAR DIARY

~~or~~

~~INTELLIGENCE SUMMARY.~~

(Erase heading not required.)

Army Form C. 2118.

Place	Date	Hour	Summary of Events and Information	Remarks and references to Appendices
			FEBRUARY 1917.	
BRONFAY	25th		Major Genl. de Lisle & Brig. Genl. Williams called at 1 o pm. Bn. practiced attack at 3.pm. & were cinematographed during the practice. Trial of new message rocket. 2/Lieut. Reade & 2 men carried out a special Patrol in No man's Land opposite the SAILLY SECTOR to ascertain the state of the ground. Point of departure: about junction of U14/9 & U8/1. Average time 43 yds. paces minute. 2/LIEUT. Bird rejoined from No 34 C.C.S. Weather Bright	H.G.
"	26th		Bn. moved to COMBLES. first company at 1pm. W. X & H.Q. by Train to TRONES WOOD. arrived COMBLES at 4.15pm. 'H.Q.' W & X. at COMBLES. Y & Z at HALLEWOOD. Heavy Artillery fire at 6pm. till 6.15pm. & 10pm. till 10.15pm. on SAILLY SECTOR. Fine	H.G.
COMBLES.	27th		Operation Orders No1. by Lt. Col. G.A. Stevens issued to Coy. Comdrs. (D.1.) D.2. & D.3.) Bn. left Combles for Sailly Sector. Order. 'X' 'W' 'Y' 'Z'. Leading Company passed Hebule at 8.pm. Companies moved forward to their battle positions. Bn. H.Q. moved forward from the Hebule at midnight to U14.8. when the Bn. came under G.O.C. Left Brigade Group. Weather fine.	B2 & 3. H.G.
SAILLY Sector Front Line	28th		Bn. attacked PALZ Trench at 5.30AM. See Report on Operations (D.4. & D.5.) (March) Weather – fine. Message from Corps Commander. E.1. (Contd.)	H.G.

T2134. Wt. W708–776. 500000. 4/15. Sir J. C. & S.

Instructions regarding War Diaries and Intelligence Summaries are contained in F. S. Regs., Part II. and the Staff Manual respectively. Title pages will be prepared in manuscript.

WAR DIARY

~~or~~

~~INTELLIGENCE SUMMARY.~~

(Erase heading not required.)

Army Form C. 2118.

Place	Date	Hour	Summary of Events and Information	Remarks and references to Appendices
			FEBRUARY 1917.	
SAILLY SECTOR FRONT LINE	28th		Officers in action:- Bn. Hd. Qrs. Lt. Col. G.A. Stevens, Lt. P.T.O. Boult, 2/Lt. Reade. "In the advance":- W. Coy. Capt. Hurle, Lts. Pape & Marsden, X Coy. Capt. Dearden, 2/Lts. Banks & Daniel Y. Coy. 2/Lts. Bently & Sutcliffe. 'Z' Coy. Lt. Wyndham, 2/Lts. Lewis, Kirkpatrick. Brigade Hd. Qrs. (Hebule) Capts. S. Thomson & Baldwin, 2/Lieuts. J. Stapleton Fleming & F.L. Thomerson. M.O. Capt. C. Russell.	

G. A. Stevens Lieut. Col.
Cmdg. 2nd Roy. Fus.

A5834 Wt W4973/M687 750,000 8/16 D. D. & L. Ltd. Forms/C.2118/13

2nd Bn. Royal Fusiliers (1)

Copy Report on Operations of 28th Feby. 1st March 1917.

28th Feb.

1. All preparations were satisfactorily completed by the night of the 27/28th Feb. dumps formed, direction tapes laid etc.

The Battn. commenced taking up its assembly position at 9 p.m. on the 27th Feb. This worked easily and no difficulties were experienced owing to all leaders being thoroughly acquainted with the ground.

The night passed quietly with rather less than the usual amount of shelling on the enemy's part.
During the night we cleared wire from our own front.

2. A few minutes before Zero the men got ready & in some places filed through the prepared gaps in our own wire ready for the assault.

At Zero the barrage came on splendidly, the men advanced keeping well up to our barrage. There was no difficulty in doing this on the left but on the right direction was lost owing to the difficulties of the ground, but only slightly.

The hostile barrage came down some four minutes after Zero, it did not interfere with our advance but was very heavy on and behind our old front line.

On arrival at the German line it was found to be well covered with thick concertina wire & some knife rests on the right. There were many good gaps through the wire & no difficulty was experienced in getting through.

3. On entering the German trench practically no resistance was encountered, the enemy surrendering readily, a good number being caught in the dugouts.

The right of the right Co. slightly lost direction and entered the German trench at [illegible] (A), the left of the Company entered the support line at the junction point B.

This Company tried to move further up to the right to gain touch with the company on the right but were prevented by continuous bombing from the right from BAYREUTH Tr. After a good deal of fighting [illegible] the battalion reached its [illegible] with great difficulty a block at the junction of [illegible] BAYREUTH trench. The [illegible] difficult owing to the trench being very wide and much commanded by German snipers who could not be located [illegible] also [illegible] machine guns.

On getting to the junction point B. parties immediately tried to [illegible] work on the strong point on either side of the road.

On the left of the road was a trench about 10 feet [illegible] [illegible] further than the road, the left of the

[illegible]

[illegible]

[illegible]

[illegible]

caught in the German line going back were killed. In one place some prisoners were killed by German machine Gun fire.
It was noticed that the machine Guns opened fire from above of the trench within a few minutes of Zero.

For many hours the Germans kept up a steady & heavy bombardment of our old front line.
About 3/4 of an hour after entering their trench the Germans bombarded PALZ Tr. about the area of the sunken road (B.)
There was a fairly strong bombing attack from BAYREUTH trench (A) which was beaten off.

6. About 3/4 of an hour after Zero telephonic Communication was opened with the left company & soon after with the right Coy.
The artillery also put out a line.
It is noteworthy that telephonic ~~[illegible]~~ Communication was maintained with the front line from Bn. H.Q. almost the whole time during the two days.

During the work of consolidation it

was found a good deal of material had
been lost in the mud and going over.
The front line was short of bombs.
Every effort was made to get things
across but great difficulty was experienced
in this owing to the shelling which destroyed
some of the dumps & the persistent sniping
from the German lines.
Dumps of German bombs were collected
in the new front line.
During the morning carrying parties were
organised & supplies of bombs etc. sent
forward. A great many of these were collected
from the old front line, support &
Strong Points.
Pigeons were released at 7 AM.
One message pocket was fixed the
remainder were lost through casualties.
All S.O.S. rockets were lost going over
but were afterwards made up.

At 10.15 AM. situation was: All
objectives held, short of bombs & material.
Our old front line & Kelly Salient
was being heavily bombarded & also part
of new front line.
We were losing a number of casualties
from snipers who commanded

the ~~Ground~~ Trench from high ground.
All Telephonic Communication to back areas broken down.
Power buzzers not working.
Wireless working.
I ordered slow barrage on German trenches.

7. At noon hostile shelling increased & became intense at 1.30 The artillery ordered to stand by for a counter attack. At 1.40 Germans commenced strong bombing attack on right from BAYREUTH & was reported to be advancing, barrage called for by wireless & S.O.S. rockets fired.

The Germans made a most determined bombing attack from BAYREUTH, at first they were held off but owing to their snipers shooting down our bombers continuously & our being unable to locate the German snipers to keep down their fire, they gradually beat our [illegible] back to beyond the bomb dump.

The Germans then through their supply

[illegible] gradually [illegible] branch of PALZ trench to a block which had been established at D.

The fighting was stubborn & many men distinguished themselves in trying to keep the enemy back.

At 2.15 we were back at D & the hostile counter attack was stopped.

We tried to counter attack again but made very little progress.

The fighting went on until about 3.30 All the time every endeavour was made to get bombs up to the front line, all H.Q. were employed except one telephonist.

Up to 9.25 pm. there were several bombing attacks but all were beaten off.

During the night the line was reorganized the remainder of the men at about D were organised into one Company under Capt. DEARDEN less about 50 men & three Lewis guns & an officer who were placed in our old front line.

During the night the Monmouths dug a trench from point E to our front line

near U14. 8.
The front D.E. was strongly wired & the trench D.E. was improved.

The question of a further counter attack was considered but this was not undertaken owing to a shortage of bombs & the difficulty of supply.
It was felt that POTSDAM trench was most important, that if an attack was undertaken supplies might run short & there might be failure to stave off a counter attack & so all advantage would be lost.

Feb. 1st

Considerable shelling all day increasing in intensity during the afternoon & evening.
Though further attacks were expected none developed until 10 p.m. when another bombing attack was made but was driven off.

The assistance rendered by the artillery was very great they were remarkably quick in bringing down their barrage

(10)

On the afternoon of the 20th a request was made to alter the barrage line & this seemed to be done in an extraordinary short time.

Signed. G. A. Stevens Lieut Col.
Comdg. 2nd Roy. Ir.

3/3/17

22.B.
(17 sheets)

N.L/13

MARCH

CONFIDENTIAL

WAR
DIARY
of
2nd Bn Royal
FUSILIERS.

VOL. 25.

Instructions regarding War Diaries and Intelligence Summaries are contained in F. S. Regs., Part II. and the Staff Manual respectively. Title pages will be prepared in manuscript.

WAR DIARY
or
INTELLIGENCE SUMMARY.
(Erase heading not required.)

Army Form C. 2118.

Place	Date	Hour	Summary of Events and Information MARCH. 1917	Remarks and references to Appendices
FRONTLINE SAILLY SECTOR	1st		See Report on Operations D4. & D5. & D6. Lt. Col. Beckwith took over command of Left Brigade Group from Brig. Genl. Williams. Casualties Appendix D7.	
			Bn. Relieved by Newfoundland Regt. Relief complete 5.30 AM. (2/3/17) Weather – Bright. Bn. moved to Fregicourt – less 'X', 'Z' & HQrs. to Monchoir Copse.	[illegible]
[illegible]COURT	2nd		Bn. left Fregicourt & marched to Combles 10 AM. Waited until 5 pm. & proceeded to Bronfay Camp by Lorry. Arrived at Bronfay 6.0 pm. Weather – Cold, Bright.	[illegible]
BRONFAY	3rd		Bn. moved to Ville by train. Left 3.30 pm. Arrived Ville at 6.0 pm. Billets good. Weather – Bright but very cold.	[illegible]
Ville	4th		Church services. 2/Lieut. Morris returned from mining course. Cold.	[illegible]
"	5th		Companies under Company Commanders' arrangements for reorganization. Brig. Genl. Williams left for England (Leave). Lieut. Col. G.A. Stevens took over command of 86th Brigade. Capt. Dearden went to 86th Brigade. Capt. S. Thomson, took over command of the Battalion. Snow	[illegible]
"	6th		Maj. Genl. De Lisle called on CO. & interviewed officers in the attack. Practice for Corps Commander's inspection 11.45 AM. Cold & bright.	[illegible]
"	7th		Corps Commander inspected the Battalion with R.D.F. at 10 AM. Very cold.	[illegible]

T2134. Wt. W708–776. 500000. 4/15. Sir J. C. & S.

WAR DIARY

~~or~~

~~INTELLIGENCE SUMMARY.~~

(Erase heading not required.)

Army Form C. 2118.

Instructions regarding War Diaries and Intelligence Summaries are contained in F. S. Regs., Part II. and the Staff Manual respectively. Title pages will be prepared in manuscript.

Place	Date	Hour	Summary of Events and Information MARCH 1917	Remarks and references to Appendices
VILLE.	8th		Specialist Classes. Very cold.	H.J.
"	9th		ditto. 2/Lts. Edgar & Allen rejoined from Works Bn & Tunnelling Coy.	
			2/LIEUT. Bird left for England (leave) Cold – Snow.	H.J.
"	10th		Specialist Classes. Lieut. Wyndham left for Base under escort of 2/Lieut. Jackson upon instructions from G.H.Q. warm.	H.J.
"	11th		Church Parade – (Drumhead Service.) a/Brigadier (Lt. Col. G. A. Stevens) & Brigade staff attended. Presentation of Military Medals by Brigadier to: – ~~Sgt.~~ Ptes. Dewy, Tregoning, Bell, Cpl. H. Langham. (Ptes. R. Osborne & Attewell away wounded.) . Warm & Bright.	H.J.
"	12th		Specialist Classes. ditto.	H.J.
"	13th		Training as per Divisional Programme. ditto.	H.J.
"	14th		Capt. Dearden awarded D.S.O. & 2/Lieut. Reade the M.C. Rain.	H.J.
"	15th		Route March with rear guard & advance guard practice. Specialist training in the afternoon. Gen. Masse met all C.O's of the Division.	H.J.
"	16th		Company training – short route march. C.O. met G.O.C. Division to choose training ground. Bright.	H.J.

Instructions regarding War Diaries and Intelligence Summaries are contained in F. S. Regs., Part II. and the Staff Manual respectively. Title pages will be prepared in manuscript.

WAR DIARY
or
~~INTELLIGENCE SUMMARY.~~
(Erase heading not required.)

Army Form C. 2118.

Place	Date	Hour	Summary of Events and Information — MARCH 1917.	Remarks and references to Appendices
VILLE	17th		Route march with outpost duties (under Company arrangements.) Drums massed with R.D.F. played at Reveille. (St. Patrick's Day.) Fine.	H.T.
"	18th		Church Parade. Billeting party left for AIRAINES. Dull.	H.T.
"	19th		Company training. Transport left for DAOURS. Draft of 121 arrived. Class: good Trained. Bright – some rain.	H.T.
AIRAINES	20th		Move from Ville to AIRAINES by Train 10.0 A.M. from Edge Hill. Arrived AIRAINES at 2.15 p.m. Billets: Officers – Good. Men, very bad & crowded. Transport at ARGOEUVES. Draft of 106 arrived. Class – good, Trained. (no trained specialists) G.O.C. Division called at 3.0 p.m. Capt. R.F. Nation joined & took over 2nd i.C. Fine.	H.T.
"	21st		Reorganization of Companies. Practice Artillery formations. Transport arrived 5 p.m. all except chargers billeted in open. 2/Lieuts. L.C. Bonne (X) B. Light (Y) J.H. Corre (W) G.W. Mills (Z.) Fine	H.T.
"	22nd		Company training in Artillery formation. Lt. Col. G.A. Stevens returned from Brigade Sns.	H.T.
"	23rd		Company training. Bright – Cold.	H.T.
"	24th		Bn. Parade 9.15 A.M. Attack (open warfare) Y. Coy. provided advance guard. Return 2.30 p.m. 2/Lieut. Penny joined. 2/Lieut. Bird rejoined from leave. Fine	H.T.

T2134. Wt. W708–776. 500000. 4/15. Sir J. C. & S.

Army Form C. 2118.

WAR DIARY ~~or~~ ~~INTELLIGENCE SUMMARY.~~

(*Erase heading not required.*)

Instructions regarding War Diaries and Intelligence Summaries are contained in F. S. Regs., Part II. and the Staff Manual respectively. Title pages will be prepared in manuscript.

Place	Date	Hour	Summary of Events and Information	Remarks and references to Appendices
			MARCH 1917.	
AIRAINES.	25th		Church Parade 11 AM. Bn. Sports & Race Meeting 1.30 pm. See Programme. F.1. Fine.	H.T.
"	26th		Divisional exercise. Attack (open warfare) Parade 9.45 AM. Return 3.45 pm. Bright — Rain.	H.T.
	27th		Brigade practice Attack. Parade 10.30 AM. Rewards Div. Order No. 1383. (E2) Capt. R. F. Nation left for Hospital. ~~2nd~~ LIEUT. Marsden rejoined from Signalling course. Snow. Cold.	H.T.
"	28th		Company parades. Fine.	H.T.
"	29th		ditto. Rain	H.T.
"	30th		Bn. Marched from AIRAINES to Berteaucourt via Hangest, Flixecourt (Halt for dinners) St. Ouen. Parade 9.30 AM. ~~X miles~~ Arrived 3.25 pm. Nobody fell out. Rain.	H.T.
			Billets good.	H.T.
BERTEAUCOURT.	31st		Company Parades. Bright — occasional showers.	

J. A. Stevens. Lieut. Col:
Cmdg: 2nd Roy: Fus

A5834 Wt W4973/M687 750,000 8/16 D. D. & L. Ltd. Forms/C.2118/13.

5b
229

23 B.
(Arkata?)

Vol 14

CONFIDENTIAL WAR DIARY

APRIL · 1917

2ND BN

THE · ROYAL · FUSILIERS

VOL · 26

Instructions regarding War Diaries and Intelligence Summaries are contained in F. S. Regs., Part II. and the Staff Manual respectively. Title pages will be prepared in manuscript.

WAR DIARY

~~or~~

~~INTELLIGENCE SUMMARY.~~

(*Erase heading not required.*)

Army Form C. 2118.

Place	Date	Hour	Summary of Events and Information — APRIL 1917	Remarks and references to Appendices
BERTEAUCOURT	1st	—	Brigade March to GEZAINCOURT via Halloy, Canaples, Montrelet, Candas. Parade 10.10 AM. arrived 2.15 PM. Billets – bad. Weather wet.	[initials]
GEZAINCOURT	2nd	—	Brigade March – 2nd R. Fus. to Pommera via Doullens. Parade 9 AM. Arrived 12.30 pm. billets – bad. Capt. Rose rejoined from England. 2/Lieut. Morris rejoined from L.G. Course. Wet & some snow.	[initials]
POMMERA	3rd	—	Company Parades. Lieut (T/Capt) Leaning left for Hospital	[initials]
"	4th	—	do. C.O's inspection of Transport loaded. Rain.	[initials]
"	5th	—	Brigade Marched to SUS ST LEGER. Start 2.10 pm. Arrived 4.45 pm. Via Lucheux. billets: Officers bad. Men Good.	[initials]
SUS ST LEGER	6th	—	Company Parades. Genl Penney called on CO. at 9.30 AM. Showery	[initials]
"	7th	—	ditto. 2/Lt. Morris to hospital. Lieut. Marsden. 2/Lieuts. Hood, Allen, Blight, J.H. Core, B.W. Penny, left for Div! Depot Battn. Showery.	[initials]
	8th	—	Brigade March. 2nd R. Fus to Humbercamp. Start 9.15 AM. Arrived 1.15 pm. Billets good. Fine.	[initials]
HUMBERCAMP	9th	—	Company Parades. Wire cutting. Bathing. 1st day of offensive. Showery	[initials]
"	10th	—	ditto Snow! (See Appendix A.)	[initials]
"	11th	—	Move to SIMENCOURT parade 5.50 pm. arrived 10 p.m. Huts. Snow.	[initials]
SIMENCOURT	12th	—	Move to Arras Start 12.41 pm. arrived 4.15 pm. billets in Citadel. bad. Fine.	[initials]
ARRAS	13th		Move to old front line at 7.45 AM. Major Nation went to Hospital.	
Trenches	14th	.	— Harfleur Trench H3c. 10 AM. 88th Brigade Attacked. 2.40 pm. moved to CHAPEL HILL, owing to heavy counter attacks. 2/Lieut. Bird wounded.	[initials]
CHAPEL HILL	15th		Making strong Points. Casualties 1 OR. wounded. Rain.	[initials]

Instructions regarding War Diaries and Intelligence Summaries are contained in F. S. Regs., Part II. and the Staff Manual respectively. Title pages will be prepared in manuscript.

WAR DIARY

~~or~~

~~INTELLIGENCE SUMMARY.~~

(*Erase heading not required.*)

Army Form C. 2118.

Place	Date	Hour	Summary of Events and Information APRIL. 1917	Remarks and references to Appendices
CHAPEL HILL	16th		Continual Shelling 8" & 5.9" H.E. 'Z' Coy. Officers & some men buried in dugout but they were dug up out unhurt. Rain Snow.	[initials]
–	17th	14 Poze Sect	2.45pm to 5 pm & 8 pm to 8.15pm. Heavy shelling on Chapel Hill & Batteries behind.	[initials]
–	18th		Relieved 16th Middlesex in front line. 'Y' Coy. Right. 'Z' Coy. left. 'W' Coy. Support & 'X' Coy. Reserve at N6a. R.D.F. on left. S.W.B. on Right. Relief complete 12.30pm. Weather dull	[initials]
MONCHY.	19th		~~At~~ 5.0AM. one man gave himself up. (17th Bav. I.R. 1st Bn. 4th Coy.) he came from Boiry notre dame. Heavy Shelling on Monchy. Rain	[initials]
–	20th		Fairly quiet night. Shelling from 7.30 – 9.30 Am. & periodically during the day.	[initials]
–	21st		Heavily Shelled. Head Qrs. ~~by~~ cellar blown in. 1 Killed 5 wounded.	[initials]
ARRAS.	22nd		Relieved by 16th Middlesex, & went back to Caves in Arras. Rest. Fine. Lieut Col. G.A. Stevens sick.	
	23rd		* Move to Brown Line (ORANGE HILL) Lieut Hamilton rejoined ^ 9.30pm. Moved up to La Fosse Farm & were then told to relieve Worcester Regt. in Front Line Trenches Monchy. No guides. Bn. relieved Worcester Regt. Complete at 3.0AM. *29th Division took part in Attack. Major Middleton took over Command of the Bn. Fine	[initials]
	24th		Attack on Blue line. (Casualties 190.) Officers Killed:- Capt. S. Thomson, 2/Lieuts. E.B. Baucells, J. Hoskie wounded 2/Lieut. L.G. Kirkpatrick, W.L. Reade, H. Edge. (Appendices:–	[initials]
	25th		Relieved by Suffolk Regt. Bn. moved back to Arras. Fine. Bn. Moved to Bernville by bus. Major Middleton sick. Capt. Rose took over command of the Battalion.	[initials]
BERNVILLE	26th		Bn. Moved to WANQUETIN via SIMENCOURT. 2/Lieuts. C.H. Hewlett & R.J. Macrigot joined also 4 officers from St. Pol:- Lieut. Marsden, 2/Lieuts. Penny, Light, Allen. Fine	[initials]
WANQUETIN	27th		Move to Souastre. Billets good. (Huts.)	[initials]
SOUASTRE	28th		Kit inspections & reorganization. Capt. P. Wilson took over Command of Bn. Bright & Sunny.	[initials]

[signature]

A5834 Wt W4973/M687 750,000 8/16 D. D. & L. Ltd. Forms/C.2118/13.

Army Form C. 2118.

Instructions regarding War Diaries and Intelligence Summaries are contained in F. S. Regs., Part II. and the Staff Manual respectively. Title pages will be prepared in manuscript.

WAR DIARY
~~or~~
~~INTELLIGENCE SUMMARY.~~
(Erase heading not required.)

Place	Date	Hour	Summary of Events and Information	Remarks and references to Appendices
			APRIL. 1917.	
SOUASTRE	29th		Bathing Parades. Draft from [illegible] arrived (30 OR) Fine — Bright.	[illegible]
"	30		Company parades. Brigadier Genl Williams left to take over 30th Div & Brig Genl Jelf took over command of 86th Brigade. Bright	[illegible]

[illegible] Wilson Capt.
Commanding 2nd Bn. Royal Fusiliers.

3rd May. 1917.

A5834 Wt W4973/M687 750,000 8/16 D. D. & L. Ltd. Forms/C.2118/13.

Operations – 24th April 1917

Left Company

Zero 4-0 pm 3 guns were heard to fire. Our first three Companies left the front line trench (Shrapnel Trench). The support Coy (Y Coy) advanced from our old front line and took up position in Shrapnel Trench. After going about 40 yds the left Coy saw some British Infantry in the trench 150 yds in front of them. These were presumed to be the Royal Dublin Fusiliers who were on our left. The trench was strongly held and men were shoulder to shoulder. They signalled to us to change direction to the right which the left Coy did to avoid crossing this trench. On coming level with the trench the left Coy dropped into shell holes as they came under heavy machine gun fire. The men in this trench were then discovered to be Worcester Regiment. The left Coy then advanced again and saw that the right Coy was temporarily held up in front of the Wood at O8 central by machine gun fire. They thereupon changed direction half right to flank the wood and take up a line of pits on the north east edge of the wood.

Here the enemy heavy artillery shelled them very heavily. All of this shelling came from the directions of the Bois-de-Sart and Boiry-Notre-Dame. There was also machine gun fire from Pole trench and a certain amount of sniping from Tool trench. This caused a considerable number of casualties. At 4-45 pm we had very little ammunition left. We filled a few empty drums for Lewis Guns and gave orders not to fire unless a good target presented itself. At 5-0 pm patrols were sent out to the right and left to get into touch with the troops on our flanks. The patrol to the right did not return. The patrol to the left proceeded over a considerable distance but could not get into touch with any troops. At 5-30 pm owing to heavy casualties reinforcements were called for. One Officer, one sergeant and 30 men arrived shortly after. One Lewis Gun was sent out well to the right to guard the flank. At 5-40 pm the Machine Gun Officer and 3 Vickers guns arrived and 2 of these were sent out to the left flank. At 5-45 pm our heavy artillery was firing short and rockets were sent up to lengthen range. This was responded to. The only remaining Officer (2nd Lieut. Bourne) counted the remaining men and found that he had 35 men left. At 6-10 pm the position became untenable. Orders were given for all wounded to be cleared back to Shrapnel Trench. At 6-30 pm the S.O.

was sent up as the enemy appeared to be working around the flanks. No artillery support was given. At about 6-00 pm orders were given to retire. This was done with very few casualties and all wounded were brought back.

Centre Company (W Coy)

There were very few casualties going over as the men got away quickly and got out of the enemy barrage. Both Officers became casualties before reaching the objective. The Coy went round the northern side of the wood and took up the position ~~that~~ was occupied by the Left Coy. The enemy were seen in the Bois-de-Vert in large numbers but were dispersed by Lewis Gun Fire. The Officer in charge of the Left Coy took over Command.

Right Company (Z Coy)

Shortly after leaving Shrapnel Trench we were held up in front of the wood by Machine Gun fire. There were a few of the enemy in the wood. Our Lewis Guns opened fire and every man fired into the wood and immediately we charged through the wood, the enemy retiring rapidly. We then took up a position in the trench east of the wood. The enemy retired to the Bois-de-Vert. Our Lewis Guns caused considerable damage and casualties during the retirement. We consolidated the position for about 20 minutes when we came under heavy artillery fire causing many casualties during which time both Officers became casualties. Large quantities of S.A.A. Lewis Gun panniers, and bombs etc, were found in this trench having been left by other ~~people~~ British Troops

---

Many dead Germans and a lot of equipment, packs and rifles were found at our objective.

PELVES
Scale 1:10000
TRENCHES (Approximate) from AIR PHOTOS up to 20-4-17 (inclusive)
Quarry
Pelves
Rœux
La Scarpe River
(Canal)
Mount Pleasant Wood
Cemetery
Pelves Lane
Chinstrap Lane
Pelves Mill
Lone Copse
FUZE TRENCH
GRENADE TRENCH
(Sunken road)
SHELL TRENCH
RIFLE TRENCH
BOMB TR.
BAYONET
CARTRIDGE TRENCH
HAVERSACK TRENCH
TREE TR.
WOOD TRENCH
Keeling Copses
Sunken Road
B. des Aubepines
B. du Sart
Twin Copses
Arrow Head Copse
Monchy le Preux
Sword Lane
Gardens
13°20 1917

MAP No1. SCALE 1:10,000
TOP4 SECTION
29th DIV. 15.4.17.
35
36
31
32
5
6
2
7
8
12
11
17
18
13
14
WIRELESS &
POWER BUZZER
MONCHY-
LE-PREUX
B. DES
AUBEPINES
GUEMAPPE
LA BERGERE

(6202) W 11186/M1151 350,000 12/16 McA. & W., Ltd. (Est. 731) Forms/W 3091/3. Army Form W. 3091.

2A 3. (Ashkeld)

8M/5

6/29

Cover for Documents.

Nature of Enclosures.

CONFIDENTIAL.

WAR DIARY.

of

2nd BATTALION ROYAL FUSILIERS.

Notes, or Letters written.

VOLUME 27.

MAY 1917.

Instructions regarding War Diaries and Intelligence Summaries are contained in F. S. Regs., Part II. and the Staff Manual respectively. Title pages will be prepared in manuscript.

WAR DIARY
or
~~INTELLIGENCE SUMMARY.~~
(*Erase heading not required.*)

2nd R. [illegible]

Army Form C. 2118.

Place	Date	Hour	Summary of Events and Information — May. 1917	Remarks and references to Appendices
SOUASTRE	1st		Move to GOUY. Started 6.23 AM. arrived 10.0 AM. Billeted in huts. Good. Weather Fine	[illegible]
GOUY.	2nd		Move to Arras at 8.15 pm. arrived 11.30 pm.	[illegible]
ARRAS.	3rd		Removing refuse from streets & billets.	[illegible]
"	4th		do. do. do.	[illegible]
"	5th		do. do. do. (Inspection by Brigadier at 3 pm.)	
"	6th		do. do. do. Lewis Gun practice on the Race course. Weather Fine	[illegible]
"	7th		Company training (Strong Points.)	[illegible]
"	8th		Company Lectures in billets. Lecture by Capt. R. Gee on the Regiment at 3 pm. Rain.	[illegible]
"	9th		Company Training & Bathing. Fine	[illegible]
"	10th		do. Digging Strong Points from Arras-Cambrai Road to Blancourt during the night. (Casualties 3 O.Rs.) Very hot.	[illegible]
"	11th		Move to BERNVILLE. at 5.19 pm. arrived 7.30 pm. (via DAINVILLE)	[illegible]
BERNVILLE	12th		Shooting practice (range.) Kit inspection. Night operations.	[illegible]
"	13th		Church Parade 11.0 Am. Brigadier attended. Rain during evening & night.	[illegible]
"	14th		Company parades. 2/Lt. Hood to Hospital. Cooler.	[illegible]
"	15		Move to ARRAS. at 6.50 Am. arrived 9.0 AM. billets - men in cellars & officers in houses — good. Fine	[illegible]
"	16th		Company training & bathing. Clearing refuse from billets. Cold	[illegible]
"	17th		ditto Rain	[illegible]
"	18th		ditto Fine	[illegible]
"	19th		ditto Fine	[illegible]
"	20th		Took over MONCHY Defenses from S.W.B. Fine	[illegible]

A5834 Wt. W4973/M687 750,000 8/16 D. D. & L. Ltd. Forms/C.2118/13.

Instructions regarding War Diaries and Intelligence Summaries are contained in F. S. Regs., Part II. and the Staff Manual respectively. Title pages will be prepared in manuscript.

WAR DIARY ~~or~~ ~~INTELLIGENCE~~ SUMMARY.

(*Erase heading not required.*)

2nd R. Fus.

Army Form C. 2118.

Place	Date	Hour	Summary of Events and Information MAY 1917	Remarks and references to Appendices
MONCHY DEFENSES	21st	–	MONCHY shelled fairly heavily with 15cm. & 10.5cm. H.E. Fine.	
	22nd	–	Ditto.	
–	23rd	–	Relieved 16th Middlesex in the front line. Dispositions:– X Coy. Right & Z Coy. Left in HILL Tr. W Coy. Support in DALE Tr. Y Coy. Reserve in SHRAPNEL Tr.	
–	24th	–	Dug saps out 75x in front of HILL Tr. & moved wire entanglement out in front of these. Saps at:– O2c 9.6 & O2d 1.3. ~~[illegible]~~	
–	26th	–	Improved trenches & saps. Major [illegible] [illegible]	
–	27th	–	2/Lieuts. Rumball & Spearey joined the Bn. Quiet. Formed [illegible] in Hill Tr. at O2c 98.80, O2c 90.70 & also ~~[illegible]~~ in the two saps.	
–	28th	–	Relieved by 16th Middlesex Regt. & 1st Lancs. Fus. & took over MONCHY Defences. [illegible] [illegible] rejoined from L.G. Course.	
–	29th	–	Carrying to [illegible] dumps from E. Strong Point. Fine.	
–			Returned to Brown Line (Orange Hill) Y Coy. in Strong Points E. F. G. H. [illegible]	
BROWN LINE	30th	–	Relieved by K.O.S.B. & returned to ARRAS. Fine. Stormy.	
ARRAS.	31st	–	Bathing & cleaning up. Concert by the Number Nines. Lieut.-Col. [illegible] rejoined. Capt. Wilson left for England (Leave). [illegible]	

1/6/17

S. A. Stevens. Lieut.-Col.
Commdg. 2nd R. Fus.

A5834 Wt W4973/M687 750,000 8/16 D. D. & L. Ltd. Forms/C.2118/13.

25.B.
(5 sheets)

Vol 16

CONFIDENTIAL WAR DIARY

2nd Bn THE ROYAL FUSILIERS

JUNE 1917

No 28

Instructions regarding War Diaries and Intelligence Summaries are contained in F. S. Regs., Part II. and the Staff Manual respectively. Title pages will be prepared in manuscript.

Vol. 28.

WAR DIARY ~~or~~ ~~INTELLIGENCE~~ SUMMARY.

(*Erase heading not required.*)

2nd Royal Fusiliers

Army Form C. 2118.

Place	Date	Hour	Summary of Events and Information JUNE. 1917.	Remarks and references to Appendices
ARRAS.	1st	-	Company inspections & reorganization. Bright.	[illegible]
"	2nd	-	Move to Bernville. Started 8.50AM. Arrived 11.30AM. Huts. Lieut. Bond remained in Arras to go on leave on the 3rd. Hot.	[illegible]
BERNVILLE	3rd	-	Move to LANCHES. Start 9.45AM. entrained at BEAUMETZ at 10.45AM arrived 5.30pm. (detrained at FIENVILLERS: CANDAS) Billets – Good but very few Officers [illegible]. Hot.	[illegible]
LANCHES.	4th	-	REST. Company inspections. Hot.	[illegible]
"	5th		Parade 5 AM. digging trenches for Field Firing Practice. Breakfasts on parade ground. Hot	[illegible]
"	6th		Company Training 7.0AM. – 11.0AM. (Improving range etc. by reserve platoon.) Hot	[illegible]
"	7th		– – Drafts from St. POL:- 2 Officers 968 OR. [illegible] ETAPLE:- 1 Off. 34 OR. Capt. [illegible] & Baldwin rejoined & LIEUT. Griffiths joined. Fine.	[illegible]
"	8th		Coy. Training. Cinema in the evening. 2/Lieut. [illegible] joined – posted to 'X' Coy. –	[illegible]
"	9th		– – 2/Lieut. Twells joined – – 'Z' Coy. –	[illegible]
"	10th		Church parade. 10.45 AM. Draft 39 joined. very little training. Fine	[illegible]
"	11th		Company Training, till 10.AM. Battalion Sports at 3.pm. Lieut. Hamilton rejoined from Course. 2/Lieut. Hood rejoined from hospital. Hot.	[illegible]
"	12th/13th		Company Training. Storm from 7.pm – 10pm. on 12th. Brigade Sports on 13th. weather dull	[illegible]

T2134. Wt. W708–776. 500000. 4/15. Sir J. C. & S.

Instructions regarding War Diaries and Intelligence Summaries are contained in F. S. Regs., Part II. and the Staff Manual respectively. Title pages will be prepared in manuscript.

WAR DIARY or ~~INTELLIGENCE SUMMARY~~.

(*Erase heading not required.*)

Army Form C. 2118.

Place	Date	Hour	Summary of Events and Information — JUNE 1917	Remarks and references to Appendices
LANCHES.	14th		Company Training. Draft of 4 Officers 140 O.R. Class – Good. Regimental Concert party gave a show at 7.0pm. (2/Lts. Mr. A.H. Aspden H. Denton. C.W. Crampton. C.J. Saul.)	H.T.
"	15th		Company Training. (2 Officers joined 2/Lts. W. Merritt. S.V. Wise) Fine	H.T.
"	16th		Divisional Horse Show. Fine	H.T.
"	17th		Rest. 'Z' Coy moved to St. Hilaire. "	H.T.
"	18th		Company Training. "	H.T.
"	19th		G.O.C. Divn watched demonstration under 2/Lt. B.W. Penny. " rain later.	H.T.
"	20		Company Training. Dull	H.T.
"	21st		Brigade Field day. Parade 1.45pm. Dull with some rain	H.T.
"	22/23rd		Company Training. Brigadier lectured Officers at 7pm (22/6/17) Showery.	H.T.
"	24th		Church parade. 12.30pm. Fine	H.T.
"	25th		Bn. route march 8 AM. to 10 AM. Trench Mortar demonstration at Pernois.	H.T.
"	26th		Move to PROVEN AREA. 'Z' Coy. left at 9.30AM. & acted as detraining party at REXPOEDE. Bn. left at 11.20pm. (entrained at Candas) 2/LIEUTS. E.C. Newman & J.S. Benson joined. H.T.	H.T.
"	27th		Entrained at CANDAS at 2.15AM. & detrained at REXPOEDE at 11.40AM. Arrived at Billets at 5.5pm. (Bn. including Transport detrained in 17 mins. marched off in less than ½ hour.) Heavy rain during night.	H.T.

Instructions regarding War Diaries and Intelligence Summaries are contained in F. S. Regs., Part II. and the Staff Manual respectively. Title pages will be prepared in manuscript.

WAR DIARY

~~or~~

~~INTELLIGENCE~~ SUMMARY.

(*Erase heading not required.*)

Army Form C. 2118.

Place	Date	Hour	Summary of Events and Information	Remarks and references to Appendices
			JUNE 1917	
PROVEN AREA	28th		Rest (2nd LIEUT E.W. Parker joined) Z Coy. Heavy rain during night	CHH
	29th		Company training. 9.30 AM. Divl demonstration (Yukon Pack 1 off) 10.30 AM Divl demonstration (Company in attack 4 Officers) 5 PM. Brigade demonstration (Yukon Pack, all Officers) Lieut Boult & Rev W. E. Hodgson returned from leave. Preliminary Boxing Bouts. Rain during night	CHH
	30th		Company Training. Specialist Classes. Boxing postponed owing to Rain (Wet) 2nd LIEUT. C. F. JACKSON left for Veterinary Course (CALAIS)	CHH

[illegible] Lieut: Col.
Cmdg: 2nd Royal Fus.
30/6/17

26.B.
(9 sheets)

CONFIDENTIAL

WAR DIARY

2ND BATTALION ROYAL FUSILIERS

JULY 1917

VOL 29

Vol. 29

Instructions regarding War Diaries and Intelligence Summaries are contained in F. S. Regs., Part II. and the Staff Manual respectively. Title pages will be prepared in manuscript.

WAR DIARY

~~INTELLIGENCE SUMMARY.~~

(Erase heading not required.)

2nd Royal Fusiliers

Army Form C. 2118.

Place	Date	Hour	Summary of Events and Information	Remarks and references to Appendices
			JULY. 1917.	
PROVEN AREA	1st		Church Parade 11.AM. Boxing Contest 5-30pm. Divisional Cinema 8pm. MAJOR. J.S. HODDING joined (as second in Command.) (Dull)	CHH.
" "	2nd		Company training. Battalion Concert party gave a Concert at 8PM, (Bright)	APPENDIX C CHH.
" "	3rd		Company training Platoons attacking strong points Baths + clean clothing 2nd LIEUT. F.L. THIMERSON left for leave to England. G.O.C's Conference at Brigade H.Q. at 10.45AM. C.O. + Coy. Commanders. Capt J.F. Harden rejoined the Battn from 88th Brigade H.Q. + resumed Command of X. Coy. 2nd Lt. C.H. Hewlett left for 3 days course with 9th Squadron R.F.C. 2nd Lt. B.W. Penny rejoined from leave. (Hot)	CHH
" "	4th		Company training. Grenadiers practised with new smoke bombs. Baths + clean clothing. C.O. lectured to Officers on Regimental exercises Dull	CHH
" "	5th		Move. X Coy. paraded at 7.15AM. + marched to PROVEN. MAP REF. F.8.d.8.6 and relieved B. Coy. NEWFOUNDLAND's. Z Coy moved off at 9.30AM. to forward area + took over ~~Huts~~ from 3 Coys Newfoundland's MAP. REF. A.11.d.8.6	

Continued

T2134. Wt. W708–776. 500000. 4/15. Sir J. C. & S.

Instructions regarding War Diaries and Intelligence Summaries are contained in F. S. Regs., Part II. and the Staff Manual respectively. Title pages will be prepared in manuscript.

WAR DIARY

~~INTELLIGENCE SUMMARY.~~

(Erase heading not required.)

2nd Royal Fusiliers

Army Form C. 2118.

Place	Date	Hour	Summary of Events and Information	Remarks and references to Appendices
			JULY 1917	
PROVEN AREA	5th	Contd	Battalion H.Q's. Lums. W. + Y Coys moved off at 6pm. to forward area Map Ref. A 11. d. 8.6 + arrived at 9.30pm. Z Coy moved into Huts at A.18.a.8.7. Dull	CHH.
WOESTEN AREA.	6th		X Coy. supplied working parties for work on Roads locally 160 including Officers + O. Ranks. W. Y + Z. Coys. working parties for XIV Corps R.E. in forward Area 360 including Officers + O. Ranks. 2nd Lt C.H. Hewlett returned from course. (Working Parties 1 officer per 40 men) (Hot)	CHH
" "	7th		Working Parties as on 6th inst 2nd Lt. H. Denton returned from course (Hot)	CHH.
" "	8th		" " " " " " 7th " Church Parades (Voluntary). (C of E. 10.AM.) (R.C. 7AM. + 10.AM.) (N.C 6pM.) (Wet)	CHH
" "	9th		Working Parties as on the 8th inst. Capt J. S. Leaming + Capt E.W. Baldwin returned from leave to England. Casualties on working parties (O. Ranks) 1. died of wounds 2. wounded (total. 3) (Dull)	CHH
" "	8th	Contd	Casualties on working parties, (O. Ranks) 1. Killed 3 wounded 1 accidentally wounded 2. O. Ranks Killed attch Div Salvage Company (Total 7) Wet	CHH

T2134. Wt. W708–776. 500000. 4/15. Sir J. C. & S.

Instructions regarding War Diaries and Intelligence Summaries are contained in F. S. Regs., Part II. and the Staff Manual respectively. Title pages will be prepared in manuscript.

WAR DIARY
or
~~INTELLIGENCE SUMMARY.~~

(Erase heading not required.)

2nd Battn
Royal Fusiliers

Army Form C. 2118.

Place	Date	Hour	Summary of Events and Information	Remarks and references to Appendices
			JULY. 1917.	
WOESTEN AREA	10th		Working parties as on 9th inst (Bright)	CHH
" "	11th		working parties as on 10th " C.O. Adjt + Coy ~~Off~~ Commanders reconnoitred L. Defences prior to relieving the Worcesters (Hot)	CHH
" "	12th		The Battn moved from A 11 d. 8.5 W. + Z Coys + Battn H.Q. relieved W. + X Coys also H.Q. in L. 2. Defences X + Y Coys proceeded to the trenches X Coy Canal Bank Y Coy Bully Trench. Q.M. Stores + Transport moved to A 14 b 9.5 Details H. Camp A. 9. b. 9.4 Casualties on working party around WOESTEN AREA 1. Killed 11 wounded. Total 12 (O.R)	
ZWAANHOF SECTOR TRENCHES	13th		X + Y Coys relieved X + Y Coys 1st Essex Regt. in Front Line Hulme Trench. Dublin Fusiliers on Left 51st Division on Right. H.Q's. W. + Z Coys moved from L. 2. defences + relieved W. Z + H.Q's in trenches. W. Coy. Canal Bank Z Coy Bully Trench Battn H.Q's CANAL BANK C. 19. c. 4.1 Casualties 2. (OR) wounded. 2ND LT. B. LIGHT returned from Course (Fine)	CHH APPENDIX A
" "	14th		Situation quiet Support's + CANAL BANK shelled occasionally during the night Casualties 2 Killed 2 Wounded Total 4. (OR) (Hot)	CHH
			A Patrol of 2 Officers + 2 NCO's went out from C. 13. b. 8.5 + worked in a NE direction nothing was heard or seen of the enemy. left at 11.40 PM and returned at 12.20 AM (Hot) heavy rain during night	CHH

A5834 Wt. W4973/M687 750,000 8/16 D. D. & L. Ltd. Forms/C.2118/13.

Instructions regarding War Diaries and Intelligence Summaries are contained in F. S. Regs., Part II. and the Staff Manual respectively. Title pages will be prepared in manuscript.

WAR DIARY
or
~~INTELLIGENCE SUMMARY.~~
(Erase heading not required.)

Army Form C. 2118.

2nd Battn Royal Fusiliers

Place	Date	Hour	Summary of Events and Information JULY 1917	Remarks and references to Appendices
ZWAANHOF SECTOR	15th		Enemy artillery quiet, our own very active on enemy Front Line Supports + Reserves with H.E. Shrapnel + Heavies. CANAL BANK occasionally shelled with Shrapnel but no Heavies. 2nd Lt. B. Light + 30. (O. Ranks) came up to the trenches from details at H. Camp. Casualties 3 Killed. 9. wounded. Total 12. (O. Ranks) A Patrol of 1. Off + 4 O.R. went out from about C.13 b 7·9 + worked along enemy wire N.E. of CAESARS NOSE for about 50yds + found wire badly damaged + formed no obstacle. no M.G. or rifle fire was heard. Patrol left at 11pm + returned about 1AM. (no casualties) Fine	C.H.H.
	16th		Enemy artillery more active. CANAL BANK shelled intermittently all day with Heavies + H.E. Several Gas Shells fell on Support lines during the night. our own artillery active on enemy's Front and Support lines also back area's. Casualties 4. (O.R.) wounded. A Patrol of 1. Off. + 10. (O.R.) left our lines about C.13 b 7.9 at 11pm + approached within 10yds of CAESAR NOSE. C.13 b 8.5. Retd 1 AM. Fine	C.H.H.
	17th		Enemy artillery active all day. CANAL BANK shelled intermittently with Heavies. relieved by 16th Middlesex Regt in the line. Battn moved back to L.2 defences + took over Bivouacs from Middlesex. Casualties 4 Wounded 3 Killed ~~total~~ 7. (O.R.). A Patrol of 1 Off. (Hat) + 11. (O.R.) left our lines at 11pm at C.13 b 7-9. Retd 12 pm. Lt Col. G. A. Stevens buried in dugout. Slight injury to foot	C.H.H.

A5834 Wt. W4973/M687 750,000 8/16 D. D. & L. Ltd. Forms/C.2118/13.

Instructions regarding War Diaries and Intelligence Summaries are contained in F. S. Regs., Part II. and the Staff Manual respectively. Title pages will be prepared in manuscript.

WAR DIARY
or
~~INTELLIGENCE SUMMARY.~~
(Erase heading not required.)

2nd Battn Royal Fusiliers

Army Form C. 2118.

Place	Date	Hour	Summary of Events and Information	Remarks and references to Appendices
			JULY 1917	
L.2 DEFENCES	18th		Working Parties. carrying to Front line + Supports. (500 men.) 2nd Lt. A.O.M. Gyems left for 3 days course with R.F.C. Casualties 1. wounded night 18th/19th Battalion Raiding Party 2 Offs. 27. (O Ranks) (Wet)	C.H.H. APPENDIX B
" "	19th		Working parties as on 18th inst relieved in L2 defences by 10th Welsh Regt. Battn moved to Camp Sheet 19, X.29.c.2.2. Q.M. Stores + transport moved from A.14.B.9.5. Details from H. Camp A.9.b.9.4 to X.29.c.2.2. a/Major F.W. Swift rejoined the Battn (Dull)	C.H.H.
Crombeke area	20th		Rest. Inspections + general clean up. Fine	C.H.H.
	21st		Kit inspections Box Respirators inspected + men exercised in marching with them on for 1 Mile 2nd Lt. A.O.M. Gyems returned from course Hot	C.H.H.
	22nd		Battn Church Parade Raiding Party lectured by Brigadier General R.G. Jelfs on successful raid. Concert in evening by R.F's. L.F's. RWF's	C.H.H.
" "	23rd		Company training Platoons attacking Strong Points, creeping barrage 6 Officers + 4 NCO's reconnoitred No's. 11 + 12 Tracks Lecture on forthcoming operations by Lt Col G.A. Stevens. Bathing Parades + change of clothing. a number of Officers viewed plan of enemy trenches on XIV Corps front at A.2.C.9.0. 1 Officer 52 (O. Ranks) Hot attached 41st Siege Battery for fatigue	C.H.H.

A5834 Wt. W4973/M687 750,000 8/16 D. D. & L. Ltd. Forms/C.2118/13.

Instructions regarding War Diaries and Intelligence Summaries are contained in F. S. Regs., Part II. and the Staff Manual respectively. Title pages will be prepared in manuscript.

WAR DIARY
or
~~INTELLIGENCE SUMMARY.~~
(Erase heading not required.)

Army Form C. 2118.

2nd Battn Royal Fusiliers

Place	Date	Hour	Summary of Events and Information	Remarks and references to Appendices
			JULY 1917	
PROVEN AREA	24th		Battn moved from Camp at X.29.C.2.2 to Camp at X25.C.8.5 reorganisation of Platoons (Hot)	CHH.
" "	25th		Battalion marched to Brigade area EAST NE. HERZEELE and carried out Brigade exercise 1 off. 25 (O.R.) RE Fatigues (Very Wet)	CHH.
" "	26th		Company Training, Inspections Wire cutting (Warm)	CHH
" "	27th		Battalion marched to Brigade Training Area E.N.E. HERZEELE and carried out Brigade exercise in the attack. Conference for all Officers of 86th Brigade after tactical scheme by Divisional Commander and Brigadier General 86th Brigade. Draft of 39 men (Ptes) arrived. 3 to 4 months service (Very Hot)	CHH.
" "	28th		Company Training Specialist Classes 4 officers + 4. O.Ranks reconnoitred tracks 11 + 12. LIEUT. A.G. PAPE rejoined from England (Very Hot)	CHH.
	29th		Church parade cancelled owing to weather. Conference for all Officers by Lt Col. G.A. Stevens on forthcoming operations (Wet)	CHH.
	30th		Coy Training Firing Rifle Grenades practice under Barrage BATTN. less ~~XIV Corps~~ 10%. moved to Camp at X.27.a.3.2. Battn H.Q. and Transport at X26.b.0.5. Dull	CHH.

A5834 Wt. W4973/M687 750,000 8/16 D. D. & L. Ltd. Forms/C.2118/13.

WAR DIARY
or
~~INTELLIGENCE SUMMARY.~~
(Erase heading not required.)

Instructions regarding War Diaries and Intelligence Summaries are contained in F. S. Regs., Part II. and the Staff Manual respectively. Title pages will be prepared in manuscript.

2nd Battn Royal Fusiliers

Place	Date	Hour	Summary of Events and Information	Remarks and references to Appendices
			JULY. 1917.	
PROVEN AREA	31st		Coy Training. Inspections etc. Lecture by Divisional Gas Officer to All Officers + O. Ranks in the Battn. Conference for C.O. and Coy Commanders by Divisional General on forthcoming operations. (Dull) Heavy rain during night.	C.H.H.

L. A. Stevens. Lieut: Col.
Cmdg: 2nd Roy: Fus:
31 VII 17.

Note.

1. The XIV Corps Chief Engineer wrote to 29th Div: H.Q. expressing his appreciation of the excellent work done by men of the Battn: on working parties in forward area.

2. On the 19th July the Div: Cmdr: Major Gen: Sir H. de B. de Lisle, K.C.B. congratulated the C.O. on the fine work of the raiding party on the night of 18/19 July & the valuable information and identification they obtained. The G.O.C. further said he knew if he required any work done if he called on the Royal Fusiliers he had complete confidence it would be done well. L.A.S. Lt. Col.

A5834 Wt. W4973/M687 750,000 8/16 D. D. & L. Ltd. Forms/C.2118/13.

27.B.
(10 sheets)

~ CONFIDENTIAL ~

WAR DIARY

~ 2ND BN ~

THE · ROYAL · FUSILIERS

~ VOL: 30 ~

AUGUST · 1917

Vol. 30

Instructions regarding War Diaries and Intelligence Summaries are contained in F. S. Regs., Part II. and the Staff Manual respectively. Title pages will be prepared in manuscript.

WAR DIARY
~~or INTELLIGENCE SUMMARY.~~
(Erase heading not required.)

2nd Battn
Royal Fusiliers

Army Form C. 2118.

Place	Date	Hour	Summary of Events and Information	Remarks and references to Appendices
			AUGUST. 1917	
PROVEN AREA	1st		Rest. Lecture by Coy Comdrs to Platoon Comdrs + NCO's on forthcoming operations. About 30% Officers + Other Ranks of the Battn. were conveyed by Motor Lorries to PROVEN to see Divl Concert Party.	C.H.H. (Very Wet)
" "	2nd		Rest. No parades owing to heavy rain. (Very Wet)	C.H.H.
	3rd		Battn moved to Camp at A.11.a.1.8 accomodation for Battn very bad. Camp taken over from 1st K.O.S.B. (Very Wet)	C.H.H.
	4th		General clean up. Rifle inspections. Z Coy moved from Camp 16 to Camp 11. 2nd Lieut E.W. Parker awarded Military Cross for Conspicuous bravery on night 18th/19th July whilst in charge of Battn Raiding Party. (Very Wet)	C.H.H.
" "	5th		Battn less 10% Q.M. Stores + Transport moved to Camp at B.7.d.5.3 + took over from 2nd Battn Scots Guards (Fine)	C.H.H.
FORWARD AREA	6th		Battn moved into the Trenches + relieved 1st Battn Grenadier Guards in Support lines BOESINGHE SECTOR. RIGHT SUB SECTOR of Brigade. W. Coy. Rt. Z Coy Left. X Coy Reserve to W. Co. Y Coy Reserve to Z Coy. CAPT. F.W. SWIFTE. 2nd LT. E.C. NEWMAN (Wounded)	C.H.H. (C.H.H.)

Army Form C. 2118.

Instructions regarding War Diaries and Intelligence Summaries are contained in F. S. Regs., Part II. and the Staff Manual respectively. Title pages will be prepared in manuscript.

WAR DIARY

~~or INTELLIGENCE~~ SUMMARY.

(Erase heading not required.)

2nd Battn Royal Fusiliers

Place	Date	Hour	AUGUST 1917 Summary of Events and Information	Remarks and references to Appendices
BOESINGHE SECTOR.	6th	Contd	2nd LIEUT R.W. ASPDEN died of Wounds (Other Ranks) 2 Killed 15 Wounded (total Casualties (20)) Battn HQ's C.2.b.0.5. (Dull)	CHH
"	7th	night	Battn relieved 1st Grenadier Guards in Front Line Trenches X Coy Rt Front Z Coy Left Front 20th Division on Rt 1st R Dublin Fusiliers on left Y Coy Left Support W Coy Rt Support Battn HQs CAPTAINS FARM U.26.b.2.7. (Casualties) O.R 1 Killed 4 Wounded (Total 5) (Fine)	CHH Appendix "A"
"	8th		Situation Quiet. GREEN LINE + Reserves shelled intermittently with Shrapnel HE + 5.9's CAPTAINS FARM heavily shelled with 5.9's from 9.10pm till 9.45pm. WORK Improving parapets consolidating + deepening trenches established one post + dug in on far side of STEEN BEEK about U.21.C.9.4. Casualties [struck through] CHH 2/Lt A.D.M. GJEMS wounded (O.R.) wounded 6 Total 7. (Heavy rain during night)	CHH
"	7th	Contd	A Patrol of 1 Officer + 9 (OR) left our lines night 7/8th at 1.30 AM about U.21.C.90.25. + returned without Casualties 2.45 AM (Fine)	CHH Appendix "A"
"	9th		Situation Unchanged enemy artillery active on Front Line Supports + reserves Casualties 2nd Lt L.C. BOURNE Wounded (O Ranks) Killed 9 Wounded 23. (Total 33) Battn was relieved by 1st Lan Fusiliers + moved back to Camp at B.7.d. (Fine)	CHH

WAR DIARY
~~or~~
~~INTELLIGENCE SUMMARY.~~
(*Erase heading not required.*)

Army Form C. 2118.

Instructions regarding War Diaries and Intelligence Summaries are contained in F. S. Regs., Part II. and the Staff Manual respectively. Title pages will be prepared in manuscript.

2nd Battn Royal Fusiliers

Place	Date	Hour	Summary of Events and Information	Remarks and references to Appendices
			AUGUST 1917	
WOESTEN AREA	10th		Battn moved from Camp at B.7.d. and took over Huts from S.W.B.: at DUBLIN CAMP A 11 C. (Fine)	CHH.
	11th		Rest. General clean up Inspections etc. (Dull) Heavy rain during night	CHH
	12th		Battn Church parade in field adjoining Camp (Showery)	CHH.
	13th		Company Training, Saluting and Arms Drill. [illegible] 21 (O.R.) were conveyed by Lorry to Divisional Cinema at 3pm and Divl. Concert Party at 6pm. at INTERNATIONAL CORNER. (Fine)	CHH
	14th		Bathing parade all Coys at Baths B.7.d. Clean clothing issued. 1 Officer per Coy reconnoitred No. 11 TRACK as far as BOESINGHE POSITION. Battn moved to Camp at B.8.C. + took over from 2nd Hants Regt. (Stormy) [illegible] at 9.30 p.m.	CHH.
BOESINGHE [illegible] August	15th		after completing fitting out with bombs, tools etc: the Bn: left camp at 9.30 p.m. via track 12 for the assembly position preparatory to the action to-morrow. Dispositions as follows: Bn: H.Q. in HEY WOOD. Y & Z. Cos: in area GABLE Ho: & de BARRIERE Ho: W & X. Cos: in area [illegible] and GENERALS FARM. The Co: Cmdrs: were W. Co. ~~[illegible]~~ Capt: LEAMING.	[illegible]

A5834 Wt W4973/M687 750,000 8/16 D. D. & L. Ltd. Forms/C.2118/13.

Instructions regarding War Diaries and Intelligence Summaries are contained in F. S. Regs., Part II. and the Staff Manual respectively. Title pages will be prepared in manuscript.

Army Form C. 2118.

WAR DIARY or INTELLIGENCE SUMMARY.

(*Erase heading not required.*)

2nd Royal Fusiliers.

August 1917

Place	Date	Hour	Summary of Events and Information	Remarks and references to Appendices
BOESINGHE SECTOR:			X. Co: 2nd Lt: BENSON. Y. Co: Capt: BALDWIN. Z Co: Lieut: GRIFFITHS.	
August	15th		(Continued). Owing to the darkness it was difficult taking up positions. The 88th Bde: are to attack on the right, 87th Bde: on the left, 86th Bde: in Divisional reserve. The 2nd R.F. are attached to 88th Bde from Zero hour; our role is in case of things going wrong with LANGEMARCK to attack that place from the W & secondly as a reserve to cover the right flank if necessary after the attack reaches the line of the BROENBEEK. All night our guns heavily shelled the enemy, chiefly with gas shells, there was a good deal of hostile shelling but it was not severe. 20th Divn: on our right. Dublin Fusiliers on our left with the French beyond them.	
August	16th		Zero hour was at 4.45 a.m. The attack of the 29th Divn: was entirely successful & it is reported that the final objective was secured within two minutes of the advertised time. Owing to the success of the attack the Bn: was not called on to support the 88th Bde: & during the afternoon again came under the orders of the 86th Bde (now commanded by Lieut Col: NELSON Dublin Fusiliers) established at SAULES FARM. During the afternoon orders were received that the Bn: should relieve the 1st ESSEX Regt: after dusk in the right Bn: sector. Just before the relief two shells came in to Bn: H.Q. severely	

A5834 Wt. W4973/M687 750,000 8/16 D. D. & L. Ltd. Forms/C.2118/13.

Instructions regarding War Diaries and Intelligence Summaries are contained in F. S. Regs., Part II. and the Staff Manual respectively. Title pages will be prepared in manuscript.

WAR DIARY ~~or~~ INTELLIGENCE SUMMARY.

(Erase heading not required.)

2nd Royal Fusiliers

August 1917.

Army Form C. 2118.

Place	Date	Hour	Summary of Events and Information	Remarks and references to Appendices
BOESINGHE			SECTOR) wounding 2nd Lt. HEWLETT and killing Co: S. M. ROLFE	
August	16th	(Cont.)	and causing several other casualties. S. M. Rolfe is a great loss to the Battn: he has always carried himself in action with the most conspicuous gallantry. Relief commenced 7.45 p.m. guides being furnished by the Essex Rgt: at TUFTS FARM. The relief was very difficult owing to guides losing their way (they had only been over the ground during the attack), the darkness of the night and considerable hostile shelling. The Bn: took over the area in the triangle formed by the LANGEMARCK – STADEN railway LANGEMARCK – KOKUIT road & the BROENBEEK. Z & Y Cos: formed the front line W & X the support line about 100 yds in rear. The front line was just in front of the old German trenches with posts pushed out in front. Bn: H.Q. in an old German emplacement near MARTINS MILL. Relief was not completed until dawn. A Battn: of the K.O.Y.L.I. was in touch on the right, the 1st Dublin Fusiliers on the left.	Appendix B Appendix B
August	17th		The Battn: remained in the front line. From time to time there was heavy German shelling; work on trenches was very much interfered with. 2nd Lt. PENNS mortally wounded during the afternoon.	

A5834 Wt. W4973/M687 750,000 8/16 D. D. & L. Ltd. Forms/C.2118/13.

Instructions regarding War Diaries and Intelligence Summaries are contained in F. S. Regs., Part II. and the Staff Manual respectively. Title pages will be prepared in manuscript.

WAR DIARY or INTELLIGENCE SUMMARY.

(Erase heading not required.)

2nd Royal Fusiliers.

August 1917.

Army Form C. 2118.

Place	Date	Hour	Summary of Events and Information	Remarks and references to Appendices
BOESINGHE SECTOR.	August 18th		In the early morning two of our men unarmed who had lost their way carrying water to an advanced post encountered a German patrol of three men, they immediately attacked it & captured all three. The Bn: remained in the front line. Hostile shelling less than usual (tho' severe at times) but increased again at night. 2nd Lt. Perry died from wounds in DOZINGHEM. C.C.S. ~~[illegible]~~	R.A.S.
Aug:	19th		Battn: remained in front line, shelling by day considerably below normal, at dusk it increased becoming violent at times during the night. The 1st Essex Regt: relieved the Lancashire Fusiliers in support & the 4th Worcesters the Dublin Fusiliers on our left. The 37th Divn have relieved the 20th on our right.	R.A.S.
Aug:	20th		In front line all day, relieved after dusk by the Hampshire Regt: when the Battn: moved into bivouac W. of BOESINGHE near BLEUET Farm. All into camp by 4. a.m. The total casualties whilst in the line this tour 2 Officers & 82. O.R. killed & wounded.	R.A.S.
Aug:	21st		Moved at 2. p.m. from BLEUET Farm to BEDFORD camp. Sheet 28. A.12d. Day spent reorganising and cleaning up.	R.A.S.

A5834 Wt. W4973/M687 750,000 8/16 D. D. & L. Ltd. Forms/C.2118/13.

Instructions regarding War Diaries and Intelligence Summaries are contained in F. S. Regs., Part II. and the Staff Manual respectively. Title pages will be prepared in manuscript.

WAR DIARY
or
INTELLIGENCE SUMMARY.
(*Erase heading not required.*)

2nd Royal Fusiliers

August 1917.

Army Form C. 2118.

Place	Date	Hour	Summary of Events and Information	Remarks and references to Appendices
WOESTEN Area				
August	22nd		Battn: at BEDFORD Camp. Men had baths. Divn: band played during the afternoon in camp.	f.Cd.
"	23rd		Battn: at BEDFORD camp. In afternoon all men employed at work on mending track 11 between WOESTEN & Bedford Camp.	f.Cd.
"	24th		Battn. at BEDFORD Camp. Mending track 11. Fine	
"	25th		" " " Move to EATON CAMP (B9c4a) Sunny.	
"	26th		" EATON CAMP. Work on road from ELVEDINGHE to BOESINGHE. Cold.	
"	27th		" " ditto ditto wet.	
"	28th		Move to PRIVETT CAMP. (Proven) Entrained at Elvedinghe 1 pm. Arrived 3.45pm. Wet	
	29th		Battn at PRIVETT Camp. General clean up, inspections etc. smartening up drill. All N.C.Os instructed in Guard Mounting by R.S.M. The following new officers joined the Battn from the Base:- 2/Lts. H. Branford, J.H. Abbott, J. Barr, H.L. Meghan, P.G. Brain, W.C. Batterbury, P.H.R. Mason, R.M. Shaw, P.L. Sparks & C.W.G. Burton. 2/Lt Hood & Hornby rejoined the Battn from Corps 10%. A draft of 132 new O.R. arrived - large proportion middle aged men. Fair to dull very windy	

A5834 Wt. W4973/M687 750,000 8/16 D. D. & L. Ltd. Forms/C.2118/13.

Army Form C. 2118.

Instructions regarding War Diaries and Intelligence Summaries are contained in F. S. Regs., Part II. and the Staff Manual respectively. Title pages will be prepared in manuscript.

WAR DIARY
or
INTELLIGENCE SUMMARY.
(Erase heading not required.)

2nd Royal Fusiliers
August 1917

Place	Date	Hour	Summary of Events and Information	Remarks and references to Appendices
PROVEN AREA				
August	30th		Battn at PRIVETT Camp. Company training, saluting, arms & squad drill specialists classes. Afternoon - all Companies bathed at X.26.a.1.6. Colonel Stevens proceeded on leave. Maj Stodding taking over command of Battn.	A.W.D.
"	31st		Battn at PRIVETT CAMP. Company training, close order drill, musketry and bombing - specialists classes - Heavy downpour of rain interfered somewhat with training. 2/Lt. Sant & 25 O.R. rejoined Battn from R.E. working party. Fair to dull - windy. Showery & unsettled.	A.W.D.

List of appendices :- Maps :- Appendices "A" & "B"

Award to 2/Lt. L.C. Bourne for bravery — Appendix "C"

List of men granted awards for bravery }
" " " commended " } — " — "D"

Letter of appreciation — " — "E"

Copies of Field Returns for August — " — "F"

J. Stodding Major
O.C. 2 R. Fus.

A5834 Wt. W4973/M687 750,000 8/16 D. D. & L. Ltd. Forms/C.2118/13.

86/59 28.B. (9 sheets)

~ CONFIDENTIAL ~

Vol 19

WAR ~

~ DIARY

~ 2ND BN ~

THE · ROYAL · FUSILIERS ~

~ VOL. 31 ~

~ SEPT 1917 ~

Vol. 31.

Instructions regarding War Diaries and Intelligence Summaries are contained in F. S. Regs., Part II. and the Staff Manual respectively. Title pages will be prepared in manuscript.

WAR DIARY ~~or INTELLIGENCE~~ SUMMARY. 2nd Royal Fusiliers.

(Erase heading not required.)

September 1917

Army Form C. 2118.

Place	Date	Hour	Summary of Events and Information	Remarks and references to Appendices
PROVEN ~~[illegible]~~ AREA. (PRIVETT CAMP)				
September	1st		Battn. at PRIVETT Camp. Company Training – Close order drill, musketry, Company in attack, Specialists Classes. Capt. J. C. Pearson proceeded on leave to England. Dull & Showery.	H.D.T.
"	2nd (Sunday)		Battn. Church Parade. Capt. Baldwin proceeded to Boulogne rest camp for 14 days. 2/Lt. H. Denton & E. W. Crampton rejoined Battn. from 14th Corps Infantry School Course. Bright.	H.D.T.
"	3rd		Battn. rehearsed for G.O.C's inspection – Afternoon men played football & practiced running for the coming sports. Lt. F. J. Hamilton proceeded on 10 days leave to England. Bosch aeroplanes very active round this camp at nights. Sunny & warm	H.D.T.
	4th		Battn. marched to ground just outside camp & formed up with Brigade for the Brigadier's & G.O.C's inspection & distribution of medals. Inspected at 10 a.m. by Brigadier General Cheape & again at 11 a.m. by General de Lisle after which the latter presented medals to men from the various units of the Brigade – Military Crosses were presented to 2/Lts. Parker & Rumbolt & one D.C.M. & several M.M's to N.C.Os & men of this Battn. (See appendice 'D' August) Afternoon men played football. Sunny & warm	H.D.T.

A5834 Wt. W4973/M687 750,000 8/16 D. D. & L. Ltd. Forms/C.2118/13.

Vol 31

Instructions regarding War Diaries and Intelligence Summaries are contained in F. S. Regs., Part II. and the Staff Manual respectively. Title pages will be prepared in manuscript.

WAR DIARY 2nd Royal Fusiliers
or
INTELLIGENCE SUMMARY. September 1917
(Erase heading not required.)

Army Form C. 2118.

Place	Date	Hour	Summary of Events and Information	Remarks and references to Appendices
PROVEN AREA (PRIVETT CAMP.)				
September	5th		Company training - Attack - section rushes - fire orders. Specialists Classes. Afternoon football. at 4.30 pm 20th Divisional Concert Party gave a free show in this camp to the Battn. 2/Lt. A.L. Mephan proceeded on a 4 days musketry course. Sunny & warm.	H.V.W.
	6th		Morning:- Battn. bathing parade at X.26.a.1.6. Afternoon:- 2 officers per Coy & Battn & Coy scouts & snipers attended a lecture given by the Brigadier at Brigade H.Q. Brigadier very keen on this work! 2 Officers 2/Lts Benson & Parker, 1 N.C.O. & 2 men per Coy proceeded on a days outing by Motor Lorry to Coast near Dunkirk. 2/Lt G. Ware joined Batt. Fine & warm - evening thunder.	H.V.W.
	7th		Battn paraded 7 a.m. & marched to PROVEN Station & entrained for ELVERDINGHE. Left PROVEN 8.6 a.m. arrived ELVERDINGHE 8.35 a.m. detrained & marched to OXFORD Camp relieving the K.R.R.s (MAP REF. B.9.d.8.8). Commenced work on roads E of Canal at 6 o'clock same evening. Drums & specialists classes left behind at PRIVETT Camp in charge of Capt Leaning. Dull to bright.	H.V.W.

T2134. Wt. W708-776. 500000. 4/15. Sir J. C. & S.

Vol. 31

WAR DIARY 2nd Royal Fusiliers

or

~~INTELLIGENCE SUMMARY.~~

(Erase heading not required.)

September 1917

Army Form C. 2118.

Instructions regarding War Diaries and Intelligence Summaries are contained in F. S. Regs., Part II. and the Staff Manual respectively. Title pages will be prepared in manuscript.

Place	Date	Hour	Summary of Events and Information	Remarks and references to Appendices
BOESINGHE AREA. (OXFORD CAMP.)				
September	8th		Battn at night work on roads E of Canal & up as far as the Steenbeek River. 2/Lt. Hood proceeded on 10 days leave to England. Casualties 8 O.R. slightly wounded. Bright & warm	HWW
"	9th		Battn at night work on roads E of Canal. 2/Lt. R. A L. Billson joined the Battn from Base. 2/Lt. Mephan rejoined from Musketry Course Bright & warm	HWW
"	10th		Battn left OXFORD CAMP 7.15 a.m. & entrained at ELVERDINGHE. Arrived at PROVEN 9.15 a.m. & marched back to PRIVETT Camp arriving there 10 a.m. At 5 p.m. Lewis Gunners & bombers went through a practise on the 30 yds range & bombing pit at F.4. 6.9.4. Afternoon - football with 1st Battn R.F. result 1-1. Fine. 2/Lt. E. J. Allen proceeded on 10 days leave to England.	HWW
APPRECIATION.			Received letter of appreciation from Brigadier for work done on roads E of Canal, during the last 3 nights.	See appendix "A"
			Brigade Cross Country Run took place - 2nd R.Fus. 4th on list; but men were sent down from forward area specially to run in this race.	

1577 Wt. W10791/1773 500,000 1/15 D. D. & L. A.D.S.S./Forms/C. 2118.

Vol 31

Instructions regarding War Diaries and Intelligence Summaries are contained in F. S. Regs., Part II. and the Staff Manual respectively. Title pages will be prepared in manuscript.

WAR DIARY or ~~INTELLIGENCE SUMMARY~~. 2nd Royal Fusiliers

(Erase heading not required.)

September 1917.

Army Form C. 2118.

Place	Date	Hour	Summary of Events and Information	Remarks and references to Appendices
PROVEN AREA (PRIVETT CAMP)				
September	11th		Company training & Specialists Classes. Afternoon Brigade Sports took place. Our Battn were a close 2nd on the list with 121 points as against 124 points scored by the Royal D. Fus. who leaded the list. Bright & warm.	[illegible]
"	12th		Company training & Specialists Classes. Afternoon, lecture for all Officers at Brigade H.Q. by Comdr. of Flying Corps. Evening preliminary boxing contests of Battn Boxing Tournament. Bright & cool.	[illegible]
"	13th		Company training & specialists. Bathing parades. Evening finals of Battn boxing tournament took place. Dull & cool.	[illegible]
"	14th		Company training - attacking strong points, advancing under barrage etc. Lewis Gunners & Snipers fired on 30 yds range at F.4 b.9.4. Capt. Baldwin rejoined from 14 days at Boulogne rest camp. 2/Lt Sparks returned from 7 days signalling course. Bright & warm.	[illegible]
"	15th		Company training & Specialists Classes. Evening - concert given by 89th F.A. Col. Stevens rejoined from leave in England. Dull & bright.	[illegible]

A5834 Wt. W4973/M687 750,000 8/16 D. D. & L. Ltd. Forms/C.2118/13.

Vol. 31.

Instructions regarding War Diaries and Intelligence Summaries are contained in F. S. Regs., Part II. and the Staff Manual respectively. Title pages will be prepared in manuscript.

WAR DIARY or INTELLIGENCE SUMMARY. 2nd Battn. Royal Fusiliers

(Erase heading not required.)

Army Form C. 2118.

September 1917.

Place	Date	Hour	Summary of Events and Information	Remarks and references to Appendices
HERZEELE				
September	16th		Battn paraded 2.30 pm. + marched to HERZEELE, arriving there 5.30 pm. "Z" Coy + BHQ billeted in Town, remainder scattered in farms round the village - Billets good + plenty of room. Capt Rawson + Lt. Hamilton returned from 10 days leave in England. Bright + warm	H.W.N.
"	17th		Company training in specially allotted training area - attacking strong pts. + advancing under barrage. Dull to bright - cool	H.W.N.
"	18th		Battn paraded 8.30 am. + practiced a tactical scheme viz:- Battn in attack, capturing strong points, concrete dug-outs etc. Dull - slight rain.	H.W.N.
"	19th		Battn paraded with Brigade + practiced Brigade in the attack - meeting counter attacks etc. Our Battn. carried their part out very successfully. Paraded again at 3.30 + marched back to PRIVETT CAMP arriving there 7 pm. Evening an impromptu concert was arranged for the men. 2/Lt. A.L. Chalker joined from the Base. Fine + warm	H.W.N.
PROVEN AREA			(PRIVETT CAMP) Battn paraded 2 pm. + marched to PROVEN STATION, where they entrained	
September	20th		for ELVERDINGHE, arrived there 3.30 pm. + marched to ABINGLEY CAMP (28/B.7.c.6.6) relieving the 2nd Scots Guards. Very good billets (under canvas + dug outs) 2/Lt Parker returned from L.G. Course. Corps 10% party left for BOLLEZEELE + Div 10% for ROUNDSLOW CAMP. Dull to bright	H.W.N.

A5834 Wt. W4973/M687 750,000 8/16 D. D. & L. Ltd. Forms/C.2118/13.

Vol. 31

Instructions regarding War Diaries and Intelligence Summaries are contained in F. S. Regs., Part II. and the Staff Manual respectively. Title pages will be prepared in manuscript.

WAR DIARY 2nd Bn. Royal Fusiliers
or
INTELLIGENCE SUMMARY.
(Erase heading not required.)

September 1917.

Army Form C. 2118.

Place	Date	Hour	Summary of Events and Information	Remarks and references to Appendices
ELVERDINGHE AREA.			(ABINGLEY CAMP)	
September	21st		Company training - specialists classes; Rifle grenade firing - Lewis Gun instruction Scouts & Signallers special classes. Bright & cool	H.W.
"	22nd		Company training & specialist classes, as yesterday. Bright & warm	H.W.
	23rd		Battn paraded 9.30 am & proceeded to work repairing track 11 - from road junction on the Woesten-Elverdinghe Rd. to Boesinghe; Work finished 12 Noon. Scouts & Signallers special classes. Bright to dull	H.W.
	24th		Battn working on track 11 as yesterday. Scouts & Signallers special classes. 2/Lt. Chaplan left to work with R.E. party. Bright & warm	H.W.
	25th		Battn working on track 11 as yesterday - Special classes for signallers & scouts. Capt. Leaning left to take charge of Div. 10% party at HOUNDSLOW Camp. Bright & warm	H.W.
	26		Battn working on track 11 as usual. Afternoon, baths. Bright & warm	H.W.

A5834 Wt. W4973/M687 750,000 8/16 D. D. & L. Ltd. Forms/C.2118/13.

Vol 31

Instructions regarding War Diaries and Intelligence Summaries are contained in F. S. Regs., Part II. and the Staff Manual respectively. Title pages will be prepared in manuscript.

WAR DIARY or ~~INTELLIGENCE SUMMARY~~. 2nd Battn Royal Fusiliers

(Erase heading not required.)

Army Form C. 2118.

September 1917

Place	Date	Hour	Summary of Events and Information	Remarks and references to Appendices
ELVERDINGHE AREA			(ABINGLEY CAMP)	
September	27th		Battn (less "Z" Coy) Company training - Special classes for Scouts & Signallers. "Z" Coy working on track 11. Bright & warm.	HVD
"	28th		Battn (less "W" Coy) Coy training - Special classes scouts & sigs. "W" Coy on track 11. 2/Lt Burton left for General Course at 5th Army School. Bright & warm	HVD
"	29th		Battn (less "X" Coy) Coy training. Special classes for scouts & signallers. "X" Coy working on track 11. Fatigue party of 40 men (10 per coy) working at RUGBY DUMP (2 shifts - day & night) Bright & warm	HVD
"	30th		Battn church parade - Usual fatigue parties at RUGBY DUMP, sustained following casualties "W" Coy 1 O.R. "Y" Coy 2 O.R. & "Z" Coy 2 OR - all wounded. Bright & warm	HVD
LIST OF APPENDICES.				
Appendix	"A"		Letter of appreciation from Brigadier for work on tracks.	
"	"B"		An account of a minor operation carried out by an officer of the 1st Battn R.F. who was previously a NCO in this Battn.	
"	"C"		Records the presentation of the "Croix de Guerre" to Lt A. G. Pape.	
"	"D"		Field returns for September 1917.	

L. A. Newnes
Cmdg: 2nd Roy Fus
30/9/17

A5834 Wt. W4973/M687 750,000 8/16 D. D. & L. Ltd. Forms/C.2118/13.

86/39

29.B.

~ CONFIDENTIAL ~

Vol 20

WAR ~ DIARY

~ 2ND BN ~

ROYAL · FUSILIERS

~ VOL·32 ~

OCT·1917

Vol 32

Instructions regarding War Diaries and Intelligence Summaries are contained in F. S. Regs., Part II. and the Staff Manual respectively. Title pages will be prepared in manuscript.

WAR DIARY or INTELLIGENCE SUMMARY.

(Erase heading not required.)

2nd Royal Fusiliers

October 1917.

Army Form C. 2118.

Place	Date	Hour	Summary of Events and Information	Remarks and references to Appendices
ELVERDINGHE AREA (ABINGLEY CAMP)				
October	1st		"Z" Coy working on track 11. Rest of Battn "Coy training". Special classes for Scouts & Signallers. Usual fatigue party at RUGBY DUMP. Bosch Aeroplanes very active night bombing in this area – All Coy Lewis guns mounted (16 in all) to cope with them. Bright & warm	H.O.W.
"	2nd		"X" Coy on track 11. Rest of Battn coy training – All the Battn were bathed during the day. Scouts & Sigs. special classes. Bright & warm	H.O.W.
"	3rd		"W" Coy on track 11. Rest of Battn coy training – practice in crossing streams with specially made bridges. Dull & cool	H.O.W.
"	4th		"Y" Coy on tracks. Rest of Battn coy training. "W" Coy (Capt Pearson) left camp at 5.30 pm. to reinforce the 1st Royal Dublin Fus. in the line who successfully attacked early this morning in front of LANGEMARK. This Coy arrived at the Dublin's B.H.Q. (in Langemark) at 10 pm. without casualties. They proceeded from there with guides to EAGLE TRENCH where they remained in support to the 1st R.D.Fus. Dull & showery.	H.O.W. Appendix "A"

A5834 Wt. W4973/M687 750,000 8/16 D. D. & L. Ltd. Forms/C.2118/13.

Vol 32.

Instructions regarding War Diaries and Intelligence Summaries are contained in F. S. Regs., Part II. and the Staff Manual respectively. Title pages will be prepared in manuscript.

WAR DIARY
or
INTELLIGENCE SUMMARY.
(Erase heading not required.)

2nd Royal Fusiliers
October 1917

Army Form C. 2118.

Place	Date	Hour	Summary of Events and Information	Remarks and references to Appendices
ELVERDINGHE AREA (ABINGLEY CAMP)				
October	5th		X Coy working on tasks. Y & Z Coy training specialists classes for Scouts & Signallers. W Coy were relieved in EAGLE TRENCH at twelve midnight & marched back to the above camp, having sustained no casualties. Dull & showery	H.O.?
"	6th		Battn practiced an attack in conjunction with the 1st Lancs Fusiliers. Showery & cold	H.O.?
"	7th		Battn moved to ROUSSEAU FARM CAMP for one night, being relieved by the Irish Guards. 2/Lts Benson & Hine with guides from each Coy proceeded up the line to 't GOED-TER-VESTEN FARM (U.17.d.7.2) & laid tape marking out Battn assembly line preparatory to attack. Showery & cold	H.O.?
"	8th		AT ROUSSEAU FARM. Morning – Battn drawing Battle stores & preparing generally to go into action. At 5.30 pm. Battn left camp & started for the line with guides. Although the night was very dark, the assembly on the tape laid the previous night was carried out most successfully & all Coys were in position by midnight, ready for the attack tomorrow morning. Dull & cold	H.O.?
"	9th		Battn in action } See appendix	App A
"	10th		" }	

A5834 Wt. W4973/M687 750,000 8/16 D. D. & L. Ltd. Forms/C.2118/13.

Vol 32

Instructions regarding War Diaries and Intelligence Summaries are contained in F. S. Regs., Part II. and the Staff Manual respectively. Title pages will be prepared in manuscript.

WAR DIARY 2nd Royal Fusiliers

or

INTELLIGENCE SUMMARY.

(Erase heading not required.)

October 1917.

Army Form C. 2118.

Place	Date	Hour	Summary of Events and Information	Remarks and references to Appendices
October	11th		With the exception of a few stragglers, most of the Battalion arrived at ELVERDINGE STATION from the line, at 5.30 am where they entrained for PROVEN arriving there at 7 a.m. marched to POONA CAMP & settled down to rest. Bright - cold	H.O.W.
"	12th		Battn generally cleaning up. The following new officers arrived from the Base Camp :- 2/Lts C.F. Harley, H.S. Piper, J.W. Watts, J. Thomas, H. Sinclair, C.T. Long, J. Steel & F. Wilson. Showery - cold	H.O.W.
"	13th		Battn generally cleaning & smartening up. 2/Lt Wise & 2 N.C.Os left for BLAIRVILLE France, billetting. Bright - cold	H.O.W.
"	14th		Battn inspected by Brigadier General, who also gave a speech of appreciation for good work done by the Battn in last push. Bright - cold	H.O.W.
"	15th		Battn preparing to leave for FRANCE. Left camp at 12 midnight for railhead. Dull - cold	H.O.W.
"	16th		Battn arrived at Railhead about 3 am. & entrained for BEAUMETZ, FRANCE. Train left at 4.45 am. sharp, & arrived at destination at 3 pm. Battn detrained & marched (5 Kilos) to BLAIRVILLE No 2 CAMP, arriving 5 pm. Bright cool	H.O.W.

A5834 Wt. W4973/M687 750,000 8/16 D. D. & L. Ltd. Forms/C.2118/13.

Vol. 32

Instructions regarding War Diaries and Intelligence Summaries are contained in F. S. Regs., Part II. and the Staff Manual respectively. Title pages will be prepared in manuscript.

WAR DIARY
or
INTELLIGENCE SUMMARY.
(Erase heading not required.)

2nd Royal Fusiliers

October 1917.

Army Form C. 2118.

Place	Date	Hour	Summary of Events and Information	Remarks and references to Appendices
October	17th		AT BLAIRVILLE CAMP.	
			Battn. arranging & cleaning up camp – Inspections. Bright & cool	[illegible]
"	18th		Companies smartening up drill. Bright & cool	[illegible]
"	19th		Battn. parade under R.S.M. Lecture by C.O. to all Officers. Bright & cool	[illegible]
	20th		Battn. parade under R.S.M. 2/Lt Watts transferred to T.M.B. Rev. took several Officers & N.C.O.s for a days outing to DOULON. Bright & cool. Lt. Thomson left for 14 days rest at BOULOGNE. Capt Leaning made Town Major of HENDECOURT.	[illegible]
"	21st		Voluntary Church parade. Doctor left for leave in England. Bright & warm	[illegible]
"	22nd		Adjutant's parade – Coy training & Specialists classes – All Coys had a cross country run. Maj. Hodding appointed Commander of 6th Army Corps Reinforcement Camp at Achiet. 2/Lts Allen & Saul left for 4 days rest as guests of a C.C.S. Mess. Fine & cold	[illegible]
"	23rd		Parades washed out owing to rain. All Coys had a cross country run. Capt. H. Hebdon joined the Bn. from the Reinforcement Camp. Raining & cold	[illegible]

Vol 32.

Instructions regarding War Diaries and Intelligence Summaries are contained in F. S. Regs., Part II. and the Staff Manual respectively. Title pages will be prepared in manuscript.

WAR DIARY 2nd Royal Fusiliers
or
~~INTELLIGENCE SUMMARY.~~
(Erase heading not required.)

October 1917.

Army Form C. 2118.

Place	Date	Hour	Summary of Events and Information	Remarks and references to Appendices
BLAIRVILLE No 2 CAMP	24th		Specialist training. Bn cross country run. Cold & wet.	PRoB
"	25th		No parades owing to rain. Cross country run for all. Wet.	PRoB
"	26th		Brigade practise for ceremonial parade at 10. AM "	PRoB
"	27th		Brigade practise ceremonial @ 10 AM. Sports in afternoon Wet.	PRoB
"	28		Church parade @ Divn Cinema. Fine.	PRoB
"	29th		R.S.M.s parade. Specialist training. 2Lt W. DIMMOCK joined. Cool.	PRoB
"	30th		Baths in morning. a little musketry & specialist training. Drizzly	PRoB
"	31st		Brigade Practise ceremonial from 10–11.30 AM. Rest party returned.	PRoB.

C. A. Stevens [illegible]
Cmdg 2nd Roy Fus:

A5834 Wt. W4973/M687 750,000 8/16 D. D. & L. Ltd. Forms/C.2118/13.

REPORT ON ACTION of 9th Oct.1917.

2nd Battalion, Royal Fusiliers.

1. The approach march was successfully carried out with very few casualties.
The forming up in the assembly position was also successfully performed under considerable difficulties, due to darkness and weather.
The previous reconnaissance and laying of tapes being so well done , there was no confusion of any sort.

2. During the wait after fitting into assembly formation, the enemy shelled fairly heavily but consistantly between 2.30 a.m. and zero hour, very few casualties were incurred & the line only had to be placed a little further forward.

3. At zero hour the men got well off the mark & closed up. The ~~fixingxwasxheavy~~ going was very difficult owing to the slippery ground and the large numbers of shell craters but at the same time was not as bad as might have been expected considering the weather

4. The enemy barrage came down about 5 minutes after zero and thickened up about 8 minutes after. The barrage was never very formidable. The enemy seemed quick in following up the attacking waves with his guns, but never seemed to quite get his target.

5. The advance proceeded normally until OLGA HOUSE was approached The dispositions of the Battalions were as follows:-

1st Wave Y. Co. (<u>Lieut Hood</u> on right) X. Co.(Capt GRIFFITHS on left.)

2nd wave. Z. Co. (Capt ANGEL on right.) W. Co. Capt. PEARSON on left.)

(a) On the right.

Y. Co. had two Platoons in support of the 1st Lancashire Fusiliers, the third Platoon following on behind. When approaching OLGA HOUSE the line was held up for about 15 minutes, there were then about two Companies of the L.Fs. in front of the two Platoons of Y. Co. The barrage went forward and was lost.

After about 15 minutes delay the L.Fs. went on about 100 to 150 yards followed by Y. Co. and Z. Co. behind them the whole two Companies of L.Fs. less about 30 men seemed to swing to the left the 30 men keeping straight on followed by the R.F. The barrage was then halted on the CONDE HOUSE line in front of first objective.

The 30 (roughly) men of the L.Fs. halted on the line of the real first objective i.e. between OLGA HOUSE and CONDE HOUSE, for the time the barrage halted.

Capt HOOD who was with his front two Platoons noted the time for the advance to the second objective and observed the thickening of the barrage beforehand, preparing to advance.

2/

The L.Fs. were not seen to advance, and Lieut.RUMBALL was sent forward to see what help was required.

2/Lieut RUMBALL found that about 20 men had advanced beyond the CONDE HOUSE POELCAPPELLE Road and that about that 10 or 15 men were lying in shell holes west of the Road.

Capt. HOOD then pushed forward to reinforce with his two Platoons as the two Platoons advanced they came under severe Rifle fire. After crossing the above named Road, the fire coming from the direction of SENEGAL FARM. Further progress was made to about 200 yards East of this Road by advancing from Shell hole to Shell hole. When after suffering about 20 casualties from Rifle fire, h the further advance was brought to a halt.

The few L.Fs. in front observed firing off to the left, nobody could be seen on the right XXXXXXXXXXXXXXXXXX the right of these two Platoons was about MILLERS HOUSES.

A Patrol(under CORPL- FLOYD) sent out to the right, reported a gap of 300 yards to the nearest troops of the 4th Division. Capt. HOOD then consolidated the line he was on, viz:- from about 250 yards in front of CONDE HOUSE to about 100 yards north of MILLERS HOUSE. Capt. HOOD did not advance to the attack of the 3rd objective

1st. Because the second objective had not been made good.
2nd. There were no supports.
3rd. Prevented from advancing by reason of Rifle fire.

Z. Co. from the start followed behind Y. Co. 2nd Lieut SAUL commanded right Platoon. 2nd Lieut. PARKER left Platoon of first line.
2/Lt. WARE commanded the third Platoon following in rear .
Capt. ANGEL, 2/Lt. WARE and 2/Lt. PARKER are casualties, and no account cah as yet be obtained from them.
2/Lieut SAUL followed Capt. HOOD, after the 15 minutes halt at OLGA HOUSE, he passed through one or two groups of L.Fs. in Shell holes, was then drawn off to his right about the huts at (v.13 a.7.7) where he was held up by Rifle fire.

(B) On the left.

X. Co. followed by W. Co. got on all right up to about the line of OLGA HOUSE when the line in front of them was held up for about 15 minutes.
During this wait the Barrage got right away.
After the 15 minutes wait the L.Fs. in front advanced about 100 yards when they again halted, apparently on first objective, they-~~noticed-the-thickening-of-the-barrage-and-advanced-by-the-watch--~~
Officers commanding W. & X. Companies were together preliminary to advance on second objective. They noticed the thickening of the barrage and advanced by the watch. They passed through a line of L.Fs. in shell holes and thought another line was in front, but could neither see or get in touch with them. Their Companies halted on the line roughly U. 12.D.7.4. CONDE HOUSE where they proceeded to reorganise preparatory to advance on third objective, they were in touch with Worcesters on left but could not obtain touch with anybody in front or on the right.

The advance to third objective was commenced with the watch, The right near CONDE HOUSE was immediately held up by short shooting of our barrage, which caused some casualties and interfered with advance. The barrage was lost through this cause, advance was continued, then found that their was nobody in front and the second objective had not been taken.
The line then halted on the line TRANQUILLE HOUSE. V.7.c.3.2. consolidated and extended further to right.

Vol 33

86/79

30b

Vol 21

Confidential

WAR DIARY

NOVEMBER

2nd Bn Royal Fusiliers

VOLUME . 33

(1)

Army Form C. 2118.

Instructions regarding War Diaries and Intelligence Summaries are contained in F. S. Regs., Part II. and the Staff Manual respectively. Title pages will be prepared in manuscript.

WAR DIARY or ~~INTELLIGENCE SUMMARY.~~

(Erase heading not required.)

2nd. BN. Royal Fusiliers

Place	Date	Hour	Summary of Events and Information for NOVEMBER	Remarks and references to Appendices
BRAYVILLE CAMP	NOVEMBER 1st		Company Training advance guards etc. Lecture on Pigeons. G.O.C Divn attend all officers except in Lancs Lecture Hall.	BB
	2.		Brigade ceremonial and distribution of honours at 3 PM General Hickey (G.O.C 16th Divn) + Gen de Lisle came to tea afterwards going to Divisional Concert.	BB
	3.		Specialist training.	BB
	4.		Demonstration attack in co-operation with tanks (with fascines). Lieut-Col ARTHUR CRONSHAW - Manchester Regt - attached to BN as 2/command.	BB
	5.		Recreational training. 2/Lt W. H. S. Jewells + 25 O.R. attached to 20th Divn for work in forward area.	BB
	6.		Coy Bathing.	BB
	7.		Whole BN passed through gas chamber. Draft of 45 O.R. from Base - also 1 NCO + 20 ORs (all signallers) from Corps Depot BN. First night of our concert show.	BB
	8.		Coy training. → Final of Soccer - inter BN - cup. - Middlesex won. Presentation of prizes.	BB
	9.		BN parade.	BB
	10.		Bathing for BN. C.O saw all officers at 11.30 am re coming operations.	BB
	11		CHURCH PARADE @ 10.45 AM. - Capts H.H. HEBDEN, - W.J. HOOD, L.W. GRIFFITHS proceeded to forward area	BB
	12.		our Lt-Col G.A. STEVENS, D.S.O left to take over command of the 90th Brigade. Major J.S. Podding rejoined from depot BN and assumed command	BB

A5834 Wt W4973/M687 750,000 8/16 D. D. & L. Ltd. Forms/C.2118/13.

VOL 33

Instructions regarding War Diaries and Intelligence Summaries are contained in F. S. Regs., Part II. and the Staff Manual respectively. Title pages will be prepared in manuscript.

WAR DIARY
or
~~INTELLIGENCE SUMMARY.~~
(~~Erase heading not required.~~)

Army Form C. 2118. (2)

2nd Bn Royal Fusiliers

Place	Date	Hour	Summary of Events and Information for NOVEMBER	Remarks and references to Appendices
	NOVEMBER			
BIAIRVILLE CAMP	12th		Lieut. Col. E. A. CRONSHAW was re-posted to 1st Lancs Fusiliers & left this Bn. 2nd Lt. MAINGOT returned from leave.	
	13th		Bn rehearsed attack with Bde moving off at 7.45 AM	
	14th		Do	
	15th		Division rehearsed attack starting at 10.0 from zero position	
	16th		Company parades	
	17		Bn marched to BOISLEUX-AU-MONT and entrained for PERONNE at 11 PM. Capt LATHOM-BROWNE joined up at station and assumed position of 2nd/Command	
HAUT-ALLAINES	18th		Arrived at PERONNE at 5.30 AM and marched to HAUT-ALLAINES at 6 PM Bn marched to EQUANCOURT and billeted in huts.	
EQUANCOURT	19		Resting as much as possible and drawing battle stores.	
THE ATTACK.	20th	2.0 AM	Bn moved off and marched to DEAD MANS CORNER via FINS and GOUZEAUCOURT	
		5 AM	Ready at assembly position in Right rear of 16th Middlesex and on Right of RGLI in diamond formation with 1st Lancs in Bde Support.	
		ZERO (6.20 AM)	We moved forward as a Brigade with our W coy in front, X Right rear Y Left Rear and Z coy in Support.	

A5834 Wt W4973/M687 750,000 8/16 D. D. & L. Ltd. Forms/C.2118/13.

VOL 33

WAR DIARY
or
INTELLIGENCE SUMMARY.
(Erase heading not required.)

Army Form C. 2118. (3)

Instructions regarding War Diaries and Intelligence Summaries are contained in F. S. Regs., Part II. and the Staff Manual respectively. Title pages will be prepared in manuscript.

2nd Royal Fusiliers

Place	Date	Hour	Summary of Events and Information for NOVEMBER	Remarks and references to Appendices
THE ATTACK	NOVEMBER 20th		The following officers took part in the attack :- Major J.S. HODDING (C.O) CAPT. P.T.O. BOULT (ADJ) J.S. LEANING. C. RUSSELL (RAMC). A.G. PAPE (OC Z) L.W. GRIFFITHS (OC X) W.J. HOOD (OC Y). 2nd Lts W.L. MERRITT (I.O) H.S. PIPER (OC W) J.N. ABBOT. (W) H. BRANFORD (W) J. HORNE-PAYNE (W) H.L. NEPHAM (X) P.G. BRAIN (X) J. THOMAS (X) W. DIMMOCK (X) W.C. BATTERBURY (Z) R.A.R. MASON (W) W. SINCLAIR (Y) R.L. SPARKS (Z) C.W.G. BURTON (Z) LT. F.G. HAMILTON (T.O)	
			At Zero the Bn moved forward in diamond formation on a bearing (true) of 40° until the original English front line was reached, and halted in front of PLOUGH SUPPORT. Here our first casualty, Pte TIBBLE No 62276 was wounded by shell, subsequently dying	
		10.20	Our advance was continued on same bearing until we passed through the 6th Division, who had captured and were holding the HINDENBURG LINE. Shortly after leaving the H. Line we came under MG fire and extended advancing in two waves. With the support of numerous Tanks the advance was continued in spite of several small strong points. When nearing the outskirts of MARCOING several Germans ran forward and gave themselves up. At the cross roads at 22 D 3.5	

A5834 Wt W4973/M687 750,000 8/16 D. D. & L. Ltd. Forms/C.2118/13.

VOL 33

(4)

Instructions regarding War Diaries and Intelligence Summaries are contained in F. S. Regs., Part II. and the Staff Manual respectively. Title pages will be prepared in manuscript.

WAR DIARY
or
~~INTELLIGENCE SUMMARY.~~
(*Erase heading not required.*)

Army Form C. 2118.

2nd BN ROYAL FUSILIERS

Place	Date	Hour	Summary of Events and Information for NOVEMBER.	Remarks and references to Appendices
"THE ATTACK"	NOVEMBER 20th		The advance was temporarily chequed by M.G. and a small amount of Rifle fire, but TANKS and rifle grenades soon overcame all obstacles on outskirts of village. 2Lt BURTON was killed, Capt Leaming wounded in Bottom + 2Lt Piper had his arm smashed. a little further on 2Lt Mason was mortally wounded. Two platoons under Capt Griffiths entered the western portion of village of MARCOING and after some street fighting captured about 100 prisoners, some M Guns and other booty of military value. All this time touch had been maintained on Right flank with K.O.S.B. and with RGLI on Left. The advance continued towards Noyelles where stubborn resistance was encountered from Road running through L.17.A. Eventually we reached our final objective at 3.15 P.M. and dug in. A Patrol [illegible] was immediately pushed forward to secure the Bridge over the Canal at NOYELLES (at L6c.2.3). This was impossible as the bridge over the River ESCAUT had been blown up (L.11.b.5.7). Prior to this our scouts got within 50 yds of the wooden Bridge at L 11 D. 9.3 when it was suddenly blown up although 3 of the enemy had been sniped in the immediate area of this Bridge.	

A5834 Wt. W4973/M687 750,000 8/16 D. D. & L. Ltd. Forms/C.2118/13.

VOL 33

Army Form C. 2118.

(5)

WAR DIARY
or
INTELLIGENCE SUMMARY.
(~~Erase heading not required.~~)

Instructions regarding War Diaries and Intelligence Summaries are contained in F. S. Regs., Part II. and the Staff Manual respectively. Title pages will be prepared in manuscript.

2nd Bn. Royal Fusiliers

Place	Date	Hour	Summary of Events and Information for NOVEMBER	Remarks and references to Appendices
	NOVEMBER			
"THE ATTACK"	20th	4-0PM	At this period ~~X~~ Coy were sent forward to hold the village of NOYELLES and link up with the post at L.5.C.2-3 which was to be held by the Middlesex. X Coy dug in between River ESCAUT and the CANAL making two strong points one facing East and the other North. This had to be done as the 87th Brigade was some 500x short of its objective, thus leaving our Right flank "in the air". Shortly after 4.0PM a patrol of the 4th Dragoons passed through NOYELLES but soon returned and placed themselves under O.C.Z who posted them on Northern outskirts of village, while Z Coy held the blown up bridge at L.11.B.6.7 and the intact wooden bridge in the chateau grounds at L.11.B.8.5. During the night a Bosch patrol approached the strong point on our extreme flank, having somehow worked along the canal bank, but were repulsed by L.G. & rifle fire. Bn Headquarters was established at L.11.d.2-2.	MAP 57C N.E.4.
NOYELLES	21st	5.0AM.	A reinforcement of 40 men of the 18th Hussars reported to O.C.Z to replace the men of the 4th Dragoons who had retired in the early morning ~~…~~ because they had been fired at by enemy.	

A5834 Wt. W4973/M687 750,000 8/16 D. D. & L. Ltd. Forms/C.2118/13.

VOL 33

Instructions regarding War Diaries and Intelligence Summaries are contained in F. S. Regs., Part II. and the Staff Manual respectively. Title pages will be prepared in manuscript.

WAR DIARY
or
~~INTELLIGENCE~~ SUMMARY.
(~~Erase heading not required.~~)

Army Form C. 2118.

(6)

2nd Royal Fusiliers

Place	Date	Hour	Summary of Events and Information for NOVEMBER	Remarks and references to Appendices
	NOVEMBER		Owing to the 4th Dragoons retiring before the 10th Hussars had relieved them the posts on the outskirts of the village were temporarily abandoned consequently the enemy gradually worked their way into NOYELLES finally making a determined Counter attack at 10-30 a.m. He again attacked at 12.15 and succeeded in making his way as far as the church where he established a machine Gun. Fighting continued around this area all the day, stokes guns being employed. At 4.0PM Two tanks (BEN my chree + BULLAWAYO II) with a mopping up party behind each of Royal Fusiliers and 10th Hussars cleared the village which we handed over to C Coy of the 1st Buffs who had come to relieve us.	
NOYELLES	21st		During all the street fighting 2Lt Reed behaved with great gallantry, destroying two enemy machine guns. 2Lt R.L.SPARKS was killed. Upon relief the Battalion was billeted in MARCOING.	
			During all these operations we captured 400 prisoners, 2 light oblique MGs and 10 heavy M Guns and 3 "granatenwerfers".	
MARCOING	22nd		G.O.C. Bde visited all men in billets. Gen de Lisle called and congratulated C.O.	
			The Mayor and populace of NOYELLES personally thanked Capt Hood, Papa and	

A5834 Wt. W4973/M687 750,000 8/16 D. D. & L. Ltd. Forms/C.2118/13.

VOL 33

Instructions regarding War Diaries and Intelligence Summaries are contained in F. S. Regs., Part II. and the Staff Manual respectively. Title pages will be prepared in manuscript.

WAR DIARY or ~~INTELLIGENCE SUMMARY.~~

(Erase heading not required.)

Army Form C. 2118. (7)

2nd Royal Fusiliers

Place	Date	Hour	Summary of Events and Information for NOVEMBER	Remarks and references to Appendices
	NOVEMBER		all the men who fought in NOYELLES for their great courage etc – this was at Brigade HQ	
MARCOING	22nd			
MASNIERES	23rd		Bn re-equipped.	
		4-30 PM	moved off to MASNIERES and relieved the Middlesex who were in support in the left Bde sector. Bn HQ at catacombes at G 20D.7.2. Relief complete by 8.0 PM	
"	24th		Relieved the Middlesex in the front line which consisted of a few strong points isolated from the main line of defense.	
"	25th		Rest during day and very busy during night. Bn thus:- Right front line W coy L front. X coy: Z in left support and Y in Right support in Quarry.	RB
"	26th		Enemy shelling much more severe but few casualties. all Bn supplied with hot food 2 times daily from Bosch cookers	
"	27th		Do Do Enemy started his Trench mortars	
"	28th		Relieved by 1st Lancs & came back into support but with title of "Counter-attack Bn." with Y+Z in Sugar Factory. W in Quarry + X off CAMBRAI ROAD. We supplied Lancs with all available men for working on Trenches. CAPT. H. LATHOM-BROWNE re-joined from Division.	
"	29th		all Bn on working parties during day and night. 2Lt P. N. DEVLIN joined Bn and 2Lts Maingot and Allen re joined from Div. 10%.	
"	30		Very heavy shelling of MASNIERES from 2 – 5 AM and we "stood to" at 6.15 am.	

A5834 Wt. W4973/M687 750,000 8/16 D. D. & L. Ltd. Forms/C.2118/13.

VOL 33

Instructions regarding War Diaries and Intelligence Summaries are contained in F. S. Regs., Part II. and the Staff Manual respectively. Title pages will be prepared in manuscript.

WAR DIARY
or
~~INTELLIGENCE~~ SUMMARY.
(Erase heading not required.)

Army Form C. 2118. 8

2nd Bn Royal Fusiliers

Place	Date	Hour	Summary of Events and Information for NOVEMBER	Remarks and references to Appendices
	NOVEMBER			
MASNIERES	30th		At 7.0 AM Enemy launched a very big attack against divisions holding LES RUES VERTES and ground back to Hindenburg Line. Y and Z Coys crossed the canal at the Lock Bridge near the Sugar factory and formed a defensive flank as far as the old Brigade Rear HQ in Les Rues Vertes – while 2 platoons of X were sent to help in the street fighting. W Coy remained in Quarry. At 2.0 PM Capt Hatton Browne with 2 platoons of W + remaining platoon of X took over the defences of Les Rues Vertes. The remaining platoon of W Coy under 2Lt BRAIN was sent down to the Sugar factory to hold the Lock Bridge. During the day Capt Hood, 2Lt Sinclair, 2Lt Brain were wounded and evacuated. 2Lt Devlin was also slightly wounded but remained at duty. Bn HQ was moved to G 26. b. 50.45 house or cellar opposite to the Guernsey HQ. At 6.0 PM warning orders were issued in case the Brigade had to evacuate the area, but later congratulations and orders to hang on to the end were received from Army HQ as masses of troops and cavalry and Tanks were about to counter attack the enemy. H Hatton Browne Major Comdg. 2nd Bn Royal Fusiliers	[illegible]

A5834 Wt W4973/M687 750,000 8/16 D. D. & L. Ltd. Forms/C.2118/13.

81 B.
(6 sheets)

Vol. 34

2 RF
Vol 22

Confidential

WAR DIARY

DECEMBER
1917

2ND Bn ROYAL FUSILIERS

Instructions regarding War Diaries and Intelligence Summaries are contained in F. S. Regs., Part II. and the Staff Manual respectively. Title pages will be prepared in manuscript.

Vol. 34
for December

WAR DIARY
or
~~INTELLIGENCE SUMMARY.~~
(Erase heading not required.)

2nd R.F

Army Form C. 2118.

Place	Date	Hour	Summary of Events and Information	Remarks and references to Appendices
LES RUES VERTES	1st		Battn still holding outskirts of village. Heavy hostile barrage at 6 a.m. which continued throughout the day. At 6 a.m. a counter attack by enemy which was repulsed by our rifle and M.G. fire. At 4 p.m. a comp. of S.W.B. came up to reinforce. At 4.15 p.m. the Bosch made another heavy attack driving in our advanced posts and succeeding in entering the village. At 7 p.m. orders were received for the evacuation of MASNIÈRES and LES RUES VERTES. [illegible] was commenced at 11.15 p.m. The last post at the sugar factory was withdrawn at 12.05 p.m. and the Battn moved, in small parties, via the [illegible] at L 2 [illegible] south of the MARCOING COPSE and on to the VILLERS PLOUICH road forming up in the Hindenburgh support at L 33 d central. Here [illegible] cookers, rations and blankets. 2/Lt Dimmock missing	App. B
Hindenburgh Support	2nd		At 3 p.m. orders were received to move to the wagon lines at TRESCAULT. At 4.50 p.m. the Battn moved off arriving at TRESCAULT at 7 p.m. The men there had a hot food after which they moved to RIBECOURT, where they were billeted in cellars. Clear and cold	R.F. [illegible]

A5834 Wt. W4973/M687 750,000 8/16 D. D. & L. Ltd. Forms/C.2118/13.

Army Form C. 2118.

WAR DIARY
or
~~INTELLIGENCE SUMMARY.~~

Instructions regarding War Diaries and Intelligence Summaries are contained in F. S. Regs., Part II. and the Staff Manual respectively. Title pages will be prepared in manuscript.

Vol. 34

For December 1917 (*Erase heading not required.*)

2nd R.F.

Place	Date	Hour	Summary of Events and Information	Remarks and references to Appendices
RIBECOURT	3rd		At 9 a.m. the Battn received orders to remove from present billets back as far as the TRESCAULT wood and await further orders. These were received at 4.30 p.m. The Battn moved to HAVRINCOURT WOOD, where they bivouaced for the night. Clear and cold	
HAVRINCOURT WOOD	4th		Battn moved from HAVRINCOURT WOOD at 10 a.m. and marched to FINS. Billets fair, weather cold.	
FINS	5th		Battn moved from FINS at 1 p.m. and marched, via EQUANCOURT to ETRICOURT, where they entrained for PETIT-HOUVIN. 2/Lt RUMBALL rejoined from Bde details. 2/Lt Saul rejoined from course.	
PETIT HOUVIN	6th		Battn detrained at 4.35 a.m. and moved via MAGNICOURT & AMBRINES to LIGNEREUIL 2/Lt Wilson rejoined. Clear and cold.	
LIGNEREUIL	7th		General cleaning of clothing, equipment etc. Lt Lawson joined battn - Dull.	
	8th		Inspection of clothing arms etc. All men bathed during day. Capt Griffiths, 2/Lt Hunt and Sergt Molyneux V.C. proceeded on leave. Clear and cold.	
	9th		Church parade 11.15 a.m. raining and cold.	
	10th		Smartening-up drill. Special class for scouts and signallers. Major Hodding left for England. — Clear and cold.	

Instructions regarding War Diaries and Intelligence Summaries are contained in F. S. Regs., Part II. and the Staff Manual respectively. Title pages will be prepared in manuscript.

Vol: 34

Army Form C. 2118.

WAR DIARY

or

~~INTELLIGENCE SUMMARY.~~

(Erase heading not required.)

for December 1917 2nd R.F.

Place	Date	Hour	Summary of Events and Information	Remarks and references to Appendices
LIGNEREUIL	11th		Speech by G.O.C. at 10.30 a.m. on recent operations. Battn paraded under R.S.M. 2/Lt Barnes rejoined from Corps depot. Draft of 80 O.R. arrived from Corps depot. 2/Lt Twells proceed on leave. Clear and cold.	[illegible]
"	12th		R.S.M's parade for new draft. Special class for L. Gunners, scouts and signallers. Capt Pearson rejoined and proceeded to G.L.I. as adjutant. Fine.	[illegible]
"	13th		W and X coys on the range, also all L. Gunners. R.S.M's parade for draft. "Royalties" gave opening show. Dull and cold.	[illegible]
"	14th		No parades owing to rain. 2/Lts Harley and Denton rejoined from Corps [illegible]	[illegible]
"	15th		R.S.M's parade for drafts. Y and Z coys on range. All L. Gunners fired. Special class for scouts & signallers. All men bathed during day. Clear & cold.	[illegible]
"	16th		Battn marched to CANCHY arriving at 4.15 pm. No stragglers. Billets fair. Snowing.	[illegible]
CANCHY	17th		Battn moved from CANCHY to NAMBERCOURT-CARVON-ST MARTIN, arriving at 4.30 pm. No stragglers - billets good. Clear & cold.	[illegible]
NAMBERCOURT	18th		Battn moved to ERGNY. Roads very bad owing to snow and hard frost. Battn arrived [illegible] with the exception of 12 stragglers who arrived later that night. Billets good.	[illegible]
ERGNY	19th		General cleaning & smartening up. Clear and cold.	
	20th		Coys under coy arrangements. 3 Officers joined Battn - 2/Lts Perry, Webb and Harley. Clear & cold.	
	21st		N.C.O's under R.S.M. Coys under coy arrangements. Special class for scouts, signallers and L. Gunners. Clear and cold. Capt Barton [illegible] joined [illegible]	

A5834 Wt. W4973/M687 750,000 8/16 D. D. & L. Ltd. Forms/C.2118/13.

Instructions regarding War Diaries and Intelligence Summaries are contained in F. S. Regs., Part II. and the Staff Manual respectively. Title pages will be prepared in manuscript.

Vol 34

For Dec 1917

WAR DIARY
or
~~INTELLIGENCE SUMMARY.~~
(Erase heading not required.)

Army Form C. 2118.

2nd ROYAL FUSILIERS

Place	Date	Hour	Summary of Events and Information	Remarks and references to Appendices
ERGNY	22nd		Coys under coy arrangements. Lecture to coys on German M.G. – Special classes for scouts and signallers. ~~Capt~~ Dull and cold.	RALB
"	23rd		Lecture to Officers and N.C.O's on Gas by Bde Major (86th Bde) – 2/Lt Wilson rejoined Bn from course.	RALB
"	24th		Coy training under coy arrangements. 2/Lt Saul proceeded on leave – 2/Lt Hunt returned from leave – Dull and cold.	RALB
"	25th		Church parade 11.15 a.m. – Christmas dinners by companys. Dull and cold, all snow gone.	RALB
"	26th		R.S.M's parade – 2/Lt Denton went on leave – Heavy snow in morning.	RALB.
"	27th		Coy training – special classes for scouts and signallers. Capt Pape went to hospital, sick. 2/Lt Osborne-Parry proceeded on L.G. course. – Dull and cold.	RALB
"	28th		Coy training under coy arrangements – Lecture to Officers and scouts on sniping and scouting by Brigadier-General Cheape	RALB
"	29th		Coy training – Special classes for scouts and signallers – 2/Lt Twells returned from leave – Dull and cold	RALB
"	30th		Lecture to Officers and N.C.O's on "Esprit de corps" and leadership – 2/Lt Barry returned from leave – 2/Lt Thomas proceeded on course. 2/Lt Kirkpatrick went on leave – Dull and cold.	RALB
"	31st		Coy training under coy arrangements – Special classes for signallers and scouts. R.S.M's class for N.C.O's – Dull and cold	RALB

[illegible signature]

A5834 Wt. W4973/M687 750,000 8/16 D. D. & L. Ltd. Forms/C.2118/13.

Confidential

Vol 23

86/29

WAR DIARY

Vol. 35

2ND Bn.

THE ROYAL FUSILIERS

January 1918

Army Form C. 2118.

WAR DIARY
or
~~INTELLIGENCE SUMMARY.~~
(Erase heading not required.)

Instructions regarding War Diaries and Intelligence Summaries are contained in F. S. Regs., Part II. and the Staff Manual respectively. Title pages will be prepared in manuscript.

Vol 35 Jan: 1918. 2nd ROYAL FUSILIERS.

Place	Date	Hour	Summary of Events and Information	Remarks and references to Appendices
ERGNY	1st		Coy training under coy arrangements. Special classes for scouts and signallers. R.S.M.'s class for junior N.C.O's. Fine and cold.	RALB.
"	2nd		Bn training – Practise in attack under barrage. Fine and thawing. Billets at ERGNY good, but scattered.	RALB
"	3rd		Battn moved to QUELMES by road, leaving ERGNY at 7 a.m. and reaching the new billets at 2 p.m., a distance of 23 Km. The condition of the roads was very bad owing to heavy snow-storms, and the transport was considerably delayed. The drums marched at the head of each company alternately, the change being effected at each halt. There were a few stragglers who reached the billets shortly after the Battn. Fine and cold, with occasional heavy ~~s~~ snow storms.	RALB
QUELMES	4th		General cleaning and smartening up. Baths for all companies. Fine and cold. Billets good.	RALB.
"	5th		R.S.M.'s parade. Special classes for scouts and signallers. Capt Pape rejoined Battn from hospital. Capt Powell, 2/Lt Smith and 2/Lt Willett joined Battn and were posted to "Y", "W" and "X" coys respectively. Weather – mild and fine.	RALB
"	6th		2/Lt Harley left Battn to join R.N.D. 2/Lt Osborne-Parry rejoined Battn from L.G. course. Cold and wet.	RALB
"	7th		Company training under company arrangements. R.S.M.'s parade for junior N.C.O's. Special classes for scouts and signallers. Dull, thawing.	RALB

A5834 Wt. W4973/M687 750,000 8/16 D. D. & L. Ltd. Forms/C.2118/13.

Instructions regarding War Diaries and Intelligence Summaries are contained in F. S. Regs., Part II. and the Staff Manual respectively. Title pages will be prepared in manuscript.

Vol 35

Jan 1918

WAR DIARY
or
~~INTELLIGENCE SUMMARY.~~
(Erase heading not required.)

2nd ROYAL FUSILIERS

Army Form C. 2118.

Place	Date	Hour	Summary of Events and Information	Remarks and references to Appendices
QUELMES	8th		Inspection of all gas masks and anti-gas drill by Bde Gas Officer – Capt Pape went on leave. 2/Lt Merritt returned from leave – 2/Lt Wilson left the Battn to become Bde Gas officer – Dull and cold.	RaHB
"	9th		Coy training – Special classes for scouts and signallers. Cold, snow in afternoon.	RaHB
"	10th		Battn Ceremonial practise in morning – Bde ceremonial practise in afternoon. 2/Lt Devlin rejoined from course. 2/Lt Long left Battn for Bde Signals. Fine, thawing	RaHB
"	11th		Coy training – Special classes for scouts and signallers – RSM's parade for junior N.C.O.s – Dull and thawing.	RaHB
"	12th		Bde Ceremonial parade at 11 a.m. Presentation of New Year Honours by Major-Gen. Sir Beauvoir de Lisle. Capt and QMr E. Harding – M.C. – Cold and showery.	RaHB
"	13th		Voluntary Church services – Fine and mild.	RaHB
"	14th		Bde practise in the attack – 2/Lts Hunt and Mepham went on courses – Dull and cold	RaHB
"	15th		Coys under coy arrangements – Transport left QUELMES proceeding by road to BRANDHOEK area. Wet. Billets at QUELMES good.	RaHB

A5834 Wt. W4973/M687 750,000 8/16 D. D. & L. Ltd. Forms/C.2118/13.

Army Form C. 2118.

Instructions regarding War Diaries and Intelligence Summaries are contained in F. S. Regs., Part II. and the Staff Manual respectively. Title pages will be prepared in manuscript.

Vol 35
Jan: 1918

WAR DIARY
or
~~INTELLIGENCE SUMMARY.~~ 2nd ROYAL FUSILIERS

(Erase heading not required.)

Place	Date	Hour	Summary of Events and Information	Remarks and references to Appendices
QUELMES	16th		Battn left QUELMES at 7.30 a.m and marched to WIZERNES, where they entrained for BRANDHOEK at 11 a.m, reaching their destination at 2 p.m. They then marched to "B" Camp BRANDHOEK, where they were billetted in huts for the night. Stormy and wet.	RaxB
"B" Camp (BRANDHOEK)	17th		Battn left "B" Camp at 10.30 a.m. and marched to St Jean area which they reached at 12 noon – W and Y companies were billetted in California Camp, X, Z and H.Q. in Junction Camp. Transport remained at Transport lines in York Camp, BRANDHOEK area. Snow and rain all day.	RaxB
ST JEAN.	18th		Battle stores drawn in morning –	
		4.40 pm	Marched up to relieve the 2nd Bn Lincolnshire Regt in line of posts N.W. of PASSCHENDAELE – W coy on right sector, X coy centre and Y coy left sector. Z coy in support. Relief completed by 10 p.m, only one casualty. 33rd Division 98th Bde on right of Battn, 1st Bn Lancashire Fus. on left. 1st R.G.L.I. in Support.	RaxB
Front line	19th		Battn holding Front Line – Dull	RaxB
"	20th		" " " " Cold and dull	RaxB
"	21st		" " " " Wet.	RaxB
"	22nd		Battn relieved by 1st R.G.L.I. and proceeded into Reserve at BELLEVUE. Relief completed by 11 p.m. – Fine.	RaxB

A5834 Wt. W4973/M687 750,000 8/16 D. D. & L. Ltd. Forms/C.2118/13.

Instructions regarding War Diaries and Intelligence Summaries are contained in F. S. Regs., Part II. and the Staff Manual respectively. Title pages will be prepared in manuscript.

Vol 35

Jan: 1918

WAR DIARY
or
~~INTELLIGENCE SUMMARY.~~
(Erase heading not required.)

2nd ROYAL FUSILIERS

Army Form C. 2118.

Place	Date	Hour	Summary of Events and Information	Remarks and references to Appendices
BELLE VUE	23rd		Battn in reserve at BELLE VUE. Carrying parties to Front line. Fine.	RA&B
"	24th		Battn relieved by 1st L.F at 7p.m and moved to California Camp. Clear & fine.	RA&B
California Camp	25th		Resting all day. All Battn on working parties at night. Very fine & bright	RA&B
"	26th		Left California Camp at 11.15 a.m. and proceeded by train from WILTSE to BRANDHOEK, arriving at "B" Camp at 1p.m. The camp was taken over from the K.O.S.B.s. – Capt P.T.C. Boutt returned from leave. Dull and foggy.	RA&B
"B" Camp (BRANDHOEK)	27th		Baths for all coys. Cold and foggy	
"	28th		General cleaning and smartening – Fine and sunny. 2nd Lieut W Sinclair joined Battn	RA&B
"	29th		Cleaning up and draining Camp – Fine.	RA&B
"	30th		Coys at Coy Commanders disposal – Fine and dry.	RA&B
"	31st		Brigade ceremonial parade. – Fine and dry.	RA&B
				W.H.

[illegible signature]

A5834 Wt. W4973/M687 750,000 8/16 D. D. & L. Ltd. Forms/C.2118/13.

Instructions regarding War Diaries and Intelligence Summaries are contained in F. S. Regs., Part II. and the Staff Manual respectively. Title pages will be prepared in manuscript.

Vol 36

Feby 1918.

WAR DIARY
or
INTELLIGENCE SUMMARY.
(*Erase heading not required.*)

Army Form C. 2118.

2nd ROYAL FUSILIERS

Vol 24

Place	Date	Hour	Summary of Events and Information	Remarks and references to Appendices
BRANDHOEK "B" CAMP.	1st		Brigade Ceremonial parade and presentation of CAMBRAI honours by Divisional Commander.	
			— List of Honours. —	
			Victoria Cross :- Capt R. GEE. MILITARY CROSS:- Capt H. LATHOM-BROWNE; Lieut F.G. HAMILTON; ~~[illegible]~~; Capt C. RUSSELL (RAMC attached)	
			D.S.O. :- 2/Lt J. PEEL.	
			DCM :- 44238 C.S.M. D. LEHANE; 13595 RQMS W. THRIFT.	
			MILITARY MEDAL:- 36644 Pte G. PRINCE; 15122 Pte C. WHITE; 37257 Cpl E. COX; 15447 Pte E. CLEWS; 53174 L/c H. SAULL.	
			BAR to M.M.:- 16024 Cpl S. CAUNT.	
			MENTIONED:- 2/Lt J.S. BENSON; Lieut S.C. SHILLINGFORD; 1647 Sgt T. MATTHEWS; 13595 RQMS W. THRIFT.	
"	2nd		Training and general improvement of camp.	
"	3rd		Moved to CALIFORNIA CAMP in ST JEAN area by train from BRANDHOEK.	
CALIFORNIA CAMP.	4th		Working parties on GOUDBERG Reserve Line	
"	5th		-ditto-	
"	6th		-ditto-	
"	7th		-ditto-	

A5834 Wt. W4973/M687 750,000 8/16 D. D. & L. Ltd. Forms/C.2118/13.

33 B (8 sheets)

2

Vol 36.

Army Form C. 2118.

Instructions regarding War Diaries and Intelligence Summaries are contained in F. S. Regs., Part II. and the Staff Manual respectively. Title pages will be prepared in manuscript.

WAR DIARY or INTELLIGENCE SUMMARY. 2nd ROYAL FUSILIERS.

February 1918. (Erase heading not required.)

Place	Date	Hour	Summary of Events and Information	Remarks and references to Appendices
CALIFORNIA CAMP.	8th		Working parties on GOUDBERG Reserve Line. 2nd Lieuts M.G. WHYTE, G.S COOK; J.T SMITH; W.E. STOKES; D. NEISH; G.V.R KENNY-SIEVEWRIGHT and 220 O Ranks joined from 20th Royal Fus. on disbandment. 1 O Rank wounded	
"	9th		"Y" and "Z" Coys moved to reserve line BELLE VUE. "W" and "X" Coys working parties	
"	10th		In reserve – quiet	
"	11th		Relieved by 23rd Bde. Moved to HASLAR CAMP. 1 O R wounded	
HASLAR CAMP	12th		Working parties on Army Battle Zone under orders of VIII Corps. 2nd Lieuts E.G. ANDREWS and H. NORWELL joined. 1 OR died of wounds	
"	13th		Working parties.	
"	14th		-ditto-	
"	15th		-ditto- 2nd Lieuts W.J. WARE; R.H. LOVERIDGE; M.S. EKINS & P.S. CUBLEY joined.	
"	16th		-ditto- 2nd Lieut W.T GOULD joined.	
"	17th		-ditto-	
	18th		-ditto-	
	19th		Relieved by 4th WORCESTERSHIRE REGT and moved to billets in EECKE area by train from WIELTJE to GODEWAERSVELDE then by march route to EECKE.	[signature]

D. D. & L., London, E.C. (A7883) Wt. W1011/M1672 350,000 1/17 Sch. 52a. Forms/C/2118/14

Vol 36 3

Army Form C. 2118.

Instructions regarding War Diaries and Intelligence Summaries are contained in F. S. Regs., Part II. and the Staff Manual respectively. Title pages will be prepared in manuscript.

WAR DIARY or INTELLIGENCE SUMMARY.

(Erase heading not required.)

February 1918. 2nd ROYAL FUSILIERS.

Place	Date	Hour	Summary of Events and Information	Remarks and references to Appendices
EECKE	19th		Billets good but very scattered. 2nd-Lieut C.W. CHILCOTT joined	
"	20th		Baths for all companies – cleaning up of equipment. Capt P.N.W. WILSON joined and assumed command of Battn. 2nd-Lieuts J.H.B. GILES and F.J. CRYER joined.	
"	21st		Coy training under Coy arrangements. Specialist training. Capt C.B. CATCHPOLE and 2nd-Lieut R.O. DARKER joined.	
"	22nd		Coy and specialist training. Lieut T.H. HARRISON joined	
"	23rd		-ditto-	
"	24th		Divine Service. 2nd-Lieut F.J. CRYER sick to Hospital	
"	25th		Coy & specialist training. 2nd Lieut J. FRASER joined. 2nd-Lt A.L. CHALKER rejoined	
"	26th		Practice Brigade Ceremonial Parade. Lecture – "MINOR TACTICS" by G.O.C. Divn.	
"	27th		Brigade Ceremonial Parade and presentation of medal ribbons by G.O.C. Divn. Recipients:- Belgian Croix de Guerre – 1817 Sgt J. MOLYNEUX V.C. and 1200 Pte G. TEDDER. D.C.M. Military Medal:- 9633 Pte J. KELLY. Bar to M.M.:- Pte E. MARTIN (No 52340).	
"	28th		Tactical exercise. Battn Troupe "RUFFLES" gave show to R.F.C.	

P.N. Wilson Lieut Col
Commdg 2/Royal Fusiliers

D. D. & L., London, E.C. (A7851) Wt. W8o/M1672 350,000 4/17 Sch. 52a Forms C/2118/14

CONFIDENTIAL

34.B.
(8 sheets)

WO 95

WAR DIARY.

2ND BATTN ROYAL FUSILIERS.

MARCH 1918.

VOL 37.

Instructions regarding War Diaries and Intelligence Summaries are contained in F. S. Regs., Part II. and the Staff Manual respectively. Title pages will be prepared in manuscript.

Vol 26

WAR DIARY or INTELLIGENCE SUMMARY.

(Erase heading not required.)

March 1918

2nd Royal Fusiliers

Army Form C. 2118.

(1)

Place	Date	Hour	Summary of Events and Information	Remarks and references to Appendices
(Ecke)	1st		Coy training. Lieut L B Solomon joined. Cold & windy weather	
ECCKE	2nd		Coy training " "	
	3rd		Lecture to Officers & N.C.O's by C.O. " "	
	4		Coy training practice raids. Wet Cleared up about 12 noon	
	5		Coy training	
	6		Brigade tactical exercise	
	7		Battn moved to Brandhoek by train left Godewaersvelde 11 AM detrained at BRANDHOEK fine & warm weather Billets good	J H B G
Brandhoek	8th		Baths specialists training Blankets & great coats disinfected	
BRANDHOEK	9th		Coy arrangements & specialists training Weather warm	
	10th		Vol Church parade. football match inter Coy. "	
	11th		At 6 AM. Battn was ordered to stand to, order was cancelled half an hour afterwards. Battn lined road to say goodbye to Major Gen Sir Beauvoir de Lisle	
	[illegible]		Specialists training Coy arrangements Y Coy practice raiding weather fine, warm	

D. D. & L., London, E.C. (A7883) Wt. W803/M1672 350,000 4/17 Sch. 52a Forms/C/2118/14

Vol 26

Instructions regarding War Diaries and Intelligence Summaries are contained in F. S. Regs., Part II. and the Staff Manual respectively. Title pages will be prepared in manuscript.

March 1918

WAR DIARY
or
INTELLIGENCE SUMMARY.
(Erase heading not required.)

Army Form C. 2118.

2nd Royal Fusiliers (2)

Place	Date	Hour	Summary of Events and Information	Remarks and references to Appendices
Hasler Camp	12		Battn marched to HASLER CAMP via YPRES. Billets good but crowded C.O, Adjt, Coy Comrs Sigs Officer & I.O. visited Battl Sec of line weather fine. Y Coy raid party remained BRANDHOEK	
	13		Y & Z Coys working parties to PICKLEHOBE KEEP	
			W & X " " " to BOSEART KEEP	
			C.O Adjt Coy Comrs & I.O. And Second i/c attended Conference at Bgde H.Q. Y Coy Raid party reformed at HASLER CAMP weather fine warm	J.H.B.G.
Passchendaele	14		Battl moved into line East of PASSCHENDAELE W Coy occupied right Coy front Y Coy left front Z Coy support X Coy reserve, B.H.Q at Bellevue relief was carried out well Sgt Armitt Sgt Parish & Pte Loft being the only Casualties. The Battn relieved the Hampshire Regt Weather fine	
	15		Weather still fine L Cpl Stokes wounded Visited by Brig Gen Cheape. Y Coy sent out patrol under 2 Lt Rumble & brought good report of no man's land & Bosch patrol work.	

D. D. & L., London, E.C. (A7883) Wt. W809/M1672 350,000 1/17 Sch. 52a Forms/C/2118/14

Vol 24

Instructions regarding War Diaries and Intelligence Summaries are contained in F. S. Regs., Part II. and the Staff Manual respectively. Title pages will be prepared in manuscript.

WAR DIARY or INTELLIGENCE SUMMARY.

(Erase heading not required.)

March — 2nd Royal Fusiliers

Army Form C. 2118.

(9)

Place	Date	Hour	Summary of Events and Information	Remarks and references to Appendices
			Lt Col P Wilson arrived in the line, & took command. Capt Barton returned to transport lines.	
PASSCHENDAELE SECTOR	16th		~~Col Wilson [illegible] command of the Battn~~. C.O. visited all Coy's Capt Barton returned to CALIFORNIA CAMP weather fine very little activity. Gen Cheepe visited Battn HQrs	
"	17th		Inter Coy relief took place "Z" Coy relieved "W" Coy "X" Coy relieved "Y" Coy. "Y" Coy came to reserve, raid party went to B Camp BRANDHOEK under 2/Lt Rumble. C.O visited all Coys weather fine, M.G's active round VINDICTIVE X Rds artillery Normal	
"	18th		E. Artillery active beyond normal BELLEVUE area shelled with gas & H.E. front line & support shelled with M werfers & T Mortars weather fine, Adjt visited all Coys Capt Russell M.O. left Battn & Capt Fehily took his place at Bellevue	[initials]
	19th		Rain in morning clearing up in afternoon. Enemy artillery active on front line support & about Bellevue, gas shells fell near Bn HQ (Bellevue) C.O visited all Coy & visited front line & support of RGLI (right Bttn)	[initials]

D. D. & L., London, E.C. (A7883) Wt. W2o/M1672 350,000 4/17 Sch. 52a Forms/C/2118/14

Vol 26

WAR DIARY
or
INTELLIGENCE SUMMARY.
(Erase heading not required.)

Army Form C. 2118.

Instructions regarding War Diaries and Intelligence Summaries are contained in F. S. Regs., Part II. and the Staff Manual respectively. Title pages will be prepared in manuscript.

March 1918 — 2nd Royal Fusiliers

Place	Date	Hour	Summary of Events and Information	Remarks and references to Appendices
PASSCHENDAELE (Sector)	20th		at 4 30 AM S.O.S. ~~was~~ went up from our front line our artillery barrage replied immediately (the Battn on our Right (R.F. L.I.) sent up S.O.S. & our Battn followed suit) No enemy action was observed. Artillery & M.G. fire active more than usual. Battn was relieved by the L. Fusiliers the Battn went back to CALIFORNIA CAMP. Sgt Murgatroyd Killed. Cpl Catchpole Sent to England on Course.	
California Camp	21st		CALIFORNIA CAMP shelled between 4.30 & 6.30 AM one man killed (PTE DUFF.) Battn Bathed & general Clean up. Coy Commanders Conference. Weather fine. Lt Hamilton went to England [illegible] [illegible]	HRG
	22nd		All Coys on Working parties on Gravenstafel defence line. Rear H.Qrs (& Sp Coy) received orders to move to BRAKE CAMP & B Coy BRANDHOEK. Weather very fine. [illegible] left Coy sick 2/Lt SMITH took over (O.C.) [illegible] Coy	
	23rd		All Coys working on Gravenstafel defence line [illegible]	

D. D. & L., London, E.C. (A7883) Wt. W593/M1672 350,000 4/17 Sch. 52a Forms/C/2118/14

Instructions regarding War Diaries and Intelligence Summaries are contained in F. S. Regs., Part II, and the Staff Manual respectively. Title pages will be prepared in manuscript.

Vol 26

March

WAR DIARY
or
INTELLIGENCE SUMMARY.

(*Erase heading not required.*)

Army Form C. 2118.

2nd Royal Fusiliers

(2)

Place	Date	Hour	Summary of Events and Information	Remarks and references to Appendices
CALIFORNIA CAMP	24th		Preparations for taking over front line. Bn. Battn took over PASSCHENDAELE AREA (Right Battn) from R G L I night of 24-25 "Y" Coy front line Right Coy "W" Left Coy front line "X" Coy support "Z" Coy reserve, relief was successful no Casualties. weather fine warm	
PASSCHENDAELE AREA	25th		Battn holding the line nothing unusual happened weather fine warm. No Casualties	
"	26th		Battn holding line. ~~[illegible]~~ weather fine warm. ~~[illegible]~~ Enemy Artillery Normal during day	AHBG
"	26th		Enemy put down barrage on our front at 11.30 Pm. S.O.S went up from Battn on our left (L Fusiliers) & also on our Left Coy front, artillery replied immediately, barrage lasted about ½ an hour, no hostile movement was observed. Casualties 2 O.R. Wounded	
	27th		4 a.m. enemy put down another short barrage on same positions no S.O.S. went up from our front no hostile movement or advance was observed. Casualties 3 killed 1 wounded. Weather fine. Inter-Coy relief. "Z" Coy Relieved "W" Left front "X" Coy relieved "Y" Right front	[illegible]

D. D. & L., London, E.C. (A7833) Wt. W80/M1672 350,000 1/17 Sch. 52a Forms/C/2118/14

Instructions regarding War Diaries and Intelligence Summaries are contained in F. S. Regs., Part II. and the Staff Manual respectively. Title pages will be prepared in manuscript.

Vol 26

WAR DIARY or INTELLIGENCE SUMMARY.

(Erase heading not required.)

Army Form C. 2118.

March

2nd Royal Fusiliers

(6)

Place	Date	Hour	Summary of Events and Information	Remarks and references to Appendices
PASSCHENDAELE AREA	27th		"Y" Coy went to support line. "W" Coy reserve line. 1 man wounded weather dull no rain. Right Coy took over two posts from MIDDLESEX REGT	
	28th		Nothing unusual happened enemy artillery normal. Enemy had several O. Balloons up in front of our position. Weather Rain in afternoon & night no Casualties. E. T. Mortars active on our front line right Coy.	
	28th		2nd Lts Pearson & Clutterbuck arrived with reinforcements. 2/Lt Pearson to "X" Coy 2/Lt Clutterbuck to "W" Coy.	
	29th		Battn holding line nothing unusual happened, weather cold Raining	
	30th		Battn Relieved by K.O.S.B returned to "B" Camp. Battn entrained by Companys at SPREE FARM & detrained at BRANDHOEK 2/Lt Lovridge wounded 2. O.R at SPREE FARM. Weather raining cold.	
BRANDHOEK	31		Battn in Billets at "B" Camp BRANDHOEK. Rest in morning cleaning up etc. Weather fine.	

[signature]

D. D. & L., London, E.C. (A7833) Wt. W5o7/M1672 350,000 1/17 Sch. 52a Forms C/2118/14

2nd Bn Royal Fusiliers — No 1

Operation Order No 30

Ref Map 28 N.E. 1/20,000 & C 1/10,000 [illegible]

1 (a) On the night of 30/31st inst this Battalion will be relieved by the 1/K.O.S.B. Regt thus:-

Their	A	Coy	relieving	our Y	Coy
"	B	"	"	" X	"
"	C	"	"	" Z	"
"	D	"	"	" W	"

(b) Coys will obtain receipts for all stores etc handed over & also for all maps, papers etc. Receipts to be sent in to me by noon of the 31st.

(c) The Battalion will be accommodated in B Camp. BRANDHOEK. Trains will wait at SPREE FARM the first one leaving at midnight. Hot tea will be supplied at entraining point.

(d) One limber for Z & Y Coys will be at WATERLOO from 10 o'clock onwards.

One limber each for W & Q will be at BELLEVUE from 9 o'clock onwards.

(12)

[illegible]

1. [illegible] PLUME [illegible]

[illegible]

2. Guides

Guides for [illegible] KOSB will be at WATERLOO [illegible] [illegible] will [illegible] [illegible]. X Coy [illegible] [illegible] by X Coy.

3. The [illegible] Officer [illegible] will [illegible] Officer of the KOSB [illegible] right front Coy #6

4. The [illegible] Officer will hand over to the incoming [illegible] Officer of the KOSB [illegible]

5. [illegible] Commanders will report [illegible] to [illegible]

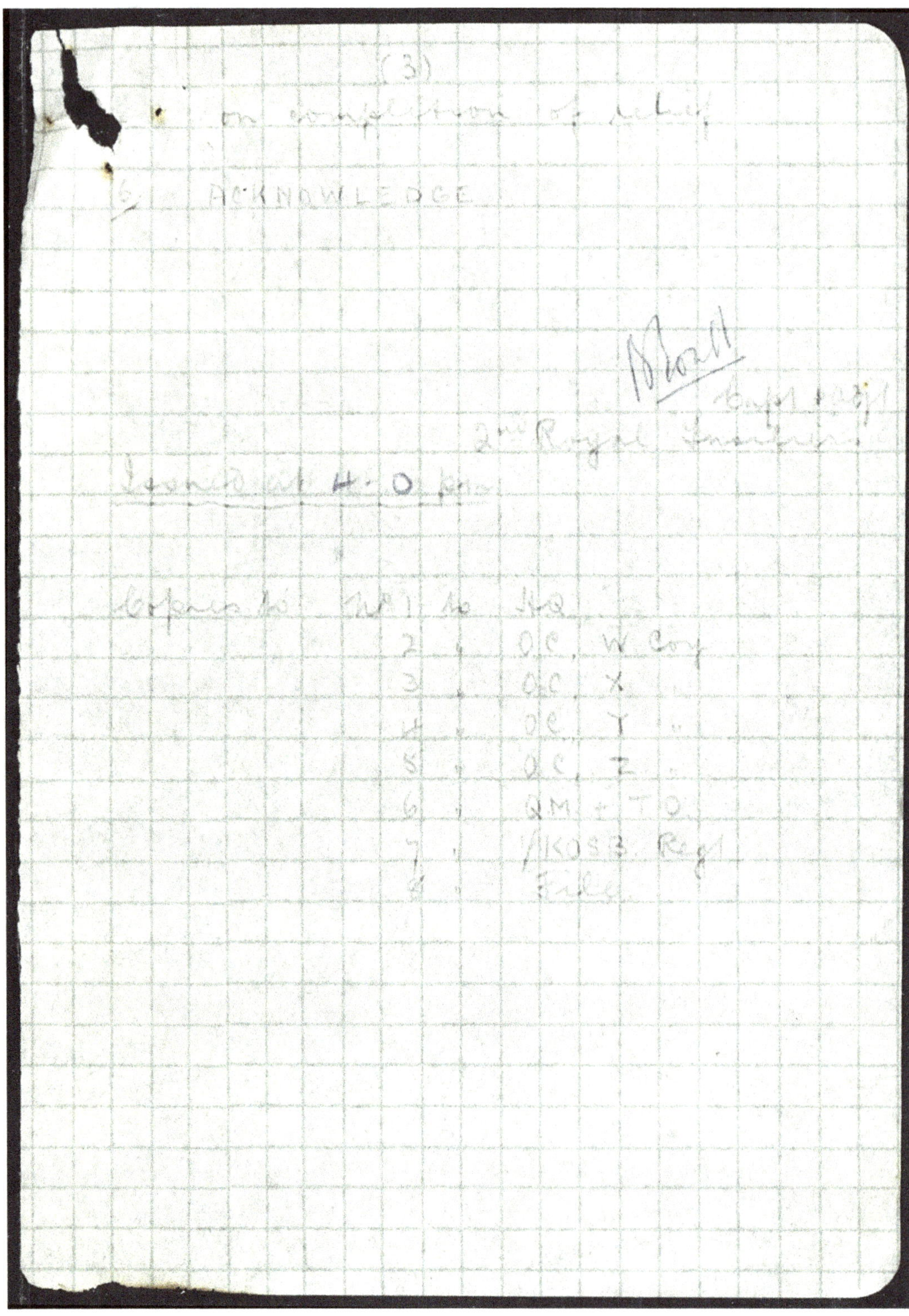

(3)

on completion of relief.

6) ACKNOWLEDGE

[illegible]

Capt & Adjt

2nd Royal Fusiliers

Issued at 4.0 pm

Copies to No 1 to HQ
2 " OC W Coy
3 " OC X "
4 " OC Y "
5 " OC Z "
6 " QM + TO
7 " 1/KOSB Regt
8 " File

Secret Copy No. 1

2nd. Bn. Royal Fusiliers
Operation Order No. 31.

The 2nd. Bn. Royal Fusiliers will relieve the 4/ Kings Liverpool Regiment tomorrow the 3rd. inst. in the Reserve line at Bellevue. be ready to

H.Q. "W" and "X" Coys. will/entrain at HAGLE Siding at 4.45 a.m.3rd. inst,& will detrain at IBERIAN D.19 b 32

"Y" and "Z" Coys. will entrain ¼ hour later.

Each Coy. to be responsible that they know HAGLE Siding

2/Lieut Pearson will be responsible for the entraining

Dress - Fighting Order.

Each Coy. will take up four Officers only inclusive of the Coy. Cmdr.

Bn. H.Q. at D. 16 b 60 25.

Guides as under will meet Units at the detraining points -

1 per Battn. H.Q., 1 each Coy. H.Q. 1 per platoon 1 for 2 sections of 2nd. Roy. Fus. in the Divisional Reserve Line.

All details of Officers left behind in "B" Camp will be under the command of Capt. Griffiths.

After detraining Coys. will in the order of H.Q. W X Y Z march to the relief in parties of not more than 20 at 300 yards interval

Lists ofall trench stores etc. taken over to be sent to Bn. H.Q. as soon as possible

Rations for 3rd. will be carried on the man,including one Tommies cooker. 8 tins of water per Coy. to be carried forward under Coy. arrangements. All water bottles to be filled before leaving Camp.

Lewis Guns will be carried to the train and onwards under Coy. arrangements.

Blankets rolled in bundles of ten,and labeled with Coy. label, packs and great coats, Officers valises etc will be stacked at the Q.M. stores before Coys. move off

Tea and rum will be issued before leaving Camp.

P.T.O.

The usual cleaning up parties will be detailed and certificates rendered to the Orderly Room that all huts and areas have been left clean.

F. P. Roland Capt.,
Adjutant,
Issued at 5 p.m. 2nd. Bn. Royal Fusiliers,

Copy to No. 1 H.Q. Officers
2 Q.M.
3. T.O.
4-8 O.C. Coys.
9 R.S.M.
10 File.

S E C R E T. Copy No. 4

86th. INFANTRY BRIGADE OPERATION ORDER NO.216.

Reference. ZONNEBEKE Sheets C.2. sheet 1/1000.

1. On the night 3/4th April the 86th Infantry Brigade will relieve the 98th. Infantry Brigade in the Left Sector of the 33rd Divisional Front in accordance with the attached relief table.

2. All details of relief will be arranged direct between Officers Comanding Units concerned.

3. The 1/Lancs.Fusiliers and 1/R.G.L.I. will each detail 1 Officer per Company to reconnoitre their Company lines.
1 Lewis Gunner per Lewis Gun of the two Companies of the 1/Lancs.Fus. and 1/R.G.L.I. who take over the Front line will also reconnoitre their gun positions before taking over.
A lorry will be at WARRINGTON CAMP at midday April 2nd to convey these Officers and men to FROST HOUSE (D.25.a.75.10). The party will remain in the line for the night of the 2/3rd April.

4. All S.A.A. Grenades and trench stores, maps, aeroplane photos, Defence Scheme, Policy of work, Intelligence notes etc, will be taken over from 98th Infantry Brigade. List of Stores and Rations taken over will be sent to Brigade Headquarters by 9 a.m. April 5th.

5. 86th. Infantry Brigade's Southern boundary will be from D.17.d.1.1. (Post 5.13 inclusive) - DERING CROSSING - D.16.c.4.3. thence JUDAH Track inclusive, to D.26.a.0.8.

6. Battalion and Company Areas and Tracks are shown on the attached map (Brigade Units only)

7. On detraining Units will move off with an interval of 150 yards between platoons.

8. Completion of relief will be reported to Brigade Headquarters.

9. Brigade Headquarters will close at BRAKE CAMP at 5 p.m. and re-open at IGNORE PILLBOX (D.20.c.5.9.) at 7-30 p.m. April 3rd.

10. A C K N O W L E D G E.

F.F. Dearden
Captain.
Brigade Major.
86th. Infantry Brigade.

1/4/1918.

Copies to :- Staff 1-3
2/Royal Fusiliers. 4
1/Lancs.Fusiliers. 5
1/Royal Guernsey L.I. 6
86th. T.M.Battery. 7
87th. Inf. Brigade. 8
98th. Inf. Brigade. 9
29th. Division "G" 10
29th. Division "Q" 11
100th. Inf. Brigade. 12
Area Cmmdt. BRANDHOEK. 13
29th. Div. M.G. Battn. 14
Diary. 15
File. 16

W Welles
Small)

X Ware

Y Rundald

Z Clark.

Darker.
Giles.
ady
C.O.

86th. INFANTRY BRIGADE ADMINISTRATIVE ORDER No.25.
(Issued in connection with Brigade Order No.216)

Sheet 28 N.E. 1/10000 and Sheet 28 N.W. 1/20000.

1. The following will be the routine during the next tour in the line.

2. Ammunition and R.E. Material.
These can be obtained on an order signed by Adjutants from SEINE Du D.18.d.3.4. and HAALEN COPSE Dump D.11.b.8.4. A quantity of R.E. material is also available at WATERFIELDS D.10.d.5.8.
SEINE Dump will be under the charge of th Brigade Dump Corporal.
The O.C. 1/Lancashire Fusiliers will detail one N.C.O. to take char of HAALEN Dump;he will report to Staff Captain 9 a.m. 2nd inst.
All Dumps forward of SEINE and HAALEN will be maintained by Regiment Sergeant Majors under the instructions of O.C.Units.

3. Supplies.
Supplies will go forward on 1st Line Transport as far as SEINE Dum

4. Trench Foot.
O.C.Units will ensure that the usual precautions are adopted. Dr Socks can be exchanged at Divisional Baths VLAMERTINGHE. Powder can be obtained from the Foot Baths at IRISH FARM.

5. Rear Headquarters.
Brigade Headquarters will be in the RAMPARTS,YPRES, I.8.a.9.4.
Battalion Rear Headquarters will remain for the present in "D", WARRINGTON,and RED ROSE CAMPS. The total number left behind including Transport is not to exceed 140 per Battalion.
Quarter Master Stores and advance Transport will be accomodated as

2/Royal Fusiliers. No, 1 advance Transport Lines		I.8.b.6.4.
1/Lancashire Fusiliers.	ditto	I.9.a.3.9.
1/Royal Guernsey L.I.	ditto	I.3.d.2.4.

The accomodation consists of 2 Nisson Huts and Standings for 20 Horses.
Details of taking over will be arranged by Quarter Masters and Battalion Transport Officers.

6. Town Majors.
Town Major will be detailed as under to take charge of and allot accomodation in the following Area:-

CREST FARM	2/Royal Fusiliers.
PRIMUS	1/Royal Guernsey L.I.

They should take over prior to arrival of Battalions.

Captain.
Staff Captain.
86th.Infantry Brigade.

2/4/1918.

2nd Bn. Royal Fusiliers.

To O.C., all Coys.

1. In continuation of Operation Order No 31, dated today, the companies will be reduced to Company Strength of 100 and no more.

2. No water tins will be taken up, but the necessary water for the companies will be drawn from the Headquarters there.

3. Cooking will be done at Battalion H.Q. under the Cook Sergt, and one cook per Company.

4. There will be no change of officers during the tour in the line. O.C., Coys will let me have a list at once of their four officers going into the line.

5. All Coy Sergt-Majors will form a party in the front part of the first train, i.e. starting at 5-O'clock, and immediately upon detraining will march ahead, one special guide being provided, and take over the company stores.

6. Companies will march in platoons, at 150 yards interval, thus, H.Q., W. X. Y. Z.

7. A C K N O W L E D G E.

Capt & Adjt.
2nd Bn. Royal Fusiliers.

2-4-1918.

86th Brigade.

29th Division.

2nd BATTALION

ROYAL FUSILIERS

APRIL 1918.

86/79 35.B.
(8 sheets)

WAR DIARY

2 R F
WO 26

April 1918

VOL. 38.

(6339) Wt. W160/M3016 1,500,000 10/17 McA & W Ltd (E 1898) Forms W3091.

Army Form W.3091.

Cover for Documents.

Nature of Enclosures.

Notes, or Letters written.

Army Form C. 2118.

Instructions regarding War Diaries and Intelligence Summaries are contained in F. S. Regs., Part II. and the Staff Manual respectively. Title pages will be prepared in manuscript.

Vol 38

WAR DIARY
or
INTELLIGENCE SUMMARY.
(Erase heading not required.)

APRIL

2nd Bn. ROYAL FUSILIERS.

Place	Date	Hour	Summary of Events and Information	Remarks and references to Appendices
BRANDHOEK	1st		Company arrangements. Specialists training. Weather fine. Kit inspections in Coys. Rifle inspections. An enemy aeroplanee flew over the camp and was shot down. 2/Lieut Darker said he was of opinion that his Lewis Gun brought it down, no proof. Battalion deloused and bathed at LAITERIE. Weather fine, a little cold.	Hazebrouck 5a Zonnebeke 28 N.E
do.	2nd		Company arrangements. G.O.C. visited Battalion and lectured Officers & Senior N.C.O's. Company Commanders visited section of the line to be taken over. Capt Wells joined and took over W Coy from 2/Lieut Smith. Football match between 1/R.G.L.I. and 2/R.F. R.F. won 2 goals to 0. Fine during day, rain at night.	
do.	3rd		Battalion equipping and resting prior to relieving the 4/Kings in Hamburg Reserve Area 10% under Capt Powell left in CALIFORNIA CAMP.	Zonnebeke 9..
Hamburg Reserve Area.	4th		Battalion entrained at HAGLE Siding (Just beside B Camp) BRANDHOEK at 5-0 a.m. and detrained at IBERIAN at about 6-30 a.m. and proceeded to relieve the 4/Kings Liverpool Regt, thus.- Headquarters at D.16.b.75.20; X Coy at D.10.d.7.4.(Reserve Company in BELLEVUE SWITCH); Z Coy at D.16.b.90.95; Y Coy at D.17.a.4.1; and W Coy at D.17.c.30.95; Relief completed by 9-0 a.m. Sector very quiet.	
	5th		Battalion working partly under 546th R.E's and partly under Divisional Scheme on local defences. 2/Lieut Barry and small party went out on patrol.	
	6th		ditto. ditto.	
	7th		Relieved by 10-30 a.m. by the 18/K.R.R. entraining from BORRY FARM back to B Camp, BRANDHOEK.	
			General cleaning up and classes.	
Brandhoek.	8th		Preparing to embus at B Camp. Busses finally arrived at 10-0 p.m. We moved off after	
do.	9th		midnight, our Transport moving off under the Brigade Transport Officer.	[signature]

D. D. & L., London, E.C. (A7883) Wt. W803/M1672 350,000 4/17 Sch. 52a Forms C/2118/14

Instructions regarding War Diaries and Intelligence Summaries are contained in F. S. Regs., Part II. and the Staff Manual respectively. Title pages will be prepared in manuscript.

WAR DIARY
or
INTELLIGENCE SUMMARY.
(Erase heading not required.)

Army Form C. 2118.

Place	Date	Hour	Summary of Events and Information	Remarks and references to Appendices
MERVILLE AREA	10th		Battalion debussed at 6-30 a.m. at VIEUX BERQUIN, marching to MERVILLE, where a meal was hastily eaten. X Coy were sent to put out an outpost line about farms K.30.d.7.5. coming under the orders of 151st Brigade, At noon the remainder of the battalion was ordered to report to the 151st Brigade, with headquarters at L.26.c.2.1 billeting in surrounding farmhouses. At 8-0 p.m. received orders to take up a position in support of troops holding ESTAIRES Ø with Z Coy and half of Y Coy in B (ii) and W Coy and half of Y Coy in reserve at B (i). By midnight 10/11th April we had relieved odd detachments of a reinforcement battalion holding a line from L.27.d.8.6. to L.29.a.5.6. exclusive of road, with Battalion headquarters at ESTAIRES on road junction at L.28.c.4.8. Rear headquarters remained at MERVILLE which was heavily shelled towards evening.	Sheet 36A Ø See B line
			Officers who moved forward were Lieut-Col P.N.W.Wilson, D.S.O.,M.C., Capt P.T.O.Boult, (Adjutant)., Capt T.Fehily,R.A.M.C; W Company- Capt H.V.Wells, 2/Lt E.T.Allen; Lieut L.B.Solomon, 2/Lt R.O.Darker, 2/Lt H.Norwell; X Company- Capt L.W.Griffiths, 2/Lt J Pearson, 2/Lt N.H.Willett, 2/Lt H.L.Mepham; Y Company- 2/Lt G.T.S.Rundall, 2/Lt J.H.B. Giles, 2/Lt J.Fraser, 2/Lt M.S.Ekins, 2/Lt W.T.Gould; Z Company - 2/J.W.Hunt, Lieut A.G.Pape, 2/Lt F.T.A.Wilson, 2/Lt W.H.E.Twells.	
			Strength of Companies.- W 147; X 168; Y 149; Z 151; H.Q.32; Total 647.	
DOULIEU & PRADELLES Area.	11th		Upon orders from 151st Brigade at 0400 we (less X Coy) handed over our positions to the 5/D.L.I. as they had evacuated ESTAIRES, and took up a position in reserve in farms about L.11. with Battalion headquarters at L.11.d.8.2. positions in yellow. At noon we relieved the 1/R.G.L.I. in the defences of DOULIEU with W Coy in front line (running through N.E. of village) Z Coy in support, and Y Coy in close support on right of Z Coy; positions in [blue]. We were unable to put a Company in BRIELLE FARM as our X Coy were permanently attached to the 151st Brigade, and the remainder of the Battalion were again under the 86th Brigade. At 3-0 p.m. the enemy became very lively and troops shewing a tendency to retire, we sent our support company (Z) to the right, and placed them under the orders of the K.O.S.Bs.at about L.12.a.1.8. Sharp fighting all that afternoon and night, when we were ordered to evacuate DOULIEU at 2-0 a.m. on the morning of the 12th inst.	
			Rear headquarters moved to VERTE RUE at 3 p.m. arriving at 5 p.m. although heavily sniped and M.Gunned when leaving MERVILLE. Again moved at 7-30 p.m. to PRADELLES arriving there at 12-30 a.m. midnight.	

D. D. & L., London, E.C. (A7883) Wt. W803/M1672 350,000 4/17 Sch. 52a Forms/C/2118/14

Army Form C. 2118.

Instructions regarding War Diaries and Intelligence Summaries are contained in F. S. Regs., Part II. and the Staff Manual respectively. Title pages will be prepared in manuscript.

WAR DIARY
or
INTELLIGENCE SUMMARY.
(Erase heading not required.)

Place	Date	Hour	Summary of Events and Information	Remarks and references to Appendices
	12th		We took up a line from L.4.Central westwards astride the NEUF BERQUIN Road (coloured red) this battalion taking up a line from L.3.d.8.8.(road exclusive) to Cross Roads at L.4.Central (inclusive) with a strong outpost at L.4.d.5.0. and also hedge at L.4.c.0.0. with Battalion headquarters at F.27.d.6.9. the 1/R.G.L.I. in position on our right; our W Coy on right, Z Coy on left, and Y Coy in support about L.4.a.5.2. Between 9-0 a.m. and 10 a.m. the enemy started pushing forward his skirmishers and M.Gs and drove back our front line, but only after the 31st Division on our left had retired a considerable distance back, thus leaving our flank in the air. Y Coy immediately formed a defensive flank on the left, and Battalion headquarters moved to F.26.b.2.3. together with the 1/Lancs Fusiliers and 1/R.G.L.I. headquarters. A light line of resistance was formed at noon along F.26.d.3.8. to F.27.a.Central, with a defensive flank thrown back to cottage at F.20.d.9.5. About 1-0 p.m. the defensive flank retired, and from then until 2-30 p.m. we were retiring on to the village of BLEU which was held by the remains of troops of the 86th and 87th Brigades until 4-0pm when the village was evacuated. As many men of the Division as possible were rounded up on railway line at F.7.a.5.0. and later under orders from the 86th Brigade the remains of this Battalion, with details of the 1/R.G.L.I., S.W.B., and Borders, were taken forward and made to dig a support line along F.18.c.9.5. to F.18.b.8.2. and on the left of the Lancs Fusiliers, who held as far as VIEUX BERQUIN. Our front line was along VIEUX BERQUIN - OULTERSTEENE Road as far as FME LABIS. Thence northward along the W. side of wood at F.7.c. The 2ndRoyal Fusiliers established headquarters in conjunction with Colonel Raikes, who was commanding all details of 29th Division. Rear headquarters moved to Q.25.c.2.0. midway between ST SYLVESTRE CAPPEL and CAESTRE at 3-30 p.m.	Sheet 36A
	13th		Early in the morning a heavy attack was launched by the enemy on our left which was finally held up. The ammunition dump at F.13.b.7.8. catching fire caused considerable confusion to the enemy who were forming up close by. A considerable number of Germans were killed with M.G. fire from our left post. Later on it was seen that the K.O.Y.L.I on our right were retiring before a heavy German attack which was being launched against the village of VIEUX BERQUIN. The Lancs Fusiliers in support on our right also retired, thus leaving our right flank in the air. The defensive flank from our right post was immediately formed towards VIEUX BERQUIN. Shortly after this the troops on our left were seen to leave their trenches and retire. They were stopped by the Staff Captain of the 86th Brigade and led forward to their original trenches.	SHEET 27

D. D. & L., London, E.C. (A7883) Wt. W803/M1672 350,000 4/17 Sch. 52a Forms/C/2118/14

Instructions regarding War Diaries and Intelligence Summaries are contained in F. S. Regs., Part II, and the Staff Manual respectively. Title pages will be prepared in manuscript.

WAR DIARY
or
INTELLIGENCE SUMMARY.
(Erase heading not required.)

Army Form C. 2118.

Place	Date	Hour	Summary of Events and Information	Remarks and references to Appendices
	13th		Meanwhile the enemy attacked our line but was held up about 800 yards from it by M.G. and rifle fire. He then proceeded to dig himself in on a line 800 yards from our position. At nightfall the Coy Commander of the Company of the 31st Division on our left informed us that his battalion had moved off and had vacated all the trenches on our left. The position then was that we were holding a line in front with both flanks in the air and with the certain knowledge that the enemy held the village of VIEUX BERQUIN. At dusk a withdrawal was duly carried out without confusion and in perfect order, and troops were found digging in on a line in rear of VIEUX BERQUIN. Rear headquarters prepared for relief of Battalion, but could get no definite instructions from either Brigade or Division.	Sheet 36A.
			Capt H.W.Persse joined the battalion.	
St SYLVESTRE ~~Cappel~~	14th		Battalion marched to Brigade headquarters where we received orders to march to BORRE Arrived at railhead near BORRE about 3-0 p.m. where tea was served and a brief rest was taken, afterwards marching to a farm/opposite Transport field, arriving there at about 10-0 a.m.	Sheet 27
			Casualties.- Officers, KILLED, Capt H.V.Wells, Lieut L.B.Solomon, 2/Lt H.Norwell, 2/Lt N.H.Willett, 2/Lt H.L.Mepham, 2/Lt G.T.S.Rumball, 2/Lt F.T.A.Wilson, Capt T.Fehily. WOUNDED, Capt L.W.Griffiths, 2/Lt M.S.Ekins, 2/Lt J.H.B.Giles, 2/Lt W.H.E.Twells, 2/Lt J.W.Hunt. MISSING, 2/Lt R.O.Darker, 2/Lt W.T.Gould. - Total 15 Officers.	
			Other ranks.- KILLED 23, WOUNDED 156, MISSING 145, Total 324 O.R.	
	15th		A composite Brigade was formed with 2/R.F. as Nº 1 Battalion, and 1/Lancs Fusiliers & 1/R.G.L.I. as Nº 2 Battalion, coming under the 87th Brigade. Lt A.G.Pape arrested for deserting the line from 4 p.m. 12th until noon 13th and 2/Lt P[illegible] put in charge of [illegible]	
	16th		Started Lewis Gun classes and continued reorganising.	
	17th		Battalion ordered to stand to under arms and be ready to move forward to Reserve positions at LE PEUPLIER if required. Moved to LE PEUPLIER at 10 a.m. to dig a line of trenches for 87th Brigade, ~~but could get no orders of any kind~~. We returned to billets at midnight.	[signature]
			Lt A.G.Pape tried by special Courts Martial.	
	18th		Continued Lewis Gun classes. Two parties of 3 Officers and 180 other ranks dug under the R.E's in LE PEUPLIER area, starting at 7 p.m. returning at 11 p.m.	

D. D. & L., London, E.C.
(A7883) Wt. W809/M1672 350,000 4/17 Sch. 52a Forms/C/2118/14

Instructions regarding War Diaries and Intelligence Summaries are contained in F. S. Regs., Part II. and the Staff Manual respectively. Title pages will be prepared in manuscript.

WAR DIARY
or
INTELLIGENCE SUMMARY.
(Erase heading not required.)

Army Form C. 2118.

Place	Date	Hour	Summary of Events and Information	Remarks and references to Appendices
HONDEGHEM	19th		The Brigade moved to billets around HONDEGHEM starting at 3-0 p.m. and arriving at about 5-0 p.m. Brigade being under half an hour's notice to move by day, and one hour's notice by night.	Sheets 27 36A 36a N.E
	20th		Work on 2nd Support Zone under 510th Field Coy R.E. reporting to 2nd Lieut Meffett at V.5.c.6.6. at 2-30 p.m. Work finished at 6-30 p.m. Battalion party about 450 men, 20 N.C.O's, and 6 Officers.	
			2nd Lieut F.J.Cryer sick to England 15-4-1918. Struck off strength 21-4-1918.	
	21st		4 Officers, 10 N.C.Os, and 200 men excavating trenches in Support Line. Rendezvous at 10-0 a.m. at V.30.c.1.7. reporting to 2nd Lieut Meffett of 510th Field Coy R.E. Worked till 1-0 p.m.	
			38 other ranks joined from Base.	
			Lieut A.G.Pape and 2nd Lieut J.Pearson to XV Corps Reinforcement Camp, LINGHEM.	
	22nd		3 Officers, 24 N.C.O's, and 400 men rendezvous at D.12.a.5.8. at 9-0 a.m. for trench digging in 2nd Zone, D.12. and E.1. under 455th Field Coy R.E. Returned about 2-0 p.m.	
	23rd		2 Officers, 5 N.C.O's, and 100 men rendezvous 9-30 a.m. at V.23.a.6.8. to 2nd Lieut Meffett of 510th Field Coy R.E. for wiring in 2nd Zone Support Line. Work ceased at 12-30 p.m.	
			6 Officers, 12 N.C.O's, and 275 men rendezvous at V.23. for trench digging under 510th Field Coy, R.E.	
			Major K.F.B.Tower joined.	
	24th		7 Officers, 17 N.C.O's, and 365 men rendezvous V.23.d.1.6. at 10-0 a.m. to 2nd Lieut Wilson, 510th Field Coy, R.E. for trench construction in 2nd Zone Support Line. Work ceased at 1-0 p.m.	[signature]
			Lewis Gun Classes.	
	25th		5 Officers, 10 N.C.O's, and 250 men rendezvous at V.29.b.5.4. at 10 a.m. to 2nd Lieut Elliott, of 510th Field Coy, R.E. for trench digging in 2nd Zone Support Line. Work	

D. D. & L., London, E.C.
(A7883) Wt. W809/M1672 350,000 4/17 Sch. 52a Forms/C/2118/14

Instructions regarding War Diaries and Intelligence Summaries are contained in F. S. Regs., Part II, and the Staff Manual respectively. Title pages will be prepared in manuscript.

WAR DIARY
or
INTELLIGENCE SUMMARY.
(Erase heading not required.)

Army Form C. 2118.

Place	Date	Hour	Summary of Events and Information	Remarks and references to Appendices
HONDEGHEM	25th		ceased at 1 p.m. 2 Officers, 6 N.C.O's, and 115 men rendezvous V.30.c.3.6. at 10 a.m. for trench construction in 2nd Zone Support Line, under 2nd Lieut Meffett of 510th Field Coy, R.E Work ceased 1 p.m. Lewis Gun Classes.	Sheets 27 36a 36a N.E
	26th		Baths at HONDEGHEM. 57 Other ranks joined Battalion from Base.	
	27th		Battalion passed through Gas Chamber at HONDEGHEM. Battalion relieved the 3rd Coldstream Guards in line at BOIS D'AVAL E.28.a.8.9 to E.28.c.4.2, with Z Coy left front line Company, Y right front line Company, X Coy in support of Z, and W Coy behind Y Coy, with battalion Headquarters at E.27.d.central. Officers who went forward were Lt-Col P.N.W.Wilson, D.S.O., M.C., Major K.F.B.Tower,MC Capt H.W.Persse, MC (in place of Adjutant at Transport lines). W Coy. - 2/LtsJ.T.Smith, E.T.Allen, D.Neish, S.A.Clutterbuck. X Coy. - 2/Lts A.L.Chulter, E.J.Barnes; J.Thomas. Y Coy. - Capt N.S.Powell, 2/Lts W.E.Stokes, W.R.Webb, E.G.Andrews. Z Coy. - Capt H.Clark, 2/Lts C.W.Chilcott, M.G.Whyte, W.J.Barry. The 10% went to SERCUS to join Divisional Reserve Battalion. Rear Headquarters and Transport moved to field at EECK-HOUT-CASTEEL.	
	28th		Quiet in the line. Slight gas shelling at night. Battalion Headquarters moved back to E.25a.8.5. A reconnoitring patrol of 20 went out under 2nd Lt E.J.Barnes, but unexpectedly came upon an enemy outpost and had to retire, leaving one Lewis Gun behind. 1 man missing and 1 wounded.	
	29th		Quiet. Improving Support line. 2nd Lt Barnes' patrol went out to try and locate the Lewis Gun, but failed.	
	30th		Situation fairly quiet.	

P.N.W. Wilson Lieut Col
Comdg 2nd Bn Royal Fusiliers

D. D. & L., London, E.C. (A7883) Wt. W809/M1672 350,000 4/17 Sch. 52a Forms/C/2118/14

86.B.
(16 sheets)

(6339) Wt. W160/M3016 1,500,000 10/17 McA & W Ltd (E 1898) Forms W3091. Army Form W.3091.

Vol 27

Cover for Documents.

Nature of Enclosures.

Confidential

Vol: 39.

2nd Battn Royal Fusiliers

WAR DIARY.

May 1918.

Notes, or Letters written.

Army Form C. 2118.

Instructions regarding War Diaries and Intelligence Summaries are contained in F. S. Regs., Part II. and the Staff Manual respectively. Title pages will be prepared in manuscript.

WAR DIARY
or
INTELLIGENCE SUMMARY.
(Erase heading not required.)

May 1918.

Place	Date	Hour	Summary of Events and Information	Remarks and references to Appendices
Bois Dar[illegible]	1st	PM 1030	Battalion was relieved by 1st R.D.F. and the relief was carried out very [illegible]	56 A.
			quietly. Support Coys relieved in afternoon and on relief [illegible] and 2 Platoons	
			of X Coy went to billets at D.25 & the remaining 2 Platoons [illegible]	
			Defences. W Coy HQ and 2 Platoons on relief moved to billets D.[illegible]	
			remaining 2 Platoons in LA MOTTE Defences. 4 [illegible]	
			a [illegible] of the 1st R.D.F. at E 26. Front line [illegible]	
			back to billets at D.16.b. ~~[illegible]~~ Battalion H.Q. [illegible]	
			During the tour in the trenches casualties were negligible. [illegible]	
			farm stock left behind by the inhabitants and [illegible]	
			get these away from the front line they were killed [illegible]	
PARCTE	2nd		Battalion found working parties [illegible] for R.E. [illegible]	
			Y and Z and H.Q. Coys bathed [illegible]	
			2nd Lt. BILLSON [illegible]	
			and Capt. PERSSE returned to [illegible]	
			to C.C.S. suffering from gas.	[illegible] Col.

D. D. & L., London, E.C.
(A7883) Wt. W809/M1672 350,000 4/17 Sch. 52a Forms C/2118/14

Army Form C. 2118.

Instructions regarding War Diaries and Intelligence Summaries are contained in F. S. Regs., Part II, and the Staff Manual respectively. Title pages will be prepared in manuscript.

WAR DIARY
or
INTELLIGENCE SUMMARY.
(Erase heading not required.)

Place	Date	Hour	Summary of Events and Information	Remarks and references to Appendices
PAPOTE	3/5/18		Battalion training and working parties.	
	4/5/18		— ditto — 2/Lt BARNES severely wounded and 2/Lt J. D. QUINN slightly wounded.	
	5/5/18		— ditto — 2/Lt BARNES (Y Coy) died of wounds at 15 C.C.S.	
	6/5/18		— ditto —	
	7/5/18		— ditto — Capt Pease returned from C.C.S. & [illegible]	
	8/5/18		— ditto —	
	9/5/18		Battalion took over from 1/RDF in front line sector E.28.a.5.7. to K.4.c.4.6. 1st LANCS. FUS: on right and 88th BRIGADE on left. W and X Coys in front line X on left W on right, Z in support and Y Coy in strong point at E.20 central. Battalion H.Q. at E.25.b.1.3. Lt Col. WILSON and Capt BOVET [illegible]	[illegible] Capt

D. D. & L., London, E.C.
(A7883) Wt. W809/M1672 350,000 4/17 Sch. 52a Forms/C/2118/14

Instructions regarding War Diaries and Intelligence Summaries are contained in F. S. Regs., Part II. and the Staff Manual respectively. Title pages will be prepared in manuscript.

WAR DIARY
or
INTELLIGENCE SUMMARY.
(Erase heading not required.)

Army Form C. 2118.

Place	Date	Hour	Summary of Events and Information	Remarks and references to Appendices
PERITE [illegible]	9/5/18		Along with [illegible] MAJOR TOWER and CAPT. PEARSE [illegible] front line. Relief carried through satisfactorily.	
[illegible]	10/5/18		Quiet day. Very little shelling. A few 8 inch shells fell close to Battalion H.Q. Patrols were sent out during night and found that [illegible] E.27.a.7.6 were unoccupied.	
[illegible]	11/5/18		Quiet [illegible] day. MAJOR TOWER and CAPT PEARSE [illegible] Lt Col WILSON and CAPT BAILEY respectively. They returned to [illegible]. Patrols [illegible] sent out during night and found that [illegible] within several hundred yards of our front line [illegible]	
	12/5/18		Received instructions from Brigade to carry out a raid [illegible] with 2 [illegible] and 30 other ranks. [illegible] during the day [illegible] went down to be inoculated at Field Ambulance [illegible]	[illegible] Capt

D. D. & L., London, E.C.
(A7883) Wt. W803/M1672 350,000 4/17 Sch. 52a Forms C/2118/14

Instructions regarding War Diaries and Intelligence Summaries are contained in F. S. Regs., Part II, and the Staff Manual respectively. Title pages will be prepared in manuscript.

WAR DIARY
or
INTELLIGENCE SUMMARY.
(Erase heading not required.)

Army Form C. 2118.

Place	Date	Hour	Summary of Events and Information	Remarks and references to Appendices
Bois D'Aval	12/5/18		immediately	
Bois D'Aval	13/5/18		Patrols out again in direction of E 29.a and K 4.b.3.7. Enemy working parties were located but machine guns covering them were too well protected by hedges and dykes to be approachable. All these patrols have been carried out by 2/Lt BARRY and CLUTTERBUCK. Raid should have been tonight but was postponed. B.G.G.S. XI Corps and B.G. R.E.'s XI Corps visited Battalion H.Q. 2/Lt FRASER arrived with 30 Other ranks from 10% Camp. Rained solidly all night.	
Bois D'Aval	14/5/18	PM 1.50 AM 4.0 AM	Raid carried out by 2/Lt BARRY last night but did not achieve its purpose owing to the fact that objective contained no enemy at all (See appendix). H.Q. shelled with gas from about 11 PM till 3 AM, firing in all about 1000 shells in the vicinity of Battalion H.Q. Patrol under 2/Lt CLUTTERBUCK located working party at BEAU[illegible] but could not approach them owing to the intervening dykes.	J. H. [illegible] Capt

D. D. & L., London, E.C.
(A7883) Wt. W809/M1672 350,000 4/17 Sch. 52a Forms/C/2118/14

APPENDIX.

Instructions regarding War Diaries and Intelligence Summaries are contained in F. S. Regs., Part II, and the Staff Manual respectively. Title pages will be prepared in manuscript.

WAR DIARY
or
INTELLIGENCE SUMMARY.
(Erase heading not required.)

Army Form C. 2118.

Place	Date	Hour	Summary of Events and Information	Remarks and references to Appendices
FARM	14/5/18		Raid on night of 14/15 May. Strength of party 2/Lt BARRY 30 O.R.s [illegible]	[illegible]
BEAUVAIS		P.M. 11.30	Raiding party left Z Coy H.Q. and proceeded to No 9 POST and then out to	38 A. HE
	15/5/18	A.M. 12.30	Assembly position which was reached at 12.30 A.M. One man of the party was	
			hit by shrapnel fire slightly on the way out. The [illegible] [illegible] [illegible]	
		12.40	position by 12.40 AM. The barrage commenced [illegible] [illegible] [illegible]	
		12.56	at 12.56 AM. This barrage caused no trouble and 2/Lt BARRY [illegible] the	
			led forward the raiding party [illegible] [illegible] [illegible]	
			[illegible] satisfactory but [illegible] much [illegible] in the night [illegible]	
			The raiding party moved forward close behind the barrage [illegible]	
			immediately sent up Very lights from shell holes and [illegible]	
			[illegible] running away in front of the barrage. The [illegible]	
			200 in front of the raiding party [illegible] [illegible]	
			to direct fire on them. Some of the enemy [illegible] [illegible]	
			E.29 [illegible] and some across the road the north [illegible]	
			the raiding party reached the line of shell holes which [illegible]	
			been holding they came under very heavy trench mortar [illegible]	[illegible]

D. D. & L., London, E.C.
(A7883) Wt. W809/M1672 350,000 4/17 Sch. 52a Forms/C/2118/14

Instructions regarding War Diaries and Intelligence Summaries are contained in F. S. Regs., Part II. and the Staff Manual respectively. Title pages will be prepared in manuscript.

WAR DIARY
or
INTELLIGENCE SUMMARY.
(Erase heading not required.)

Army Form C. 2118.

Place	Date	Hour	Summary of Events and Information	Remarks and references to Appendices
FARM	17/9/18	AM.	not held as a post and there are no signs of works. The line of the	
BEAULIEU			hedge is also not held and no trenches have been dug. The enemy	
			put down a barrage along the edge of the wood and in front of	
			the wood at about Zero + 5. This barrage was, however, very thin	
			and weak and consisted chiefly of 5.9s and 4.2s. A few	
			casualties were caused by this barrage, 1 Killed and 2 Wounded.	
			Trench Mortars carried out a most successful shoot and acted as	
			a diversion drawing the enemy's fire in that direction.	
			Lt. Perrins in charge of these guns is much to be congratulated	
			on the way fire was kept up in spite of heavy hostile fire.	
			There is no doubt that the enemy expected a raid [illegible] the FARM	
			BEAULIEU as most of his fire was directed round that point.	
			The raid was very well led and ably carried out by 2/Lt BARRY	
			who kept the men well together. The whole of the plans arranged	
			were carried out and each party reached their objectives.	J H Penn Capt

D. D. & L., London, E.C.
(A7883) Wt. W803/M1672 350,000 4/17 Sch. 52a Forms/C/2118/14

APPENDIX. (Contd)

Instructions regarding War Diaries and Intelligence Summaries are contained in F. S. Regs., Part II. and the Staff Manual respectively. Title pages will be prepared in manuscript.

WAR DIARY
or
INTELLIGENCE SUMMARY.
(Erase heading not required.)

Army Form C. 2118.

Place	Date	Hour	Summary of Events and Information	Remarks and references to Appendices
FARM	15/5/18	AM	right. Hostile trench mortars were evidently firing from [illegible] along	
BEAULIEU			the road close to VERTE RUE. No casualties were, however, sustained.	
			A hostile M.G. opened fire from about E.22.c.4.2. but this was engaged	
			by the left Lewis Gun and at once ceased fire. The raiding party	
			advanced towards the farm without difficulty. Hostile T.M's switched	
			back and continued to fire on the party but most of the shells fell	
			behind the raiding party. Patrol proceeded as detailed but could	
			find no trace of the enemy. They proceeded into the farm and 2/Lt	
			BARRY went right through on to the road beyond. No trace of the	
			enemy could be found and all objectives had been [illegible]	
			searched. 2/Lt BARRY fired 2 Red Very Lights and the party withdrew	
			according to plan. A search was made in [illegible] for any	
			identification left by the enemy but nothing could be found. No [illegible] were	
			made by the raiding party.	
			The hostile wire was no obstacle at all and the raiding party had	[illegible]
			no difficulty in getting through it. The farm at E.29.c.[illegible]	[illegible signature]

D. D. & L., London, E.C.
(A7883) Wt. W809/M1672 350,000 4/17 Sch. 52a Forms/C/2118/14

Army Form C. 2118.

WAR DIARY
or
INTELLIGENCE SUMMARY.
(Erase heading not required.)

Instructions regarding War Diaries and Intelligence Summaries are contained in F. S. Regs., Part II. and the Staff Manual respectively. Title pages will be prepared in manuscript.

Place	Date	Hour	Summary of Events and Information	Remarks and references to Appendices
BOIS D'AVAL.	15/5/18		Battalion was relieved by 1st R.D.F. Relief complete by 10.30 PM and the front areas were quite quiet. Just about 10.30 the enemy heavily gas shelled Battalion HQ and created a dense gas cloud in wood. On relief W and X Coys moved back to billets and bivouacs near BROTE [?]. Y Coy reserve line at MARQUETTE [?] and Z Coy reserve line at LA MOTTE. Very few casualties during this tour in the trenches from actual shell fire.	

[illegible signature] Capt

D. D. & L., London, E.C. (A7883) Wt. W809/M1672 350,000 4/17 Sch. 52a Forms/C/2118/14

Instructions regarding War Diaries and Intelligence Summaries are contained in F. S. Regs., Part II. and the Staff Manual respectively. Title pages will be prepared in manuscript.

WAR DIARY
or
INTELLIGENCE SUMMARY.
(Erase heading not required.)

Army Form C. 2118.

Place	Date	Hour	Summary of Events and Information	Remarks and references to Appendices
PAPOTE.	16/5/18		Y and Z, the Coys at LA MOTTE and PETITE MARQUETTE supplied 106 men for work under the R.E's. Arrivals. Lt Col. WILSON came up from transport lines and 2nd/Lt. F.W. TIBALLS and 2nd/Lt. I.D. QUIN joined the Battalion. Departures Major TOWER went down to transport lines slightly gassed. 26 O.R. were sent down to the Field Ambulance with eye trouble caused by gas. X and W Coys went to the Baths.	
PAPOTE	17/5/18		The Battalion supplied 236 men for work under the R.E's. In the evening the C.O. took out the Officers of W and X for tactical exercises. The fighting strength of the Battalion is 21 Officers and [illegible] O.R.	
PAPOTE.	18/5/18		The Battalion supplied 230 men for work under the R.E's. In the afternoon preparations were made for the relief to take place on the following day. An officer from the 1st HANTS and the 2nd in Command of [illegible] came down to settle details. The 86th BRIGADE is moving into the left sector of the Divisional front and the 88th BRIGADE are taking over the	[illegible] Capt

D. D. & L., London, E.C.
(A7883) Wt. W809/M1672 350,000 4/17 Sch. 52a Forms/C/2118/14

Army Form C. 2118.

Instructions regarding War Diaries and Intelligence Summaries are contained in F. S. Regs., Part II. and the Staff Manual respectively. Title pages will be prepared in manuscript.

WAR DIARY
or
INTELLIGENCE SUMMARY.
(Erase heading not required.)

Place	Date	Hour	Summary of Events and Information	Remarks and references to Appendices
PAPOTE	18/5/18		right sector in the wood.	
PAPOTE AND GRAND MARQUETTE	19/5/18		In the afternoon the Battalion was relieved by the 4TH WORCESTERS and took over the billets of the 1ST HANTS at GRAND MARQUETTE. The relief was complete by 7.30 P.M. X.W. and Z Coys were billetted at GRAND MARQUETTE, Y Coy at LE REST.	
GRAND MARQUETTE	20/5/18		The Coys were at the disposal of Coy Commanders for training in Musketry and Lewis Guns. MAJOR TOWER came up from the transport lines and Lt Col. WILSON went down. The Battalion supplied 170 men for work under the R.E's. working at night on the Reserve line. Digging lasted under 3 hours.	
GRAND MARQUETTE	21/5/18		The Battalion supplied 170 men for work under the R.E's, work lasting from 9 P.M – 11 P.M. During the day Coys at the disposal of Coy Commanders for training. Two Coys fixed up rifle range and L.G. range and carried on with firing practice.	Capt

D. D. & L., London, E.C.
(A7883) Wt. W803/M1672 350,000 4/17 Sch. 52a Forms/C/2118/14

Instructions regarding War Diaries and Intelligence Summaries are contained in F. S. Regs., Part II. and the Staff Manual respectively. Title pages will be prepared in manuscript.

WAR DIARY
or
INTELLIGENCE SUMMARY.
(Erase heading not required.)

Army Form C. 2118.

Place	Date	Hour	Summary of Events and Information	Remarks and references to Appendices
GRAND MARQUETTE	22/5/18		Coys at the disposal of Coy Commanders. Working parties of [illegible] men under the R.E.s at night.	
GRAND MARQUETTE	23/5/18		In the morning a demonstration of the New Rifle Grenade No 36 was carried out near Z Coys billet. In the evening W Coy challenged X Coy to a Boxing match. There were 10 entries and quite a good [illegible] resulted, one or two of the men showing very good form. At night the Battalion found 133 men for work under the R.E.s.	
GRAND MARQUETTE	24/5/18		In the morning another demonstration of the New Rifle Grenade was carried out by X Coy. [struck out] [struck out] MAJOR [illegible] came back from the Transport Lines. The Battalion supplied [illegible] men to work under the R.E's.	[initials]
GRAND MARQUETTE	25/5/18		Lt Col. WILSON went to the C.C.S. and MAJOR K.F.B. TOWER MC took over command	[signature]

D. D. & L., London, E.C.
(A7883) Wt. W803/M1672 350,000 4/17 Sch. 52a Forms/C/2118/14

Instructions regarding War Diaries and Intelligence Summaries are contained in F. S. Regs., Part II. and the Staff Manual respectively. Title pages will be prepared in manuscript.

WAR DIARY
or
INTELLIGENCE SUMMARY.
(Erase heading not required.)

Army Form C. 2118.

Place	Date	Hour	Summary of Events and Information	Remarks and references to Appendices
GRAND MARQUETTE	25/5/18		of the Battalion. During the day Coys were at disposal of O.C. Coys for training. The Battalion found 130 men for work.	
GRAND MARQUETTE	26/5/18		Capt C.E. CORDNEY and Lt A.J. LITTLE joined the Battalion. Arrangements were made for the relief of the 2nd S.W.B.s on the following day. At night the Battalion found usual working parties of 130.	
GRAND MARQUETTE and SWARTENBROUCH	27/5/18		Billets of the Battalion were taken over by the 1st Lancs. Fus. Battalion started to leave GRAND MARQUETTE at 9 PM and the relief of the 2nd S.W.B.s was completed by 12.30 AM. Z and Y Coys were in the front line, X and W in support. We have taken over a very long front about 1700 yds but the Hun doesn't seem to have more than an outpost position in front of us.	Sketch of [illegible] E17 A [illegible] E22 [illegible]
SWARTENBROUCH	29/5/18		On the 28th the Germans were expected to make an attack on the Divisional front but all remained quiet.	J.H. Penn Capt

D. D. & L., London, E.C. (A7883) Wt. W803/M1672 350,000 4/17 Sch. 52a Forms/C/2118/14

Instructions regarding War Diaries and Intelligence Summaries are contained in F. S. Regs., Part II. and the Staff Manual respectively. Title pages will be prepared in manuscript.

WAR DIARY
or
INTELLIGENCE SUMMARY.
(Erase heading not required.)

Army Form C. 2118.

Place	Date	Hour	Summary of Events and Information	Remarks and references to Appendices
SWARTENBROUCK	29/5/18	–	Everything was quiet with the exception of some gas shelling. 2nd Lt CUTTERBUCK was sent down to the C.C.S. gassed. Several patrols were sent out to try and gain identification but all failed. The German Patrols were not active and were quite content to lie up and let us do all the [illegible]	
SWARTENBROUCK	30/5/18		Everything remained very quiet though many patrols were sent out to try and gain identification. Early on the morning of the 30th [illegible] who had come down to BHQ on proceeding to give evidence at a [illegible] Martial were caught by a shell in the yard. the C.S.M. and a [illegible] of Z Coy being wounded. Preparation was made for our relief by the 1st DUBLIN Fusiliers on the following day. several of their officers going round our line. On the night of the 30th 31st the Brigade on our right carried out an unsuccessful raid.	
[illegible]	31/5/18	·	In the evening a successful relief was carried out by the 1st R.D.F. they took over the left front Coy and portion of the right [illegible]	

D. D. & L., London, E.C.
(A7883) Wt. W809/M1672 350,000 4/17 **Sch. 52a** Forms/C/2118/14

WAR DIARY
or
INTELLIGENCE SUMMARY.
(Erase heading not required.)

Army Form C. 2118.

Instructions regarding War Diaries and Intelligence Summaries are contained in F. S. Regs., Part II. and the Staff Manual respectively. Title pages will be prepared in manuscript.

Place	Date	Hour	Summary of Events and Information	Remarks and references to Appendices
SWARTENBROUCK	31/7/18		the Royal Irish Rifles with a 2 PLATOON frontage on the extreme right of our former	36 A NE
			position. More patrols were sent out during the night. These succeeded in	E.23.a.3.4
			getting in touch with the enemy but were unable to capture a prisoner.	E.[illegible]
			The enemy has been doing a good deal of gas shelling lately but only	
			spasmodic efforts and no highly concentrated clouds of gas from shells	
			have been met with. He may be doing this with the intention of	
			letting us get careless and then one day put down a heavy barrage	
			of gas. Our transport arrangements whilst in the line have been	
			good and no losses by shell fire reported. Court martial cases	
			are a great nuisance. Three times have we had prisoners up	
			for CMs and each time it was postponed owing to non arrival	
			of some witness from the Base. It means taking 11 Sergts and	
			others from one company as witnesses when they were urgently	
			needed in the line.	
				[illegible signature] Capt

D. D. & L., London, E.C.
(A7883) Wt. W809/M1672 350,000 4/17 **Sch. 52a** Forms/C/2118/14

[illegible]

2nd [illegible] [illegible]

Operation Order No 7

Guards of Y and Z Coy will be at the [illegible] [illegible] [illegible] on the road at 3 p.m. this afternoon and for W and X at 8 p.m. at the same spot.

Immediately after lunch the guards of Z will be relieved by the [illegible] and Z Coy less the two platoons at PTE MARQUETTE will relieve Y Coy of the [illegible] this afternoon. 2 platoons of Y Coy [illegible] will relieve the LA MOTTE outposts.

When Y Coy relieves the [illegible] the 2 platoons on PTE MARQUETTE will be relieved.

The [illegible] [illegible] guns found the [illegible] by W and X will be [illegible] immediately after lunch.

Coys will [illegible] with

100 yards interval between platoons.

Receipts will be obtained for all ammunition etc.

Y Coy will hand over the following post [illegible]

Following are the ration arrangements.

All cookers will be in the wood at E 25 central.

Coy Q M Sgts will be with cookers. Rations will be sent up as at present to Coy Q M Sgts.

The cooked portion will be put on cookers. The remainder will be distributed.

Rations for tomorrow 10th except the cooked portion will be carried on the man.

Meals for W and X Coys will be arranged as follows commencing 10th inst.

Breakfast 4.30 am } Ready at
Supper 8.30 pm } cookers

Y Coy will detail a permanent carrying party for W.

Z will do ditto for X

[illegible] Bath carrying party
[illegible] [illegible] [illegible] [illegible]
R.S.M. [illegible] by [illegible] when
they are carrying
Working [illegible] [illegible]
for Y and X [illegible] as
usual
The [illegible] [illegible] for
men will be [illegible]
forward on the man
Officers [illegible] will be
stacked at Y Coy HQ under
a caretaker who will be
selected by O.C. [illegible]

W Coy T.F. [illegible] Z Coy R.D.F. [illegible]
X [illegible] X [illegible]
Z [illegible] Y [illegible]
Y [illegible] W [illegible]
E [illegible]

Supply of [illegible] food boxes
[illegible] [illegible] will be [illegible]
cookers

Capt
Adj. [illegible] Bn Roy [illegible]

9/3/18

Secret P20

2nd Bn Royal Fusiliers
Operation Order No 39.

Ref. Map 36A May 18 - 1918

1. The Battn will be relieved on night of 19/20 May by 4/Worcesters Regt (except W Coy).
W Coy will not be relieved but will march at 1-15 p.m. to GDE MARQUETTE FME and relieve "Z" Coy of 2/Hants Regt

2. X Coy will be relieved by "Z" Coy of 4/Worcester Regt about 4-30 p.m. and on relief will move to E.1.d.4.1 and take over from W Coy. 2/Hants Regt.
Y Coy will be relieved by X Coy 4/Worcester Regt about 6 p.m. & on relief will move to LA RIEST & take over billets vacated by "Y" Coy. 2/Hants Regt. who will have moved out earlier in the day.
Z Coy will be relieved by Y Coy Worcester Regt about 5.30 p.m. & on relief move to D.12.a.2.1 and take over billets vacated by "X Coy of 2/Hants Regt.
Batt HQ relieved about 7 p.m. & move to D.6.d.95.85

3. Coys will arrange to send an advance

party of 1 Off. and 4 O.R. to their opposite numbers to arrange details of inter-company reliefs, taking over trench stores, billets etc. These parties must move off by 9 a.m. Platoon guides for W & X Coys will be mutually arranged also times and place.

4. Parties must move by Platoons.

5. The 4/Worcester Regt is sending advance parties to their opposite numbers.

6. Lists of Trench Stores handed and taken over to be rendered to Orderly Room by 12 noon, 20th inst.

7. Limbers (an extra limber for valises) and horses for cookers & watercarts will be sent to Coys about one hour before they are due to be relieved.

8. Code words for relief complete "WILL SEND HIM NOW."

9. Acknowledge by wire.

10. On arrival in new area Coys will send guides to locate Bn. H.Q.

Capt.
Adjt. 2nd Royal Fusiliers

Army Form C. 2123
(In books of 100.)

"C" FORM.

MESSAGES AND SIGNALS.

No. of Message..................

Prefix ... Code EACR 56 Words ...	Received.	Sent, or sent out.	Office Stamp.
£ s. d. Charges to Collect	From QUQA By A Boardman Cpl	At..........m.	NOBA 18/8/18
Service Instructions		To .... By	

Handed in at QUQA Office 5.7 p.m. Received 5.35 p.m.

TO NOBA

*Sender's Number.	Day of Month.	In reply to Number.	AAA
C 147	18		

All guards on bridges etc posted to protect demolitions at bridges etc will be withdrawn and not handed over to incoming unit

Repeated to OC 4th Bn 18/8/18

FROM QUQA

PLACE & TIME

* This line should be erased if not required.

(11199.) W528/M1970. 25,000 Pads. 10/4/17. A.H. & S., L.

Secret

2nd Royal Fusiliers No. 8
Operation Order No. [illegible]

Sheet 36 A — May 25 1918

1. The 1/London [illegible] will move into the trenches at present occupied by this Battalion tomorrow night 27/28 May. The exchange will be as follows:–

W Coy relieved by D Coy L.F.
X " " B "
Z " " C "

A Coy 1/London Fus. will be billeted at LE BOULEVARD.

W and X Coys will each send 1 guide to Canal Bridge at D.G. 95 20 at 9 P.M.

The advance party of 1 Officer + 1 N.C.O. per Coy of 1/London Fus. will arrive during the afternoon.

2. Tomorrow night the 27/28 May the Batt. will relieve the 1/[illegible] [illegible] as follows:–

W Coy will relieve C Coy [illegible]
X " " B "
Y " " A "
Z " " D "

Army Form C. 2123.
(In books of 100.)

"C" FORM.

MESSAGES AND SIGNALS.

No. of Message.................

Prefix.........Code...... Words............	Received.	Sent, or sent out.	Office Stamp.
£ s. d. Charges to Collect	From................ By....................	At.................m.	
Service Instructions		To.................. By....................	

Handed in at..Office...............m. Received...............m.

TO	

* Sender's Number.	Day of Month.	In reply to Number.	AAA

FROM PLACE & TIME	

* This line should be erased if not required.

(19629) Wt528/M1970. 300,000 Pads. 4/17. McC. & Co. Ltd (**E1213**).

(2)

3. Guides for Z and X Coys will be at Road Junction E.9.c.7.2 at 10 p.m.
Guides for W and Y Coys will be at Bn H.Q. of 4/S.N.B. at E.14.d.6.4 at 10 P.M.
Z Coy will move in rear of X Coy and Y Coy in rear of W Coy.
Coys will march by Platoons at 200 yards interval.

4. Advance Party of 1 Off. 1 Sgt and 2 other ranks for W, X, Z Coys & H.Q. will report to Coy H.Q. of their opposite numbers during the afternoon of 27th. Advance Party for Y Coy as soon as it is dark enough to go forward

5. The aid post for Right Coys is at E.21.a.4.5. Relay aid post for left Coys at E.15.c.70.95.

6. Lists of Stores handed & taken over to be sent to Bn H.Q. by 12 noon 28th inst.

7. All billets will be handed over clean.

8. Code word for relief complete is FLINT

9. ACKNOWLEDGE

Issued to:
No 1 O.C. W Coy
2 " X
3 " Y
4 " Z
5 4/S.N.B.
6 1/L. Fus
7 H.Q.
8 File

Capt
Adjt 8/Royal Fusiliers

Army Form C. 2123.
(In books of 100.)

"C" Form.

MESSAGES AND SIGNALS.

No. of Message..................

Prefix.........Code...... Words............	Received.	Sent, or sent out.	Office Stamp.
£ s. d. Charges to Collect	From................ By	At...... ....m.	
Service Instructions		To................. By..................	

Handed in at..Office...............m. Received...............m.

TO	

* Sender's Number.	Day of Month.	In reply to Number.	AAA

FROM PLACE & TIME	

* This line should be erased if not required.

(19629) Wt528/M1970. 300,000 Pads. 4/17. McC. & Co. Ltd. **(E1213).**

All Coys
[illegible]
[illegible]

Warning Order

The Battalion will relieve the 1/S.W. Borderers in the Left Brigade front on the night 27th/28th May, with 2 Coys in the front line and 2 Coys in support

Y Coy Right front Coy

Z Coy Left front Coy

W Right Support Coy

X Left Support Coy

The two front line Coys at present have only 3 platoons each of a strength of about 36 men

O.C. Coys will reconnoitre tomorrow evening 25th inst & will report at Bn HQ 2/S.A.B. SWARTENBROUCH E14d6.4 at 9pm where guides will take them to their Coy HQ. O.C. W & X Coys will also reconnoitre positions of platoons at E16a & E10c respectively & will obtain a guide from HQ ~~2nd~~ 1st K.O.S.B. at E7b7.7. The platoon comdrs of these two platoons ~~shall~~ will also reconnoitre these positions.

Y & Z Coy will each form
their Coys into 3 platoons.

W Coy will have 3 platoons in
the Support Line taking over from
Right Support Coy 7/S.W. Borderers
and one platoon at about E16a
taking over from one platoon 1/K.O.S.B.

X Coy will have 3 platoons in
the Support Line taking over from
Left Support Coy 7/S.W. Borderers.
and one platoon about FME MOLENHEIM
E10c
taking over from one platoon 1/K.O.S.B.

86th Inf.Brigade No. G.2/87.

2/Royal Fusiliers.
~~1/Lancs.Fusiliers.~~
~~1/R.Dublin Fusiliers.~~
~~86th T.M.Battery.~~

~~29th Division 'G'.~~)
~~87th Inf.Brigade.~~) ~~For information.~~

WARNING ORDER.

1. The 86th Infantry Brigade will probably relieve the 87th Inf.Brigade in the Left Sector of the Divisional Front on the night of the 27/28th May 1918.

2. The Left Sector is at present held by the 87th Inf. Brigade as shown on the attached tracing. (Units only).

3. Battalions will probably be distributed as under:-

(A). 2/Royal Fusiliers.
(1) The whole of the front line and immediate support posts to be held with 2 Coys.
(2) The support linez from E.21.d.15.85. to E.15.b.20.90. to be held with six platoons.
(3) Two platoons in immediate support about E.16.a. north of the road and FME MOLEGHEIN (E.10.c.).

(B) 1/R.Dublin Fusiliers.
(1) One Coy. in area SWARTENBROUCH.
(2) One Coy. in Reserve Line about E.13.d. - E.14.a. - E.8.d.
(3) One Coy. in support line about E.9.b.
(4) One Coy. in PT SEC BOIS Defences.

(C) 1/Lancs.Fusiliers. Battalion in Brigade Reserve.
(1) One Coy. at E.7.b.3.9.
(2) One Coy. at E.7.a.1.8.
(3) One Coy. at D.12.a.25.10.
(4) One Coy. at LE RIEST (D.10.c.3.7.).

Battalions will arrange to reconnoitre these areas as soon as possible.

23rd May 1918.

J.F. Deakin Captain,
Brigade Major,
86th Inf.Brigade.

E1617

S E C R E T.

86th Inf.Brigade No. G.2/91

2/Royal Fusiliers.
1/Lancs.Fusiliers.
1/R.Dublin Fusiliers.
86th T.M.Battery.

29th Division 'G'.) for information.
87th Inf.Brigade.)

86th Inf.Brigade No. G.2/87 of 23/5/18 is cancelled and the following WARNING ORDER is substituted.

1. The 86th Infantry Brigade will relieve the 87th Infantry Brigade in the Left Sector of the Divisional Front on the night of the 27/28th May 1918. The Brigade will do a tour of 16 days in the line.

2. The Left Sector will be taken over by the 86th Infantry Brigade as shown on the attached map.
The 1/Lancs.Fusiliers will be in Brigade Reserve and will be distributed as under:-

(1) One Coy. at E.7.b.3.9.
(2) One Coy. at E.7.a.1.8.
(3) One Coy. at D.12.a.1.8.
(4) One Coy. about AU SOUVERAIN.

Battalion Headquarters will be as under:-

2/Royal Fusiliers.	E.14.d.5.4.
1/Lancs.Fusiliers.	D.6.d.8.9.
1/R.Dublin Fusiliers.	E.7.d.72.79.

The 86th T.M.Battery will take over the Battn. Headquarters at present occupied by the 1/K.O.S.B. at E.7.b.73.80. and will make that their Headquarters. They will also take over the present Headquarters of the 87th T.M.Battery at E.12.b.67.57.

3. A C K N O W L E D G E.

24th May 1918.

J. F. Dearden Captain,
Brigade Major,
86th Inf. Brigade.

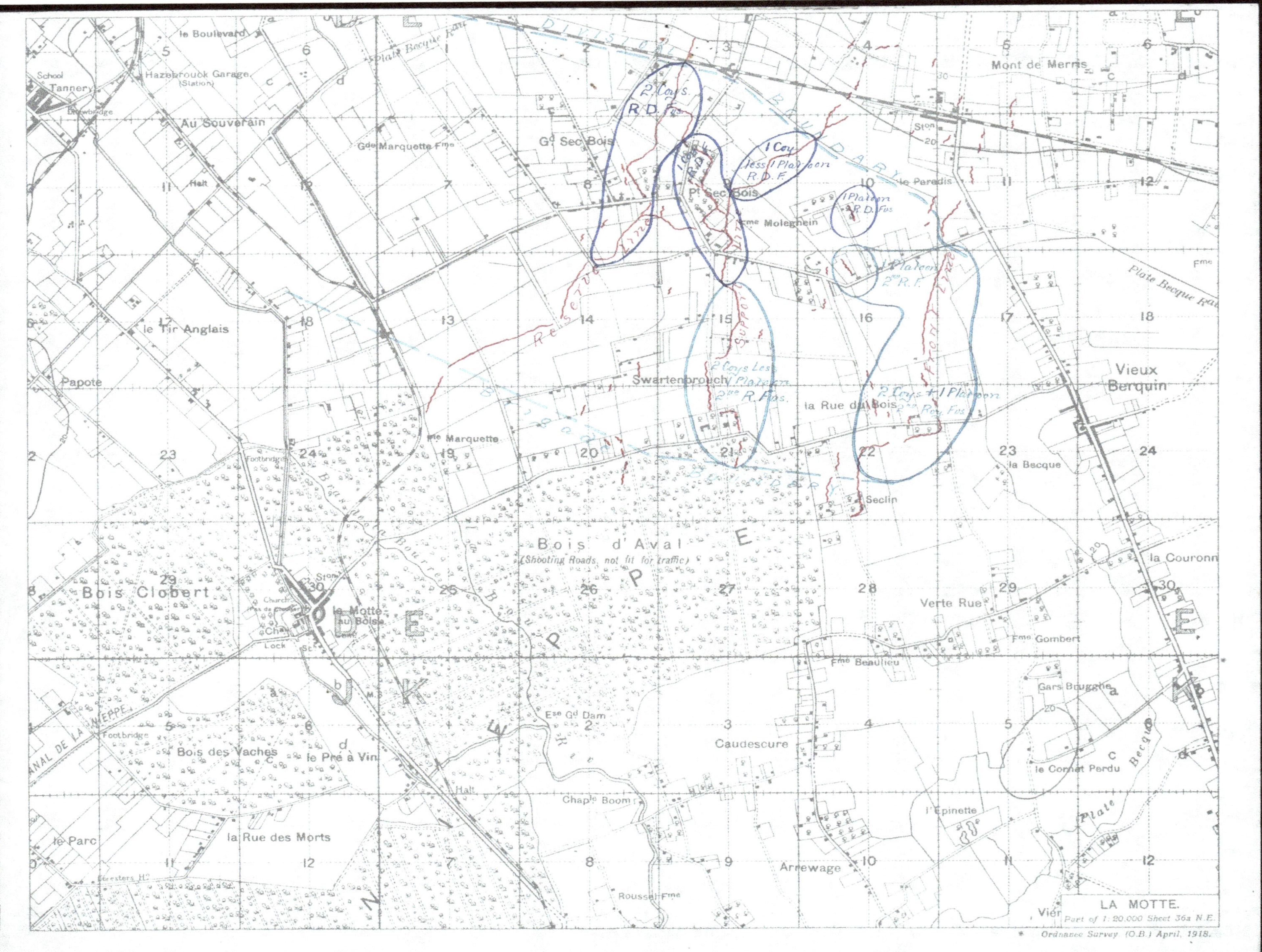
LA MOTTE.
Part of 1:20,000 Sheet 36a N.E.
Ordnance Survey (O.B.) April, 1918.
Mont de Merris
le Boulevard
Hazebrouck Garage (Station)
School
Tannery
Au Souverain
Gde Marquette Fme
Gd Sec Bois
Pt Sec Bois
Fme Molegnein
le Paradis
Plate Becque
le Tir Anglais
Papote
Swartenbrouck
la Rue du Bois
Vieux Berquin
Fme Marquette
la Becque
Seclin
Bois d'Aval
(Shooting Roads, not fit for traffic)
Bois Clobert
la Motte au Bois
Church
Lock
la Couronne
Verte Rue
Fme Gombert
Fme Beaulieu
Gars Brugghe
le Cornet Perdu
Ese Gd Dam
Caudescure
Bois des Vaches
le Pré à Vin
Footbridge
Halt
Chaple Boom
l'Epinette
le Parc
la Rue des Morts
Foresters Ho
Arrewage
Roussel Fme
Canal de la Nieppe
2 Coys. R.D. Fus.
1 Coy less 1 Platoon R.D.F.
1 Platoon R.D. Fus.
1 Platoon 2nd R.F.
2 Coys less 1 Platoon 2nd R. Fus.
2 Coys + 1 Platoon 2nd Roy. Fus.
Reserve Line
Support Line
Front Line
Divisional Boundary

Identification Trace for use with Artillery Maps.

SECRET

D E

DIVISIONAL BOUNDARY

3 Platoons 21 men each
Coy H.Q.
3 Platoons 21 men each.
1 Platoon 21 men
1 Platoon 21 men
Bn. H.Q.
Bn. H.Q.
RESERVE LINE
3 Platoons / 44 men each
SUPPORT LINE
Coy H.Q.
4. Platoons.
3 of 36 men each.
1 of 4 L.G's.
LINE
6 Platoons of 36 men each.
Coy H.Q.
Bn. H.Q.
Coy H.Q.
3 Platoons 44 men each.
BDE. BOUNDARY
Coy H.Q.

SWITCH
D E
J K
LINE
CORPS BOUNDARY
RESERVE
SUPPORT
FRONT

TO SUPERIMPOSE ON SHEET
36 A N.E. & LA MOTTE
1.20.000
No 628. TOPO SECTION 29th DIV.

NOTE.—(1). These traces are intended to facilitate the communication of information as to the position of targets, which have been located on a squared map.

(2). The squares on this trace are 500 yards in length on the 1/10,000 scale, 1,000 yards in length on the 1/20,000 scale, and 2,000 yards in length on the 1/40,000 scale.

(3). The squares on the trace are fitted to the squares of the map showing the targets, which are then drawn on the trace. Sufficient letters and numbers must also be added to enable the recipient to place the trace in the correct position on his own map. A little detail may also be traced, but this is not essential. The name and scale of the map to which the trace refers must be always given. The trace can be used for the 1/10,000, 1/20,000, or 1/40,000 scale.

G.S.G.S. 3023.

Tracing taken from Sheet..............................

of the 1:.................. *map of*..............................

Signature.............................. *Date*..................

SECRET

O.C. BMR 24

2nd Royal Fusiliers

The 88th Infantry Brigade is carrying out a raid on the [illegible] night 30/31 May.
Zero hour 12.30 a.m.
Objective about E 22 d. 75.15
There will be Artillery barrage involving squares E 28 & E 29 & E 23 c & d & E 22 d.

The SOS barrage on the Divisional front will be suspended from 12.15 a.m. to 12.30 a.m. on May 31st

30.5.18

H Parker
Major
Bde Major
86th Infantry Bde

37.B.
(not sel)

Vol 28

(6339) Wt. W160/M3016 1,500,000 10/17 McA & W Ltd (E 1898) Forms W3091. Army Form W.3091.

Cover for Documents.

June 1918

Nature of Enclosures.

CONFIDENTIAL

WAR DIARY

Vol 40

Notes, or Letters written.

2ND BN ROYAL FUSILIERS

Army Form C. 2118.

WAR DIARY
or
INTELLIGENCE SUMMARY.
(Erase heading not required.)

Instructions regarding War Diaries and Intelligence Summaries are contained in F. S. Regs., Part II. and the Staff Manual respectively. Title pages will be prepared in manuscript.

JUNE 1918.

Place	Date	Hour	Summary of Events and Information	Remarks and references to Appendices
SWARTENBROUGH	1		Lieut Col E.M.Baker, D.S.O. arrived and took over command of the battalion. Major Tower arranged details of the attack which is to take place tomorrow. He and the two Company Commanders concerned went to Brigade to attend a Conference. The attack is to be carried out by 2 Companies of the 1st Royal Dublin Fusiliers who are to attack ANKLE FARM and BRICKSTACKS (E.23.a.70.45) and one Company (Y Coy) 2nd Royal Fusiliers to attack LUG FARM, who will be supported by 2 Lewis Guns from W Company. The enemy shelled our Support Line fairly heavily during the night with Gas and H.E. No casualties.	Sheet 36A.N.E.
	2		The day spent in arranging further details of the attack for tonight. C.R.A. of Division came in during the morning and gave us all details of the artillery barrage. Major TOWER is carrying on with his arrangements and formed his battle H.Q. at E.10.c.9.0. Major TOWER and 2nd Lt W.E.STOKES (O.C. Y Coy) went out as soon as it was dark and taped out the assembly point for attacking troops. See appendix for narrative of attack.	
	3		Attack took place at 1 a.m. and at 1-27 a.m. the light signal was seen to go up from LUG FARM which indicated that the objective had been captured by Y Coy and about an hour later prisoners began to arrive at Battalion H.Q., and in all one Machine Gun and 15 Other Ranks were taken prisoner at LUG FARM. The resistance put up by them seems to have been slight. Everything worked as per programme and the artillery barrage was very good. By daylight the objective had been consolidated and our men were comfortably dug in on the eastern and southern edges of the farm. Our casualties were, 4 Officers wounded - Major K.E.B TOWER, M.C. Lt W.L.A.C.READE,M.C. 2nd Lieuts E.G.ANDREWS and H.BRANFORD. (The latter was in charge of the 2 Lewis Guns of W Coy.) Other ranks - 5 Killed, 16 Wounded, and 1 Missing. Our signallers ran out a line behind the attacking troops and communication was maintained during the day back to Battalion H.Q. The 1st R.D.F. on our left also gained their objectives, capturing 2 Machine guns & about 20 prisoners. Congratulatory messages were received from the Corps, Division & Brigade Commanders, as follows:-	

D. D. & L., London, E.C.
(A7883) Wt. W10/M1672 350,000 1/17 Sch. 52a. Forms/C/2118/14

Instructions regarding War Diaries and Intelligence Summaries are contained in F. S. Regs., Part II. and the Staff Manual respectively. Title pages will be prepared in manuscript.

Army Form C. 2118.

WAR DIARY
or
INTELLIGENCE SUMMARY.
(Erase heading not required.)

JUNE 1918.

Place	Date	Hour	Summary of Events and Information	Remarks and references to Appendices
SWARTENBROUGH	3rd		From Corps Commander:- My congratulations on your well conducted enterprise this morning. Please convey to QUQA and all Units concerned my warmest congratulations. From Divisional Commander:- Please convey the Divisional Commander's congratulations to all concerned in this morning's most successful operations. From Brigade Commander:- Please convey to your Battalion my congratulations on last night's advance, and the subsequent reorganising of the defence. It upholds the finest traditions of your regiment.	Sheet 27A. N.E.
			X Coy relieved Y Coy in LUG FARM directly after dark. A party of the Pioneer Battn 1st Monmouthshire Regt, were sent upto wire round LUG FARM, but owing to enemy machine gun fire, very little wiring was done, and a number of casualties were suffered by the wiring party.	
			At 11-30 p.m. the enemy put down a very heavy barrage on our old front line and just in rear which lasted for 40 minutes. Fortunately no casualties were suffered by us, but the 1st R.D.F. suffered a few. The S.O.S. Signal went up from the 1st R.D.F. and immediately our guns put down a very heavy barrage on their S.O.S. line and no attack was made on LUG FARM, but small parties of the enemy attacked the 1st R.D.F but were driven off by Lewis Gun fire, and 10 of the enemy were killed in front of one post. Our casualties during the past two days have been – [illegible] Officers wounded. Other ranks, 10 killed, [illegible] wounded, and 1 missing.	
			The relief of Y Coy in LUG FARM was carried out without any hitch, and Y Coy on relief went back to the Reserve Line. During the night the Lewis Gun posts were pushed forward from the eastern edge of LUG FARM to conform to the general line across to CHIMNEY STACK at E.23.a.70.45 and gained touch with the right post of the 1st Lancs Fus.	
			Lieut LITTLE was wounded on the night of the 3rd/4th but not badly.	
	4th		X Coy continued the consolidation of LUG FARM and wire was put out in front of posts and pits dug for Lewis Guns. The enemy were quite quiet during the night, but for spasmodic bursts of machine gun fire. A patrol was sent out to LA BECQUE and located a large working party. Enemy snipers crawled along up to one of our posts	

D. D. & L., London, E.C.
(A7883) Wt. W203/M1672 350,000 4/17 Sch. 52a Forms C/2118/14

Army Form C. 2118.

WAR DIARY
or
INTELLIGENCE SUMMARY.
(Erase heading not required.)

Instructions regarding War Diaries and Intelligence Summaries are contained in F. S. Regs., Part II, and the Staff Manual respectively. Title pages will be prepared in manuscript.

JUNE 1918.

Place	Date	Hour	Summary of Events and Information	Remarks and references to Appendices
SWARTENBROUCH	4th		and killed 2 of our men, but the Coy Commander, Capt SMITH, immediately sent out men to occupy the sniper's post and prevent him crawling up to our lines again.	Sheet 36A, N.E.
			Y Coy took over the SWARTENBROUCH Defences from a Company of the 4th Worcestershire Regt, 88th Brigade. The 87th Brigade relieved the 88th Brigade on our right, the 1st Border Regt being on our right flank.	
	5th		Perfect weather has prevailed for the past few weeks and still continues. Things have quietened down on our front now and normal conditions pertain.	
			A strong patrol under 2nd Lt R.W.KIRKE went out to LA BECQUE and located a large working party of the enemy but they were too well screened by sentry posts to be attacked with any chance of success.	
			Dispositions of Coys as follows:- X Coy in LUG FARM, W Coy in Support near the front line, Z Coy in Support line, Y Coy in SWARTENBROUCH Defences.	
			Strength of the battalion:- 33 Officers, [illegible] other ranks. A number of Officers keep proceeding on and returning from Courses of varying duration.	
			Leave has now opened again but the allotment is very small, and to be qualified a man must have been out of England for over 1[illegible] months, and an Officer over 5 months.	
			The men are very cheerful and the success achieved has had a very good effect.	
			The enemy system of defences is maintained by an outpost line of snipers and machine guns. These have their posts in shell holes, and the bottom of the shell hole is scooped out round the sides and shored up with timber so that the men can take shelter in and lie concealed. At first glance looking into these shell holes, one would suspect that they were unoccupied. The same shell holes do not seem to be occupied more than once every three or four days. By this means it is the greatest difficulty to locate the enemy, who do not offer any targets for our snipers and machine guns, in contrast to our own system of building conspicuous breastworks.	
	6th		The Commanding Officer, with the Commanding Officer of the 1st L.F. went up to inspect the junction of our battalion fronts. The night was very quiet, but during the day LUG FARM was shelled by about 20 rounds of 5.9 but no casualties were suffered. The enemy still continues to gas back areas and battery positions.	

D. D. & L., London, E.C. (A7883) Wt. W609/M1672 350,000 4/17 Sch. 52a Forms/C2118/14

Instructions regarding War Diaries and Intelligence Summaries are contained in F. S. Regs., Part II. and the Staff Manual respectively. Title pages will be prepared in manuscript.

WAR DIARY
or
INTELLIGENCE SUMMARY.
(Erase heading not required.)

Army Form C. 2118.

JUNE 1918

Place	Date	Hour	Summary of Events and Information	Remarks and references to Appendices
SWARTENBROUCH	7th		The Battalion is now holding the line with one company, plus one Lewis Gun team in addition. At night time there is a good deal of machine gun fire, and during the day FANTASY and LUG FARMS are heavily shelled. Our Lewis Gun posts in the front line were pushed forward into shell holes to avoid the shelling. X Coy were relieved by Z Coy in the front line.	Sheet 36A. N.E
	8th		The Divisional Commander came round to Battalion H.Q. this morning, but only stayed a short time. Major O'REILLY, 2nd in Command of the 2nd Hampshire Regt, went round our line preparatory to taking over. A carrying party from Y Coy was shelled by gas shells last night, and had 8 men wounded but none killed.	
	9th		We have fixed up a rifle range at Battalion H.Q. where firing practices can be carried out. W Coy's H.Q. hit by a gas shell and the whole place filled with gas, but no casualties. The front line is shelled heavily during the day, but we have been very lucky in having only two casualties so far.	
	10th		Z Coy were compelled to move their headquarters owing to continuous shelling. The actual front line posts do not appear to be shelled, as most of the shells drop into LUG FARM.	
	11th		All arrangements were made to evacuate our front line trenches for a depth of about 500 yards as it is intended to send over a discharge of gas. The evacuation was duly carried out but at the last minute, wind conditions being unfavourable, the project was abandoned and our trenches were reoccupied.	
	12th		There is now an epidemic of influenza prevailing. The symptoms are - high temperature and feverishness, but it only lasts for two or three days. FANTASY & LUG FARMS were shelled the whole day without ceasing, but no casualties suffered. The 2nd Hampshire Regiment came up and relieved us with 2 Coys, plus 1 Coy of the 2nd Leinster Regt. The relief was carried out expeditiously and the night was abnormally quiet.	
	13th		The battalion moved back into camp at MORBECQUE into bivouacs and tents.	

D. D. & L., London, E.C. (A7883) Wt. W809/M1672 350,000 4/17 Sch. 52a Forms/C/2118/14

Army Form C. 2118.

WAR DIARY
or
INTELLIGENCE SUMMARY.
(Erase heading not required.)

Instructions regarding War Diaries and Intelligence Summaries are contained in F. S. Regs., Part II. and the Staff Manual respectively. Title pages will be prepared in manuscript.

JUNE 1918.

Place	Date	Hour	Summary of Events and Information	Remarks and references to Appendices
MORBECQUE.	13th		Companies were all in by 2 a.m. On the way back a shell landed in the middle of a platoon of Z Coy, killing 11 and wounding 7 including Capt Small, R.E. who has been attached to us for 6 weeks, and was to have returned to take up an Infantry Commission today. It was exceedingly bad luck that this Coy should suffer these casualties, as they had been continuously heavily shelled for the last 5 days and had only had 2 casualties.	Sheet 36A. N.E
			During this last tour in the trenches our casualties have been - Officers, 6 wounded. Other ranks, 22 Killed, 65 Wounded, 1 Missing., including the attack on the 2nd/3rd inst.	
			The weather has been extraordinarily fine, with no rain.	
			Battalion in Divisional Reserve, available to man B and D lines Second Zone of Defence in case of enemy attack.	
	14th		Baths at Le GRAND HASARD.	
	15th		Battalion paraded at 4-15 a.m. while sentence of DEATH was carried out on Nº 3D5 Pte W.SPRY. Owing to prisoners' report of enemy attack on 16th inst, battalion to be ready to move at half an hour's notice.	
	16th		2/Lt A.E.Rand to hospital SICK. Influenza still prevalent. Battalion still under half an hour's notice.	
Bois D'AVAL	17th		Battalion relieved the 2/S.W.B. in the left of the right sub-sector of Divisional front on night of 17/18th, Y Coy in front line, X Coy in close support, W Coy in strong point at E.20. Central, Z Coy in Reserve. Front of BOIS D'AVAL from SECLIN to BEAULIEU. Very short of Officers owing to influenza. 1/R.D.Fus relieved the 1/K.O.S.B. on our right.	
	18th		In line with only 9 Officers owing to influenza. 2/Lt E.N.Wardell left for England to join M.G.Corps. Capt P.T.O.Boult struck off strength - ordered a Medical Board in England. 2/Leinster Regt retook LUG FARM on our left. Two wounded prisoners were found by a patrol of Y Coy in a shell hole, and brought in.	

D. D. & L., London, E.C. (A7883) Wt. W809/M1672 350,000 4/17 Sch. 52a Forms/C/2118/14

Army Form C. 2118.

Instructions regarding War Diaries and Intelligence Summaries are contained in F. S. Regs., Part II. and the Staff Manual respectively. Title pages will be prepared in manuscript.

WAR DIARY
or
INTELLIGENCE SUMMARY.
(Erase heading not required.)

JUNE 1918.

Place	Date	Hour	Summary of Events and Information	Remarks and references to Appendices
MORBECQUE	19		Battalion was relieved by the 2/S.W.B. the relief being carried out successfully & the night was very quiet. The battalion went back to the old camp at MORBECQUE and Companies were all in by about 1 a.m. The casualties during the two days tour in the line were O.R., 1 Killed 8 wounded. The Battalion Transport was inspected by Col. WRIGHT, from D.A.D.O.S. who gave an excellent report on it.	Sheet 36A NE
	20		Company Training. The 50 yards range at Le GRAND HASARD was available for the use of the battalion. Weather was very fine. Received warning orders of Divisional relief on 20th-21st-22nd inst, but 86th Brigade will remain in Divisional Reserve to the 31st Division. 2/Lt A.B.Walton joined battalion and was posted to X Coy for duty.	
	21		Training continued at MORBECQUE. A performance was given in the evening in H.Q.Coy barn by the Divisional Concert Troupe.	
	22		Platoon Commanders received Bayonet Fighting instruction before breakfast. Companies carried on with training during the morning. Football during afternoon. The Drums beat RETREAT in the evening, and the battalion orchestra played selections to the troops.	
	23		Major Persse, M.C. and the Medical Officer visited Major Tower, M.C. and other wounded officers at BOULOGNE and found them all progressing favourably.	
	24		Company training in morning. Moved about 2 p.m. to Camp at D.13.a.9.7. Accommodation satisfactory. Raining heavily. The remainder of the Brigade moved to BLARINGHEM Area but this battalion remained behind in Divisional reserve under the orders of G.O.C., 31st Division. 2/Lt G.A.Watson of 1/Northumberland Fusiliers joined and was posted to X Coy for duty.	
E.7.&7.7	25		Weather clear. After dinner we came under orders of G.O.C., 93rd Brigade. At 2 p.m. we received orders to relieve the 15th West Yorks in left sub-sector of left Brigade front same night. Relief completed by midnight. W Coy and one platoon of X Coy in front line, remainder of battalion in support. Relief was carried out quietly. Front extends from PRESIDENT CROSS to West of ANKLE FARM.	

D. D. & L., London, E.C.
(A7883) Wt. W809/M1672 350,000 4/17 Sch. 52a Forms/C/2118/14

Army Form C. 2118.

WAR DIARY
or
INTELLIGENCE SUMMARY.
(Erase heading not required.)

Instructions regarding War Diaries and Intelligence Summaries are contained in F. S. Regs., Part II. and the Staff Manual respectively. Title pages will be prepared in manuscript.

JUNE 1918.

Place	Date	Hour	Summary of Events and Information	Remarks and references to Appendices
E.7.6.7.7	26		Day fine and quiet. Major PERSSE, M.C. was wounded severely in the abdomen about 11 p.m. by M.G.fire whilst making tour of battalion with the Commanding Officer, near MOLEGHEIN FARM.	SHEET 36A
	27		At 12-30 a.m. a minor operation was carried out by the 93rd Brigade on our immediate right. ANKLE FARM was retaken yielding some prisoners and 8 machine guns. Our right hand posts conformed to the barrage and to final consolidation line of battalion on right. One slightly wounded prisoner came into our line.	
SEDIMENT HOUSE			On the night of 27th battalion was relieved by the 13/Yorks & Lancs. Relief quiet. Moved back to reserve in B and D lines Second Zone. Came under orders of G.O.C., 86th Brigade, remainder of which had moved up into reserve to 31st Division. Casualties during the two days in line were., 1 Officer wounded, 7 O.R. wounded.	
	28		Major PERSSE, M.C. died of wounds at № 2 Australian C.C.S, BLENDECQUES. Brigade is in reserve for the operation known as BORDERLAND carried out by 31st and 5th Divisions. All objectives were taken and held against counter-attacks.	
	29		From midnight 28/29th inst, under orders of the 93rd Brigade, in case of heavy counter attack at dawn, being under half an hour's notice to move. Back under orders of 86th Brigade about midday.	
BLARINGHEM			Received orders to proceed to BLARINGHEM Area after dinner. Moved at 5 p.m. Halted for tea at Transport lines en route. Arrived at BLARINGHEM at about 9-30 p.m. Billets very scattered. Battn H.Q. at B.24.a.5.2. (36 A.NW.) Received warning order to move on 30th inst to LA SABLONre Area. The first time the battalion has been out of the line since April 27th.	
LA SABLONRE	30		Moved at 2 p.m. to LA SABLONre. arriving at about 4 p.m. Billets good but rather cramped. One Company (Z) under canvas. Weather perfect.	

Eu Baker
Lieut-Col.,
Commanding 2nd Battn. ROYAL FUSILIERS.

D. D. & L., London, E.C. (A7883) Wt. W803/M1672 350,000 4/17 Sch. 52a Forms/C/2118/14

Instructions regarding War Diaries and Intelligence Summaries are contained in F. S. Regs., Part II. and the Staff Manual respectively. Title pages will be prepared in manuscript.

Army Form C. 2118.

WAR DIARY
or
INTELLIGENCE SUMMARY.
(Erase heading not required.)

APPENDIX. JUNE 1916.

Place	Date	Hour	Summary of Events and Information	Remarks and references to Appendices
			Account of Minor Operation of 2nd Bn. Royal Fusiliers on night of 2/3 JUNE.	
			In conjunction with other minor operations on the left against ANKLE FARM and THE FACTORY, the Battalion attacked on a one company front. Y Coy attacked supported by W Coy who pushed forward Lewis Gun patrol on either flank and assisted in the consolidation. The objective of the attack was LUG FARM and the three enclosures round the same. Zero time was fixed for 1 a.m. on the 3rd JUNE. An excellent artillery barrage was put down at Zero in front of the objective, and crept forward by 50 yards each minute to 100 yards the enemy side of the objective. It then lifted 200 yards on the S.O.S. lines. The Company attacked in the following formation:-	[initials]
			Rifle Section. 1 Officer. Rifle Section.	
			1 Officer. 1 Officer.	
			Lewis Gun Section in file. Lewis Gun Section in file. Rifle Section in file. Lewis Gun Section in file.	
			Company Commander. Runners.	
			Lewis Gun Section in file. Lewis Gun Section in file. Lewis Gun Section in file.	
			Stretcher Bearers & Signallers.	

D. D. & L., London, E.C. (A7883) Wt. W809/M1672 350,000 4/17 Sch. 52a Forms/C/2118/14

Instructions regarding War Diaries and Intelligence Summaries are contained in F. S. Regs., Part II. and the Staff Manual respectively. Title pages will be prepared in manuscript.

WAR DIARY
or
INTELLIGENCE SUMMARY.
(Erase heading not required.)

Army Form C. 2118.

Place	Date	Hour	Summary of Events and Information	Remarks and references to Appendices
			The Company were formed up on a tape line which was put out at ZERO minus two hours, on the position marked on attached map. The barrage fell punctually, and the Company moved forward close under it, advancing in 50 yard rushes with it. The extended Rifle Section advanced right through to the far side of the objective, Section in file in rear mopping up the near hedges, which afforded most of the prisoners.	
			The objective was reached at ZERO plus 10 minutes, and consolidation under cover of patrols pushed forward commenced immediately at points chosen.	
			A Signal of XXMXXXX, 1 Red, 1 Green, and 1 Red, Verey Lights fired in quick succession to indicate reaching of objective. Immediately on this a previously arranged carrying party started forward with ammunition, bombs and supplies of wire, etc. Extra Lewis Gun panniers were also brought forward.	
			The position was immediately consolidated, 6 Lewis Guns being used for the defence.	
			W Coy consolidated on the right with two Lewis Guns, Leinster Regt pushed out three posts on the right to conform with new line.	
			Major K. F. B. TOWER, M.C. in Command.	
			2nd Lieut W.E.Stokes. Commanding Y Company.	
			Capt J.T.Smith. Commanding W Company.	
			Prisoners. 2 N.C.Os and 13 Privates, 1 Light Machine Gun, Rifles, Revolvers, Equipment, ammunition, etc. All of 208th R.I.R.	
			Casualties. 8 wounded.	

D. D. & L., London, E.C.
(A7883) Wt. W809/M1672 350,000 4/17 Sch. 52a Forms/C/2118/14

Bn. will now hold the
line from EXETER [illegible] to K.S. [illegible]

X & Y Coys of 1st [illegible]
will take over the front
held by 'Z' Coy tonight
31/1 Jan.

[illegible]
[illegible] Z will be on
Road [illegible] MERE FARM [illegible]
at 10-30 P.M.

One for C H Q }
One for Left Platoon } To meet X Coy at [illegible]
One for Centre Platoon }

One for Right Platoon → to meet Y Coy [illegible]

[illegible]
will march [illegible] [illegible]
[illegible]

one Platoon of Z Coy RDF will relieve the left Platoon of Y Coy. OC Z Coy RDF will share CHQ with OC Y.

A guide will be in readiness at Y CHQ at 10-30 PM to meet the Platoon of RDF. this platoon together with CHQ of Z RDF will be conducted to that point by guides from BHQ. these guides to be at SANCTAS CORNER E15a 10-15 PM

Emphasis [illegible]

will be [illegible] in these

A [illegible] Code word

"SHN SATNE"

O. G. Y. [illegible]

[illegible] in the

Pocket [illegible]

[illegible]

Receipt for [illegible]

[illegible]

Sent [illegible] B.H. [illegible]

D [illegible]

S E C R E T.

Copy No.________

86th Infantry Brigade Order No. 227.

Ref. Map Sheet 36 A, N.E., 1/20,000, (Edition 7A). 1/6/1918.

1. The 86th Infantry Brigade will carry out a minor operation on a day and time to be notified later.

2. OBJECT.

The object of the operation is to advance our line from the present front line to a line conforming generally to the line of the BEEK namely from the Northern Divisional Boundary at E.11.c.7·0. to the BEEK at E.17.a.central thence along the BEEK Southwards to the point where the road crosses it at E.23.a.85.15. (road inclusive) thence to the South-Eastern Corner of LUG FARM ENCLOSURE – THENCE TO THE SOUTH-Eastern Corner of SECLIN where it will join the present front Line.

3. Posts have already been established about E.11.c.65·05., E.17.a.75.85. and E.17.a.00·75.

4. BRIGADE OBJECTIVES.

The attack will be directed against 2 objectives.

'A' Objective - LUG FARM.

'B' Objective. - Line of the BEEK from E.17.c.67.50 to E.23.d.85.35.

5. TROOPS AND METHOD OF ATTACK.

(a) 'A' Objective. will be taken by two Companies of the 2nd Royal Fusiliers.

The attack will be made on a Company Front by one Company with 6 Lewis Guns, one platoon being detailed to take each of the three portions of the Objective marked "A", "B" and "C". (See attached Map "A"). The 4th Platoon will protect the right flank of the attack and will deal with enemy hostility in close proximity to the right of the objective.

The Company in Support will keep close touch with the Company in front and will carry Consolidation Material, Ammunition, etc. If heavy resistance is met with this Company will be prepared to assist in the capture of the objective.

(b) 'B'. Objective. will be taken by two Companies with 6 Lewis Guns of the 1st Royal Dublin Fusiliers.

The attack will be made on a two Company Front. The Inter-Company Boundary is shown on the attached Map 'A'.

Each Company will attack with two platoons in front. The Left Company will be protected on the left flank by a platoon moving on the north side of the hedge marking the left edge of the objective. This platoon will be prepared to co-operate with flanking fire if necessary.

The Right Company will be similarly protected by one platoon moving on the south side of the road running from FANTASY FARM to the right of the objective. Each Company will have one platoon in support which will carry material for consolidation and Ammunition.

A party of R.E. with 6 Bangalore torpedoes will be attached to the leading troops taking "B" Objective, (three torpedoes to each company with two R.E. personnel to each torpedo), in order to destroy any obstacles that there may be to the advance.

The six approximate places where the use of torpedoes is anticipated are marked on attached map "A" and numbered one to six.

The platoon working on the North flank will take one of the torpedoes in order to destro the heavily wired gate on the road leading to ANKLE FARM Enclosure at E.17.c.4.4.

Five light bridges will be carried forward by each company of the assaulting troops on "B" Objective.

/ASSEMBLY

6. ASSEMBLY POSITIONS.

The assaulting troops will take over the portion of the present front line shown on the attached Map "A" on the evening prior to the attack.

Troops detailed to garrison the present front line during and after the assault will be closed to a flank but will be re-distributed where necessary on the assaulting troops leaving the trenches for the attack.

7. GAPS.

Suitable and sufficient gaps will be cut in our wire on the evening preceding the attack, to enable the assaulting troops to get through.

8. TIME TABLE.

Fifteen minutes before Zero	Assaulting troops will move to position on tape lines.
Zero.	Artillery, Trench Mortars and Machine Guns open fire on GREEN Line. Troops move as close as possible to the barrage.
Zero plus two. (objective "A" only)	Artillery barrage lifts to yellow line. Other barrages remain on green lines.
Zero plus four.	Artillery barrage lifts to Red line. Machine Guns switch to East side of BEEK.
Zero plus ten.	Artillery barrage lifts to blue line.
Zero plus twenty to Zero plus Forty.	Artillery carries out searching fire.

Trench Mortars detailed for barrage tasks will conform to times and lifts of artillery.

Troops will endeavour to keep up to the barrage and press forward as the barrage lifts.

9. ACTION OF ARTILLERY.

Details of tasks and lifts are shown in Appendix

10. ACTION OF TRENCH MORTARS.

One Trench Mortar will accompany each Battalion in the Assault and will be prepared to assist in the capture of the objective and afterwards to deal with any Machine Guns or snipers located beyond the objectives.

8 Trench Mortars will thicken the barrage conforming to Artillery times and lifts.

11. ACTION OF MACHINE GUNS.

The following Machine Guns will take part in the operation.

(1) 4 Guns about E.28.c.5.9. These guns will remain silent during the assault but will be prepared to put down a barrage on line gun positions to LA BECQUE on the event of threatened hostile action.

(2) 2 Guns to the East of VOLLEY FARM. These guns will put down a continuous barrage from Zero hour to Zero hour plus 4 after which time they will deliver bursts of fire on the line VOLLEY FARM LA BECQUE.

(3) 2 Guns about E.17.a.60.75. From Zero hour to Zero hour plus 4 these guns will cover, with continuous fire, the West Bank of the BEEK about AMBLE FARM and CHIMNEY STACK in E.23.a. after which time they will switch on to the east bank of the BEEK forming a belt of fire across the front of the objective.

(4) 4 Guns in E.10.a. These Guns will be prepared to deliver indirect fire on any hostile movement.

/Consolidation.

12. CONSOLIDATION.

(a) On reaching the objective 'A' covering parties with Lewis Guns will move forward in advance of the objective and on the flanks. In the case of Objective 'B' covering parties with Lewis Guns will take up positions on the BERM and on the flanks of the Objective.

(b) Patrols will get into touch with the Battalion on the right or left flank as the case may be and liaison will be established.

(c) The 80th Infantry Brigade will construct a line of posts from the Southern Corner of SECLIN to join up with LUG FARM and will be to assist with Lewis Guns on that flank.

(d) On the second night the objectives will be linked up together and the new line will be linked up with the present front line in accordance with the intention of the operation.

(e) As soon as the objectives have been taken troops will be organised in depth with Lewis Guns and snipers in the front posts.

13. LIGHT SIGNALS.

The S.O.S. Signal will be RED over RED over RED.

Flares will be used when called for to communicate with aeroplanes.

14. DRESS AND EQUIPMENT. See S.S. 135.

Fighting Order.

Wire cutters. Those available will be distributed between Front Line and Support troops in the proportion of 2 to 1.

Picks and Shovels. 50 % of the men will carry shovels.

Sharpened Bill-hooks. 2 per Section.

S.O.S. Signals. 12 will be carried by each company.

Bombs and Rifle Grenades. Bombs 2 per man. 2 men per platoon will carry Rifle Grenades.

Very Pistols. 2 per Company.

Platoon scouts will be equipped as lightly as possible and will carry sharpened bill-hooks.

Bridge carriers should follow up scouts very closely.

15. HEADQUARTERS.

(1) Advanced Battalion Headquarters will be established by both attacking Battalions at the present Company Headquarters about H.22.b.00.75.

(2) Headquarters of Companies forming the attacking troops will be established prior to the attack in the present front line.

16. COMMUNICATIONS.

Power Buzzers will be installed at Advanced Battalion H.Q. (2 Telephone lines).

On the objective being reached a message to that effect will be sent back to Advanced Battalion Headquarters.

Pigeons and dogs will also be arranged at Advanced Battn. H.Q. and pigeons will be sent forward with the attacking troops.

Telephone wires will be run back to Company H.Q. as soon as established in the objectives.

Flares will be carried in order to communicate with Aeroplanes if called for.

17. INTELLIGENCE.

No secret maps, documents or letters which would supply information to the enemy if captured will be carried by Officers or other ranks of the assaulting troops.

18. MEDICAL ARRANGEMENTS.

Units will arrange to establish advanced Regimental Aid Posts.

19. FORWARD DUMPS.

Forward Dumps will be established at E.21.b.0:3. (Ammunition) and E.15.c.9.7. (R.E. material) for Right Battalion, E.16.a.3:6. (Ammunition and R.E. Material) for Left Battalion.

Each Dump will contain :-

AMMUNITION.

S.A.A.	40 boxes.
S.A.A. Bundle packed for L.Gs.	46 boxes.
Grenades, Hand, No. 5.	30 boxes.
Grenades, Rifle, No. 23.	20 boxes.
"P" Bombs.	2 boxes.
Very Lights.	2 boxes.

In addition the O.C. 86th Trench Mortar Bty. has established a dump at ~~E.10.a.~~ E.2.b. containing rounds of Trench Mortar Ammunition.

R.E. MATERIAL.

	2/Royal Fus. Dump.	1/R.Dublin Fus. Dump.
Shovels.	50.	100.
Picks.	25.	25.
Bill-hooks.		21.
Hand axes.	10.	11.
Tape.	4 coils.	4 coils.
Wire, barbed, Coils,	100.	70.
Wire, French with Staples.	30.	34.
Pickets, Screw Long.	30.	34.
Pickets, Screw Medium.	160.	200.
Sandbags.	1950.	2530.
Bridges.		

In addition the 2/Monmouthshire Regt. which assisting in consolidation will have a forward R.E. Dump at E.22.b.5:5. as follows :-

Wire, barbed coils.	50.
Pickets, Screw Long.	170.
Pickets, Screw Medium.	350.

20. CARRYING PARTY.

O.C. 1st Lancashire Fusiliers will detail 2 ~~xxxxxxx~~ platoons for each of the assaulting Battalions to act as carrying parties to move the forward dumps to dumps to be selected by attacking Battalions in the vicinity of the present front line on the evening of 1st/2nd June.

21. SYNCHRONIZATION OF WATCHES.

Synchronised watches will be sent to Battalion H.Q. at 8 p.m. on Zero night by Brigade,

86th Trench Mortar Bty. and Machine Gun Companies engaged in the Operation will send an Officer to 86th Infantry Brigade H.Q. to synchronise at 7.30 p.m. on Zero night.

21. A C K N O W L E D G E.

H Pack[signature]

Major,
Brigade Major,
86th Infantry Brigade.

Issued at ____________

Copies to :-

1-4 Staff.	9. 29/M.G. Bn.	14. C.R.E.
5 2/Roy. Fus.	10. 88/Inf. Bde.	15. 455/Fld. Coy. R.E.
6 1/Lancs. Fus.	11. 3/Austn. Bde.	16. 29/Div. Arty.
7 1/R.Dublin Fus.	12. 87/Inf. Bde.	17. Diary.
8 86/T.M.Bty.	13. 29/Div. "G".	18. File.

S E C R E T.
- - - - - -

AMENDMENT NO. 1. to 86TH INFANTRY BRIGADE ORDER NO. 227.

Ref. Map Sheet 36A, N.E., 1/20,000. (Edition 7A). 1/6/18.

1. Cancel para 8, TIME TABLE, and substitute TIME TABLE attached.

2. Add to para 12 (c) "Plans for the defence will be organised so as to be completed before dawn".

3. Para 12 (d) after "On the 2nd night" add "3/4th June the consolidation of the captured positions and the extension of the posts between SOLIN and LUG FARM will be continued".

4. To para 12 add :-

(f) 50 men of the 1/2nd Monmouthshire Pioneer Battalion have been detailed to assist in the consolidation by wiring in front of LUG FARM between roads E.23.c.4.7. and E.23.a.50.45 (= 400 yards) with a double apron barbed wire fence with gaps every 100 yards, on night 3/4th June.

A dump of wiring material will be formed along the road East of LUG FARM consisting of :-

90 coils barbed wire.
150 Long screw pickets.
300 Short or medium pickets.

The garrison of the front to be wired will find a covering party.

(g) The 88th Infantry Brigade will establish posts on the line SOLIN FARM and LUG FARM and gain touch with troops of the 86th Infantry Brigade at the Southwest Corner of LUG FARM.

(h) One Battalion of the 87th Infantry Brigade will be in position in GRANDE MARQUETTE Area by midnight 2/3rd June.

5. Add Appendix 1. issued herewith.

6. Delete tracing "B" and substitute attached Tracing "B".

Major,
Brigade Major,
86th Infantry Brigade.

Copies to all recipients of 86th Inf. Brigade Order No. 227.

TIME TABLE

15 minutes before Zero: Assaulting troops will move to positions on Tape Lines.

"A" Objective.

Zero. Artillery, Medium and Light Trench Mortars and Machine Guns open fire on Green Line 50 yards in front of LUG FARM. Troops move as close as possible to the barrage.

Zero plus 1 minute. Barrage creeps forward at the rate of 50 yards per minute.

Zero plus 3 minutes. Barrage settles on Red Line where it remains until Zero plus 20 minutes with the exception of one How. Battery which moves on to Black Line at Zero plus 6 minutes.

Zero plus 20 minutes. Barrage lifts to Blue Line, and searching fire is carried out until Zero plus 40 minutes.

"B" Objective.

Zero. Artillery, Medium and Light Trench Mortars and Machine Guns open fire on Green Line where it remains stationary for three minutes.

Zero plus 3 minutes. Barrage creeps forward at the rate of 50 yards per minute.

Zero plus 7 minutes. Barrage settles on RED line where it remains stationary until Zero plus 20 minutes.

Zero plus 20 minutes. Barrage lifts to Blue Line carrying out searching fire until Zero plus 40 minutes.

Light Trench Mortars detailed for barrage tasks will conform to times and lifts of Artillery.

Troops will endeavour to keep up to the barrage and will push forward as the barrage creeps and subsequently lifts. Careful observation will be kept on the barrage on its initial line for the commencements of the creep.

S E C R E T.

APPENDIX NO. 1. to 86TH INFANTRY BRIGADE ORDER NO. 227.

1. The attached Tracing marked "B" gives the various barrages to be made by batteries of the 29th Divisional R.F.A.

In addition the Heavy Artillery will be given tasks.

2. Rates of fire of artillery will be :-

Zero to Zero plus 15 minutes INTENSE.
Zero plus 15 minutes to Zero plus 20 minutes RAPID.
Zero plus 20 minutes to Zero plus 40 minutes Bursts of fire averaging NORMAL RATES.

3. Rates of fire of Medium Trench Mortars will be :-

Zero to Zero plus 3 minutes - 5 rounds per minute.
Zero plus 3 to Zero plus 20 minutes - 1 round per minute.
Zero plus 20 to Zero plus 40 minutes - 5 rounds.

If enough ammunition is available the above rates will be doubled but at least 20 rounds must be kept for an S.O.S.

20 rounds in all will also be fired on TERN FARM and neighbouring enclosures.

4. At Zero plus 40 minutes the S.O.S. lines will be as shown on attached tracing "C" until further orders.

5. <u>Tasks during daylight on 1st and 2nd June.</u>

(a) The 119th Brigade, R.F.A., will cut gaps in the hedge about E.17.c.5.5.

(b) The 15th Brigade, R.H.A., will cut two or three gaps in the hedge running from E.23.a.70.55. to E.17.c.65.10. by desultory shooting, and will carry out short concentrations on LA BECQUE, the BEEK in E.23.a. and other points.

(c) The 17th Brigade R.F.A. will carry out short concentrations on BEAULIEU FARM and LUG FARM with a view to cutting gaps in the hedges.

6. <u>LIAISON.</u>

Artillery liaison officers to maintain touch with Os.C. attacking troops will be furnished as under :-

2/Royal Fusiliers by the 17th Brigade, R.F.A.
1/Royal Dublin Fusiliers by the 119th Army Brigade, R.F.A.

Copies to all recipients of 86th Infantry Brigade Order No. 227.

Secret Operation Order No. by Copy No.
Major K.F.B. Tower, M.C.
Comdg 2nd Bn Royal Fusiliers

June 2nd 1918

1/ The 2nd R. Royal Fusiliers will carry out a minor operation on night of 2/3rd June in conjunction with 1st Royal Dublin Fusiliers on our left.

2/ The object of this operation is to advance our present front line to the line of the BEEK from E.22.a.8.5 [illegible] thence to S.E. corner of LUG FARM inclusive, thence to S.E. corner of SECLIN.

3/ On night 2nd/3rd June the first part of this operation will be carried out, i.e. the capture of LUG FARM and on night of 3rd/4th June the operation will be completed by joining up the line by posts on each side.

4/ Y Coy will carry out the attack on LUG FARM supported by W Coy holding our present front line & pushing forward patrols to support the flanks of the attack.

5/ Assembly. A tape line will be laid in the earlier part of the night on E.22.d.1.c. Y Coy will be assembled on the tape line at Zero - 15 minutes

6 Method of Attack (A) Attacking Company
Y Coy will attack with 6 Sections in the front line and 3 Sections in the second line in column of sections. 3 Lewis Guns will be in front line and 3 Lewis Guns in second line.
1 Stokes mortar will accompany the attacking Coy + will move on the left flank of the Coy with the 2nd Line + will be prepared to come into action in the event of the enemy offering any resistance from the farm.
(B) Support Coy. W Coy will form the Support Coy. The Coy will take over the front line from Y Coy as soon as it is dark.
At Zero – 15 the Coy will withdraw from the 3 posts east of E.22.b.6.2. + the garrisons of these posts will be redistributed in the remainder of the present front line.
W Coy will provide 2 strong fighting patrols, each with a Lewis Gun, who will form up on the tape on the right of the attacking Coy. These patrols will move forward with the attacking Coy + will form a defensive flank on the right. These patrols will be

from different directions to form post to the SW of LUG FARM. They will dig in on their posts & will be prepared to support the attack on LUG FARM & to repel any counter attack from the S or SE

The Leicester Regt on our right are pushing out 3 posts from SEC[illegible] POST joining up with these posts at Zero + 5 minutes. Posts of W Coy will get in touch with these posts.

7 Artillery

Details of Artillery Barrage have been explained to all concerned.

8. Time Table

Zero – 2 hours. Tape will be laid for place of assembly.

Zero – 15 minutes. Attacking troops
Y Company
2 parties of W Coy
1 Stokes mortar
will form up on tape

Zero . Barrage drops.

Zero – Zero + 3 mins. Attacking troops move up as close to barrage as possible

Zero + 3 to Zero + 7 mins. Barrage moves forward 50 yards every minute. Attacking troops move forward

under the barrage
Zero + 7 Barrage lifts off objective to 200 yards beyond
attacking troops reach LUG FARM
Zero + 7 to Zero + 20 Barrage continues.
Zero + 20 to Zero + 45 Artillery fire bursts on S.O.S. line

9. Consolidation. As soon as the objective is captured O.C. X Coy will at once decide where he will dig posts & will start work at once, pushing out a patrol in front to give warning of any hostile counter attack.
Concertina wire will be put out in front of posts as soon as possible.
Arrangements are being made to wire the front of LUG FARM on night of 3rd/4th June.

10. Carrying parties. As soon as possible after the objective is captured a carrying party of 25 men from X Coy will move forward from our present front line carrying wire, screw pickets, sandbags, ammunition & bombs.

11. Headquarters. The headquarters of attacking Coy will be in post at E 22 A 8 3 at Zero hour & will later move to LUG FARM.

(5)

Advanced Batt Headquarters will be at Farm E.16.c.9.0

12. Zero hour will be notified later

13. ACKNOWLEDGE

Major
Comdg 2/Royal Fusiliers

Copies to:

No 1	to	O.C.	W Coy
" 2	"	"	X "
3	"	"	Y "
4	"	"	Z "
5	"	"	86 Bde
6	"	"	1/R.D.F.
7	"	"	2/Leinster Regt
8	"	"	File

Time table at [illegible] on
Opp. [illegible]
is cancelled & the following substituted

Zero – 2 hours Tape line laid
Zero – 15 mins Attacking troops
Y Coy
1 Section [illegible]
2 platoons W Coy
form up on tape line
Zero [illegible] Barrage [illegible] falls
for [illegible] 30 yds enemy [illegible]
attacking party moves forward
as close under barrage as possible
Zero + 5 mins Barrage lifts off [illegible]
and attacking troops [illegible] at
Zero + 5 mins to Zero + 20 mins Barrage
continues 200 yards beyond
objective

9·6·1918 Major
Comdg 2/Royal [illegible]

File

Secret — Copy No 6

2nd Royal Fusiliers
Operation Order No 44

Ref Map 36A. N.E. — June 6. 1918

1. On the night of 7/8 June X Coy [less 1 Platoon with 2 L Guns] will be relieved by 'Z' Coy in front line and on relief will take over their ~~HAZEBROUCK defences~~ old position in support line.

2. The 1 Platoon of X Coy with 2 Lewis Guns will relieve the whole of W Coy [illegible] 1 Lewis Gun team in front line remaining in immediate support at W Coy's present HQrs.
This platoon will be under direct orders of O.C. Z Coy & will be available for immediate counter attack.

3. Y Coy will remain as at present ~~[illegible] will move up to support line at E.15 [illegible]~~

4. W Coy on relief will move back to their old positions in Support line at present occupied by 'Z' Coy.

5. All posts in front & old front line will hand over lists of trench stores to incoming parties.
W Coys will send one small party to take over trench stores ~~[illegible]~~ from Z Coy

Army Form C. 2123.
(In books of 100.)

"C" Form.

MESSAGES AND SIGNALS.

No. of Message ....

Prefix.........Code...... Words............	Received.	Sent, or sent out.	Office Stamp.
£ s. d. Charges to Collect	From................ By....................	At................m.	
Service Instructions		To.................. By..................	

Handed in at..Office...............m. Received...............m.

TO	

* Sender's Number.	Day of Month.	In reply to Number.	AAA

FROM PLACE & TIME	

* This line should be erased if not required.

(19629) Wt528/M1970. 300,000 Pads. 4/17. McC. & Co. Ltd. **(E1213).**

(2)

Z Coy will leave a N.C.O. to hand over stores to X Coy on morning of 8th inst

6. No move will take place until 10 pm and then in parties of not more than 10 men

7. Relief complete will be notified by code word "BARRY"

8. ACKNOWLEDGE

W J Ware Capt
Adjt [illegible]

Copies to
No. 1 to O.C. W Coy
2 " " X
3 " " Y
4 " " Z
5 " Q.M.
6 File
~~7~~

Army Form C. 2123.
(In books of 100.)

"C" FORM.

MESSAGES AND SIGNALS.

No. of Message................

Prefix.........Code......Words............	Received.	Sent, or sent out.	Office Stamp.
£ s. d. Charges to Collect	From................ By....................	At..................m.	
Service Instructions		To.................. By...................	

Handed in at..Office...............m. Received..............m.

TO	

* Sender's Number.	Day of Month.	In reply to Number.	AAA

FROM PLACE & TIME	

* This line should be erased if not required.

(19629) Wt528/M1970. 300,000 Pads. 4/17. McC. & Co. Ltd. (**E1213**).

[illegible] Royal Fusiliers

Operation Order No. [illegible]

Ref. Map 36A NE 1/20,000
Edition XB

June 11th 1918

1. The Battalion will be relieved on night 12/13 June.
Z Coy & 1 platoon of X Coy by [illegible] Coy of Hants Regt
W & X Coys [illegible] X [illegible]
Y Coy [illegible] Leinsters
B.H.Q. by B.H.Q. of [illegible] Regt

Z Coy [illegible] at E 21 a 8.3. to lead Y Coy 2/Hants by Platoons to E 22 b 8 4 at 15 mins intervals commencing at 10 p.m.

X & Y Coys will send guides to Bn HQ E 14 d.7.2 to meet A Coy 2/Hants & C Coy of Leinsters at 10 p.m.

2. Sketches of their Coy sectors & list of all Trench Stores & R.E. material will be handed by O.C. Coys to O.C. incoming Coy & a receipt [illegible] rendered to Bn. HQ by 12 noon 13th inst.

3. On relief Coys will march to D [illegible] central where C.Q.M.S. will arrange [illegible] under R.Q.M.S. [illegible]

4. One limber per Coy for Lewis guns will be at Coy HQs W X & Y at 11.15 p.m. [illegible]

5. Completion of relief will be reported to Bn HQ by code word "CAT"

6. ACKNOWLEDGE

Copies to
No 1 W Coy
2 X
3 Y
4 Z
5 QM
6 2/Hants
7 4/Leinsters
8 File

[illegible] Capt & Adjt
[illegible]

SECRET.

O.C. 2nd Royal Fusiliers

RELIEF ORDERS

by

Major. J. W. O'Reilly.

Ref. Map. Sheet 36a. N.E. (Ed. 7a) 1/20,000.

1. On night 12/13th June 88th Inf Bde less 3 Coys 2nd Leinster Regt will relieve 86th Inf Bde in the Left Sector of the Divnl. Front.

2. Y X Coys. & Bn. H.Q. of the 2nd Hampshire Regt. plus One Coy of the 2nd Leinster Regt. will relieve the 2nd Royal Fusiliers in the Right Sub-sector. Bn. H.Q. at E14.d.75 25.
W & Z Coys. of the 2nd Hampshire Regt will be in Reserve in billets at D20 b.

3. Capt. A.J.C.W. Prendergast will be in Command and will live at Bn. H.Q.

4. Coy. dispositions will be as follows:-

Y Coy. Hampshires. relieves Z Coy R.F's in the Front Line and Close Support.

X" ... Hampshires relieves W & X Coys R.F's in Support Line

L ... 2nd Leinster Regt relieves 'Y' Coy R.F's in SWARTENBROUCK with ½ half Coy in Reserve Line

CONTD:-

5. GUIDES. 5 guides for 'Y' Coy will be at Bn. H.Q. at 10-15 pm.

1 guide for ½ Coy X at Bn HQ at 10-30 pm.

1 guide for ½ Coy X at COBLEY COTTAGE at 10-30 pm.

1 guide for C Coy, Leinsters at Bn. H.Q at 10-45 pm.

6. 1. N.C.O per platoon for Coys going into Support Line! SWARTENBRUCH and Bn H.Q will leave at 5 pm to take over.

7. Coys will leave camp by platoons at 200 yards interval in the following order.

'Y' Coy	=	8 pm.
'X' ..	=	8.30 pm.
{ 'C' ..	=	from their own camp = 8-30 pm
{ Leinsters	=	

8. All Trench Stores, Defence Schemes, work in progress and proposed, air photos, Intelligence, 'A.A. Paintings' and positions etc will be taken over and lists forwarded to this office.

Contd:.

9. RATIONS etc. Rations and 10 tins of water nightly for X Coy. will be taken up by limber to Coy H.Q. E15 d.2.0.
Rations & 10 tins for Bn. H.Q. by limber.
Rations & 20 tins for Y Coy by Pack animals to E22 a.7.8.
Y Coy will also require a good supply of Tommy Cookers.

10. WORK. Front line Coy will concentrate on Wiring and improvement of existing posts. Support Coy will provide carrying parties as required.
Reserve Coy will work on their own area.

11. REPORTS, ETC.

SITUATION - 2 am. & 3 pm.
INTELLIGENCE. - 8 am.
INDENTS FOR R.E. MATERIAL - 8 am.
BATTLE STATES. - }
CASUALTY RETURNS. - } 8 am.

Coys. will also report any shelling of their areas immediately.

Contd. :-

Relief Orders of 11-6-18. Contd :- 4.

12. Each Coy. will take 8 Lewis Guns complete, [illegible] into the line with them.

13. Relief complete will be reported by wire and by runner. The code word "PANSY" will be used.

J H Harvey [illegible]

Captain & Adjutant.

BMR. 4.

2/R Fus.
1/R D Fus
86 T M Bty.

1. The 88th Inf. Bde. will relieve the 86 Inf. Bde. tonight June 12/13.

2. If "DOG" is sent out from these H.Q. at 7 pm. tonight the withdrawal of troops will take place as on the night of June 11/12 and Batts. will be relieved in the positions taken up on completion of the withdrawal.

3. In the event of the 2/R Fus and 1/R D Fus front line Coys. being relieved after the completion of the withdrawal has taken place, one officer from each front line Coy. ~~and 2 guides~~ (who must know his Coy. line thoroughly) and 2 guides per plat. of the front line Coys. will be

left with the incoming coys. to guide them into the original front line as soon as orders are received that this is feasible.

4. In the event of BULL being sent out after midnight, relieving front line coys. will immediately be moved forward with the guides provided and as soon as the relieving coy. commanders have finished with the officers and other ranks acting as guides, these latter may rejoin their Unit in the Div. Reserve Bde. Area.

Front line coy. Commanders will wait with ~~their relieving coys.~~ coys. relieving them until 1 am. night 12/13 June so that they may be able to hand over in the original front line positions on receipt of orders BULL from Bde. H.Q. The Coy. Commanders need not wait after 1 am. but will leave it to the officer guide to hand over the front line.

5. Relief complete will be forwarded to these H.Q. by the code word "FRIEND" as soon as Coys. have been relieved in the positions taken up on evacuation.

6. Relief will take place in the ordinary way if the code word "RAT" is sent out by 7 pm. tonight.

7 ACKNOWLEDGE.

T.F. Dearden Capt
B.M. 86 Inf. Bde.

12-6-18
3.30 pm

O.C. 86 T.M. Bty. will leave 1 off. and 1 N.C.O. to put the 87 T.M. Bty guns in the original positions if relief is delayed owing to gas. Relief complete will be sent to Bde. H.Q. as soon as guns have been relieved in the rear positions
J.F. Dearden Capt.

BMR 5.

2/R Irs
1/R D Irs
86/T M Bty.

1. The same arrangements will hold as for last night for getting information of completion of withdrawal of troops to the Divl. representative (Capt. CUDDON) Lt. MERRITT will be at H.Q. 2/R Irs from 9.30 pm. in case message "DOG" is sent out at 7 pm.

T.F. Dean Capt.
BM 86 Inf. Bde.

12-6-18.

S E C R E T.

Copy No. 4

86TH INFANTRY BRIGADE ORDER NO. 233.

Ref. Map. Sheet 36A, N.E., 1/20,000.
Edition 7A Local.

June 11th, 1918.

1. On the night of the 12/13th June the 86th Infantry Brigade will be relieved in the Left Sector of the Divisional Front by the 88th Infantry Brigade, and will come into Divisional Reserve.

2. The 2/Royal Fusiliers will be relieved in the Right Sub-sector by 2 Coys. of the 2/Hampshire Regiment and Battalion Headquarters plus one Coy. of the 2/Leinster Regt.

The 1/Royal Dublin Fusiliers will be relieved in the Left Sub-sector by the 4/Worcestershire Regt.

The 88/Trench Mortar Bty. will relieve the 5 guns of the 86/Trench Mortar Bty. at present in the forward area.

The 1/Lancashire Fusiliers will be relieved in Brigade Reserve by 3 Coys. of the 2/Leinster Regt. on the afternoon of the 11th June and night of 11/12th June.

All arrangements for relief will be made between Unit Commanders concerned.

3. On relief on the night of June 11/12th the 1/Lancashire Fusiliers will move to the Right Brigade Sector of the Divisional Front and will relieve Units of the 87th Infantry Brigade as shewn on the attached table.

All details of relief will be arranged between Unit Commanders concerned.

On completion of relief the 1/Lancashire Fusiliers will come under the orders of the 87th Infantry Brigade.

4. All copies of Defence Schemes, Trench Stores, S.A.A, Grenades, work in progress and proposed, Air photos, Intelligence A.A. Mountings, etc., will be handed over and lists forwarded to this office by 6 p.m. June 14th.

5. Relief complete will be reported to this Office by the Code Word "FRIEND".

6. Camps to be occupied by Units on coming into Divisional Reserve will be notified by the Staff Captain.

7. A C K N O W L E D G E.

J. T. Dearden Captain,
Brigade Major,
86th Infantry Brigade.

Issued at 1 p.m.

Copies to :-

1-3 Staff.
4 2/Royal Fusiliers.
5 1/Lancashire Fusiliers.
6 1/Royal Dublin Fus.
7. 86/T.M.Bty.
8. 29/Div. "G"
9. 29/Div. "Q".
10. 87/Inf. Bde.
11. 88/Inf. Bde.
12. 2/Australian Bde.
13. 29/Machine Gun Bn.
14. 455/Fld. Coy., R.E.
15. 29/Div. Arty.
16 1/Border Regt.
17. 1/K.O.S.Borderers.
18. O.C. 86/Bde. Signals.
19. Diary.
20. File.

R E L I E F   T A B L E

Issued with 88th Inf. Brigade Order No. 233. dated June 11th, 1918.

Unit.	From.	To.	In relief of.	Remarks.
Headquarters, 1st LANCASHIRE FUSILIERS.	Brigade Reserve, Left Sector of Divl. Front.	FETTLE FARM.	Headquarters, 1st KINGS OWN SCOTTISH BORDERERS.	
2 Platoons, 1st LANCASHIRE FUSILIERS.	-"-	To Reserve Line along LITTLE BOURRE from K.2.a.2.2. to E.19.d.10.10.	2 platoons, 1st KINGS OWN SCOTTISH BORDERERS.	
1 Platoon, 1st LANCASHIRE FUSILIERS.	-"-	Area K.1.c.	1 platoon, 1st KINGS OWN SCOTTISH BORDERERS.	
1 Company, 1st LANCASHIRE FUSILIERS.	-"-	LA MOTTE Area.	1 Company plus 1 platoon 1st KINGS OWN SCOTTISH BORDERERS.	The defences about the Corps boundary from GD. DAM LOCK K.2.c.30.95. to the Railway at K.1.c.7.4. will be occupied by 1 platoon, 1st Lancs. Fusiliers. At present unoccupied.
1 Company, 1st LANCASHIRE FUSILIERS.	-"-	E.20.central.	1 Company, 1st BORDER REGIMENT.	
1 Company, 1st Lancashire FUSILIERS.	-"-	Reserve Line from LITTLE BOURRE D.30.b.9.9. to Brigade Boundary E.13.d.00.40.	1 Company, 1st BORDER REGIMENT.	This relief will not take place before 9 p.m.

Secret. Copy Nº

2nd Bn. Royal Fusiliers.
Operation Orders Nº 46.

Ref. Map. 36a. Edition 7A 1/20;000. 15th June 1918.

1. The Brigade will occupy the »B» and »D» line, 2nd Zone of Defence, at half hour's notice.
Dublin Fusiliers on Left, Royal Fusiliers in Centre, and Lancashire Fusiliers on Right.
Boundaries of Royal Fusiliers are D.12.d.2.8. to D.23.b.0.6. and D.11.b.5.7. to D.16.d.1.9.

2. »X» Company will hold »B» line from 12.d.2.8. to 18.a.3.3. Headquarters at 18.a.5.5.
»Y» Company will hold »B» line from 18.a.3.3. exclusive to 23.b.0.6. Headquarters at 17.a.9.1.
»W» Company will hold »D» line from D.11.b.5.7. to 17.a.3.9. Headquarters at 11.d.5.5.
»Z» Company will hold »D» line from 17.a.3.9. to 16.d.1.9. Headquarters at 17.a.2.0.
Battalion Headquarters will be in the vicinity of 10.d.3.2.

3. Battle positions will be selected in front of lines, and will be dug as soon as possible, in order to prevent the enemy's advance, but »B» and »D» lines are to be held at all costs.
Ammunition Dumps as follows:-

»B» line. 17.d.4.0. and 18.a.7.0.
»D» line. 16.b.8.4. and 11.b.2.7.

4. Loop, Wireless, and Power Buzzer Sets have been established as under:-

E.14.d.42.30.)
D.17.a. 7. 1.) Wireless,
E.1. d. 0. 3.) &
E. 3.c. 7. 1.) Loop Sets.
E.15.a. 8. 6.)

E.26.b. 6. 1. Power Buzzer.

All officers must know location of these sets, in case all other means of communication break down.

5. From midnight 15/16th June, the Battalion will be ready to move at half an hour's notice.
The R.T.O. will bringup one limber per Company to move Lewis Guns and Lewis Gun ammunition, and Company establishment of picks and shovels.
Battalion Reserve Bombs will be taken to Battalion H.Q. 10.d.3.2.

6. Dressing Station will be at 18.a.4.3.
and 10.d.9.5.

7. Acknowledge.

(Sgd). E.M.Baker, Lt.Col.
for Adjt. 2/Royal Fusiliers.

Issued at 5 p.m.

Copies to: Nº 1 to W Coy.
2 » X Coy.
3 » Y Coy.
4 » Z Coy.
5 » T.O.
6 » 86th Inf.Bde.
7 » File.

S E C R E T.

Copy Nº 9

2nd Bn. ROYAL FUSILIERS.
Operation Order Nº 47.

Ref Map. 36A. N.E. 1/20,000.
Edition 7A.

17th June 1918.

1. The 2/Royal Fusiliers will relieve the 2/South Wales Borderers, in the left of the right sub-sector, on the night of 17/18th June 1918.

2. "Y" Coy in the front line, "X" Coy in the Support line, "W" Coy in Strong Point at E.20.Central, and "Z" Coy in the Reserve line at Petite Marquette. Battalion Headquarters at E.14.c.7.0.

3. O.C. Coys will go forward and reconnoitre their new positions at once, and remain up there until their Companies arrive tonight.

4. Companies will march off at the following times:-

"X" Coy at ~~8~~-0 6 p.m.
"W" Coy at ~~8-15~~ p.m. 6.30 pm
"Z" Coy at ~~8-30~~ p.m. 7.00
"Y" Coy at 8-45 p.m.
H.Q. at ~~9-0~~ p.m. 7.30

A distance of 200 yards between platoons will be strictly observed.

5. Lists of Stores taken over will be sent in to Orderly Room by noon 18th inst.
6. On arrival, 2 runners per Company will be sent to report to L/Cpl Prince, at Battalion Headquarters.

7. Advance parties will be sent up to take over communications and trench stores, etc. in daylight.

8. Lewis Gun limbers will go with Companies as far forward as possible.

9. Relief complete will be sent to Battalion Headquarters by the Code word "ROYAL".

10. A C K N O W L E D G E.

Issued at 3-30 p.m.

[signature] Lt.
A/Adjt. 2/Royal Fusiliers.

Copies to: Nº 1 to W. Coy.
2 " X "
3 " Y "
4 " Z "
5 " Q.M.
6 " T.O.
7 " 2/S.W.B.
8 " File.

S E C R E T.
****

Copy No. 3

86th INFANTRY BRIGADE ORDER No. 234.

17th June 1918.

1. The 2/Royal Fusiliers will relieve the 2/ South Wales Borders (H.Q. E.14.c.3.0) in the left sub-sector of the 87th Brigade Front, and the 1/Royal Dublin Fusiliers will relieve the 1/ Kings Own Scottish Borderers (H.Q. FETTLE FARM D.24. a.8.2) in the right sub-sector of the 87th Brigade Front tonight June 17/18th.
   Arrangements for relief will be made direct between Unit Commanders concerned.
   Three companies of each Battalion can relieve in daylight.

2. Dispositions of 87th Brigade Units are as follows:-

   2/ S.W.B. One company - Firing line.
   One Company - Support line.
   One company - K.1.c.55.25 to GRAND DAM LOCK, thence along LITTLE BOURRE to E.25.d.55.90, thence along stream to Bridge E.19.d.1.1.
   One company - LA MOTTE Defences.

   1/K.O.S.B. One company - Firing Line.
   one company - Support line.
   One company - E.20.central.
   One company - LA MOTTE SWITCH (Reserve Line).

3. All copies of 87th Brigade Defence Schemes, work policies etc. will be taken over.
   Battalions will hand over copies of 86th Brigade Defence Schemes and ~~Instruction~~ Defence Instructions to the Battalions of 87th Brigade.

4. Relief complete will be reported to both the 86th and the 87th Brigade Headquarters by the CODE WORD "PLUM".
   On completion of relief the 2/Royal Fusiliers and the 1/Royal Dublin Fusiliers will come under the orders of the G.O.C., 87th Brigade and the 1/ K.O.S.B. and the 2/S.W.B. will come under the orders of the G.O.C., 86th Brigade.

5. A C K N O W L E D G E.

J.F. Dearden
Captain,
Brigade Major,
86th Infantry Brigade.

Issued at 2 pm.

Copies to:-

1 - 2 Staff.
3. 2/Royal Fusiliers.
4. 1/Lancashire Fusiliers.
5. 1/Royal Dublin Fusiliers.
6. 86/Trench Mortar Battery.
7. 29th Division "G".
8. 87th Infantry Brigade.
9. 88th Infantry Brigade.
10. 29th Machine Gun Battalion.
11. Diary.
12. File.

SECRET Copy Nº X

2nd. Bn. ROYAL FUSILIERS
Operation Order Nº 45

Ref. Map 36A N.E. 1/20,000
Edition 7A.

25th. June 1918.

1. The 2nd. Bn. Royal Fusiliers will relieve the 15th. West Yorks in the left Battalion sector on the night 25/26th June 1918.

2. "W" Coy. plus ~~two~~ one platoons "X" Coy. front line - "X" Coy. less ~~two~~ one platoons MOLIGHEIN FARM and Support line - "Y" Coy. ~~Left~~ right of Support line - "Z" Coy. ~~right~~ left of support line. Battalion Headquarters at E.7.b.7.7.

3. Companies will move off at the following times

"Y" Coy. at 8·15 p.m.
"Z" " " 8·35 p.m.
"X" " " 8·25 p.m.
"W" " " 8·45 p.m. + 1 platoon 'X'
H.Q. " " 8·55 p.m.

4. A distance of 200 yards between platoons will be strictly observed.

5. Lists of stores taken over will be sent in to Orderly Room by 12 noon tomorrow.

6. On arrival, 2 runners per Coy. will be sent to report to L/Cpl. Prince at Bn. H.Q.

7. Lewis Gun limbers will go with Coys. as far as possible.

8. Relief complete will be sent to Bn. H.Q. by the code word REST.

9. ACKNOWLEDGE.

[signature]
2/Lieut.,
A/Adj. 2nd. Bn. Royal Fusiliers.

Issued at 5 p.m.

Copies to: Nº 1 to H.Q.
" 2 W
" 3 X
" 4 Y
" 5 Z
" 6 Q.M.
" 7 T.O.
" 8 15th. West Yorks.
" 9 File.

"A" Form.
MESSAGES AND SIGNALS.

Army Form C. 2121.
(In pads of 100.)

No. of Message..........

Prefix.......... Code.......... m	Words.	Charge.	*This message is on a/c of:*	Recd. at.......... m.
Office of Origin and Service Instructions.	Sent		..........*Service.*	Date..........
S.D.R. Secret [illegible]	At..........m.			From..........
	To..........			
	By..........		(Signature of "Franking Officer.")	By..........

TO: 2nd Royal Fusiliers (86th Inf Bde)

Sender's Number.	Day of Month.	In reply to Number.	AAA
* 9984	25/6		

31st Div inform us that you are placed at our disposal aaa 31st Div wire that Corps Commander has approved your Battalion taking over the Left Battalion front line tonight aaa This Battalion is 15th WYR aaa Dispositions are roughly 1 coy and 2 platoons in front line remainder of second company in MOLIGHEIN Farm and Support line aaa 2 companies in Support line aaa Batt H.Q. at E 7 b 7.7 aaa Please get into touch with this Battalion at once and send Reconnoitring party up to arrange details aaa 15 WYR will come into your camp on relief aaa The code call is NOZU

From: 93rd Inf Bde
Place: 1.50 pm
Time: E 7 b 0.9

The above may be forwarded as now corrected. (Z) H. Stafford Capt.

Censor. Signature of Addressor or person authorised to telegraph in his name. Bde Major

* This line should be erased if not required.

(3796.) Wt. W492/M1647. 650,000 Pads. 5/17. H.W. & V., Ld. (E. 1161.)

Army Form C. 2123.
(In books of 100.)

"C" FORM.

MESSAGES AND SIGNALS.

No. of Message.................

Prefix SB Code BAB Words 35	Received.	Sent, or sent out.	Office Stamp.
£ s. d.	From 31 DIV	At..........m.	
Charges to Collect	By [illegible]	To	
Service Instructions VIA PRIORITY		By	

Handed in at 31 DIV Office 2 [illegible] m. Received 2 [illegible] m.

TO DOTA

*Sender's Number.	Day of Month.	In reply to Number.	AAA
G949			

authority given by ~~corps~~ corps DOTA to be put in line to right aaa WUVO to arrange all details of relief direct addressed WUVO and DOTA

FROM
PLACE & TIME 31 DIV

* This line should be erased if not required.

11199.) W528/M1970. 25,000 Pads. 10/4/17. A.H. & S., L.

S E C R E T COPY NO........

93rd. INFANTRY BRIGADE ORDER NO. 231.

25-6-18.

1. The 15th. West Yorks Regt. will be relieved to-night in the Left Front by the 2nd. Royal Fusiliers, (86th Infantry Brigade). The 2nd. Royal Fusiliers are lent to this Division and will come under orders of G.O.C 93rd. Infantry Brigade.

2. The Inter-battalion Boundary will be amended as follows :-

   E.17.c.0.4 - E.15.a.7.8.

3. Officer Commanding 18th. Durham Light Infantry will arrange to take over from Officer Commanding 15th West Yorkshire Regt. the front line from its present Northern Boundary as far as E.17.c.0.4, to-night.

4. All details of relief will be arranged between Commanding Officers concerned.

5. C.C. 15th. West Yorks Regt. will hand over all Defence Schemes, work policy and orders affecting the front to C.C. 2nd. Royal Fusiliers.

6. On completion of relief the 15th West Yorks. Regt. will move to camp at D.13.a.9.9.

7. Completion of relief to be notified to Brigade Headquarters by Code - A.W.H.A.T.

8. ACKNOWLEDGE.

I. H. Stafford

Captain,
Brigade Major,
93rd. Inf. Bde.

Copy No. 1. G.O.C.
2. B.M.
3. S.C.
4. Signals.
5. 15.W.Y.R.
6. 13.Y & L.
7. 18.D.L.I.
8. 93. L.T.M.B.
9. 'X' Comp.Coy.
10. 'Y' Comp.Coy.
11. 2nd. Royal Fus.
12. 86th. Inf. Bde.
13. 92nd. Inf. Bde.
14. 94th. Inf. Bde.
14. 3rd. Aus. Inf. Bde.
15. 12th. K.O.Y.L.I.
16. 31st. Battn. M.G Corps.
17. 31st. Division.
18. do.
19. 29th Div. Arty.
20. 15th. Bde. R.H.A.
21. 119th. Bde. R.F.A.
22. 210 Field Coy. R.E.
23. 94th. Field Amb.
24. H.Q. 31 Div. Train.
25. No. 3 Coy. Div. Train.
26 & 27 War Diary.
28 & 29 Spares.

Operation Order N 49 / 26/6/18
2nd Bn Royal Fusiliers

1 The 93rd Inf. Bde are carrying out a minor op. on night of 26/27 June. Objective ARKLE FARM and line of PLATE BECQUE Southward to Chimney

2. ZERO 12.30 A.M.

3. At Zero minus 15 min. the 3 right hand posts of front line will be withdrawn to immediate support line about E16 b 80

4. At Zero + 8 minutes these posts will be re-occupied + fire opened chiefly EAST so that the flank of the attack will be [illegible] + to engage any enemy M.G. to their front.

5. An officers patrol will be sent to gain touch with left flank of 13th Y+L Regt. at E17c 65 who are doing the attack on the signal RED over GREEN over YELLOW being sent up which will indicate the objective reached.

6. Eight Stokes mortars will be in position along immediate support line in E 16 d & will open fire at Zero hour. All posts of 2/R.F. in the vicinity must be moved northward by about 11 p.m. & then re-occupy the line as soon as the Stokes-mortars have moved back which will be about Zero + 15

7. At Zero + 40 at which time the barrage will have ceased an officers patrol will be send out under 2/Lt. NEISH & reconnoitre ground about E 17 central.
2/Lt. STOKES will also patrol line of trees at E 17 B 11 and will arrange with 2/Lt. NEISH direct as to procedure of these 2 patrols.

8 Acknowledge.

Copy No 1. O.C. W. Coy. D. Murray [illegible] Capt.
No 2 — do —
" 3 File Adjt 2/R.F

Copy No 4

Secret

2nd Bn Royal Fusiliers
Operation Order No 50

Ref Map. 36A. N.E. 1/20,000
Edition 7A. 24th June 1918

1/ The 2nd Bn Royal Fusiliers will be relieved by 13th York and Lancs and 12/Australians on the night 27/28th June 1918

2/ The front line from left to E 11 c.8.0. will be relieved by the 12/Australians, from the same co-ordinate to right by C and D Coys 13/Y and L.

The support line from left to E 9 d. 3.8. including MOLEGHEIM FARM will be taken over by 12/Australians and from same co-ordinate to right by A and B Coys 13/Y & L

3/ W Coy will prepare separate sketch maps of dispositions and lists of trench stores to hand over to the Officers of each Battalion relieving them

X Coy will prepare sketch map and list of stores for

sector to be handed over to 12th Bn. Australians including MOLEGHEIM FARM

Y Coy will prepare sketch map and list of Trench Stores to be handed over to 13/Y&L including any reserve stores at Coy H2 at E.9.a 3.6.

4/ Each Coy. will obtain receipts from relieving Officers for disposition maps and trench Stores and will render same to Bn. H2 by 12 noon tomorrow.

5/ W Coy will furnish 1 Officer and 17 guides, being 1 for each of 10 posts in front line (No 1 to 10 front line) and one for each of 7 posts in rear Support line (No 1 to 7 support line) to meet C and D Coys. 13/Y and L at E 16 a. 8.5. at 10-45 p.m.

Guides will be furnished with a slip of paper showing for which post he is guiding. The Officer will superintend distribution of guides and will

then himself guide Coy. H.2.
Y Coy will furnish 6 guides to be at E 15. d 05.60 to meet A and B Coys. B/Y and L at 11pm. This represents one guide for each platoon of relieving Coys.

6 Relief will be reported to Bn. H.2. by the code word DONE

7 Bn relief Coys. will occupy positions in second Zone as follows:-

B Line

X Coy. from Railway at D.12. C. 8.2. inclusive to canal D.12. d 2.7. inclusive with H.2. near Canal

Y Coy from Railway at D.12. C. 8. 2. exclusive to D.18.a.2.0. with H.2. about D.18 a central

D. Line

Z Coy from D. 11. C. 8. 5. to railway at D 11 b 3. 7. inclusive

W Coy. from Railway at D. 11 b. 4. 7. exclusive to D. 5. d. 8. 5.

Bn H2. SEDIMENT HOUSE D. 11. d. 4. 7.

8 Lists of Stores in Trench

if any will be sent into Orderly Room by 12 noon tomorrow.

9. Occupation complete will be sent by runner to Bn. H.Q. Code word CART.

10. Brigade H.Q. D.17 a 5.4 (le Tir Anglais)

11. ACKNOWLEDGE

[signature] 2/Lieut
A/Adj. 2nd Bn Roy Fus

Issued at

Copies to
1. X Coy.
2. Y "
3. Z "
4. H.Q.
5. W
6. Q.M.
7. T.O.
8. 13/Y+L
9. 13/Aus.
10. File.

[illegible]

[illegible]

[illegible]

[illegible] 1918

[illegible]

Route to Transport Lines 2nd Bn Royal Fusiliers

D 11. b. 3. 8. track to D10 b 85-00 Road to D 10 b. 7. 7. track to D 10 b 15. 85. Road to D 10 c. 35 60. track to TEXAS FARM. Road to D. 9 a. 85. 20. Track to D 9a 3. 2. ~~Cross roads~~ Track to D 8 b 95. 45 Road to LA GUNEWELE thence road running D 1 central C 6 central. Cross roads C. 5. d. 2. 8. Transport Lines.

Bn Starting D. 9. a. 3. 2.

Col [illegible]

[illegible]

Ref Map sheets
57 A N E 1/20000
TS 2[illegible] 1/5000

Operation Order No 68

27.6.18

1 The Battn will be relieved in the Right Sub Sector of the Bde front tonight 27/28th June by 18th DLI & on relief will take over the Left Sub Sector of the Bde front from the 2nd Royal Fusiliers

2 Dispositions C & D Coys in the front line from approximately E17 c 60 50 to E11 c 6 0 under the Command of Capt F W L HULK.

A & B Coys in Support. 'A' on the Right & 'B' on the left from approximately E15 b 0 5 to E9 d 1 8.

3. Coy Commanders of C & D Coys will arrange details of relief direct with Coy Commanders of 2nd Royal Fusiliers they are relieving. These Coys will relieve W Coy, 2nd Royal Fus.

4 A & B Coys 13 Y & L will be relieved by B Coy & 1/2 D Coy, DLI on right & left respectively, the left four posts of B Coy being relieved by D Coy DLI & the remainder of the front line by B Coy DLI. On relief A & B Coys will move back into Support trenches relieving Y Coy 2nd Royal Fusiliers

5. Advance Parties. 2/Lt WRIGLEY - RSM - Gas NCO & a proportion of Signallers from HQ will proceed at 5.0 pm to HQ, 2nd Royal Fusiliers at E7 b 7 7 to take over stores etc. 2 NCOs & 4 men from Bn HQ will also proceed at 5.0 pm to take over Stores & trenches in Support line from 2nd Bn Royal Fus., handing over to A & B Coys on the latter arrival there. These parties will report to 2/Lt Wrigley at Bn HQ at 4.45 pm

6 Guides. 1 Guide per post & Coy HQ from each of A & B Coys will ~~report~~ meet respective Coys of DLI at the junction of track & original front line at E 23. a 05 95 at 10 30 pm & guide them to their respective posts.

3 guides per Coy from 2nd Royal Fusiliers for A & B Coys will be at Jct of track & Support line at E15 d 1.6 at 11 0 pm. Lt E H TAYLOR will be at this point at 10.50 pm to meet the guides. These guides will guide A & B Coys to their new positions.

7 Rations & Water for C & D Coys will be delivered at present position at 6 0 pm & carried forward by the men. Those for A & B Coys will be taken to SANITAS Corner. These Coys will arrange to draw them on arrival in Support line. Rations & Water for Bn HQ will be taken to Bn HQ at E7 b 7 7.

8. Lewis Gun & pans will be carried by the men. The surplus of pans with A & B Coys must be brought back

9. Trench Stores. All trench stores in trenches vacated will be handed over to relieving units & those in trenches to be occupied taken over. A & B Coys will hand over the extra stores which they carried with them into the attack. Lists of trench stores handed & taken over will be forwarded to Bn HQ by 9.0 am tomorrow 28th inst, signed by representatives of both incoming & out going units.

10. Disposition Maps shewing present dispositions will be handed over by each Coy to relieving Units. Disposition maps shewing new dispositions on relief will be sent to Bn HQ by 9am 28th inst.

11 Sanitation. Trenches will be handed over as clean as possible

12 Completion of Relief will be notified to Bn HQ immediately by Code sentence "Have received stores at ...

13 Transport. 2 limbers will report at present B HQ at E.14 d 5 3 at 9.30 pm for mess, Orderly & medical stores.

14 Bn HQ will be established on relief at ...

15 Acknowledge

Copies to 1 CO. 8. 2nd R.F. (BH)
2 Adj 9 QM & TO
3-6 Coys 10. War Diary
7. 18 Div 11 File

1/Z 2
Z 2 + 10
W + 10
X + 20

2nd RF

Copy No 1

Secret

2nd Bn Royal Fusiliers
Operation Order No 52

Ref map. 36A 1/40000 30th June 1918

1/ The 2nd Bn Royal Fusiliers will march to ISLINGHEM A 22 a 30th June 1918

2/ (a) Order of march HQ W X Y Z
(b) Head of column to pass starting point B 23 b 3.3. at 2 p m.
(c) 1 Drummer with each Coy remainder of Drums with X Coy
(d) 100 yards interval between Coys
(e) Drill fighting order, caps to be worn. Shrapnel helmets to be worn slung on the right shoulder.

3/ Cookers and Coy limbers will follow behind their respective Coys.

4/ Billeting parties will meet the Battalion at road junction A 23 a 2.0.

5/ ACKNOWLEDGE

D Harvey Nash Officer
A/Adj 2nd Bn Roy Fusrs

38 B.
(4 sheets)

28031 W3125/M2250 1000m 6/17 M.R.Co.,Ltd. (1367) Forms W3091.

Army Form W. 3091.

Cover for Documents.

No 141

Natures of Enclosures.

CONFIDENTIAL

WAR DIARY

OF

2ND BN ROYAL FUSILIERS

Notes, or Letters written.

JULY  1918

Instructions regarding War Diaries and Intelligence Summaries are contained in F. S. Regs., Part II. and the Staff Manual respectively. Title pages will be prepared in manuscript.

Army Form C. 2118.

WAR DIARY
or
~~INTELLIGENCE SUMMARY~~.
(Erase heading not required.)

JULY 1918.

Place	Date	Hour	Summary of Events and Information	Remarks and references to Appendices
LA SABLONNIERE.	1st		Companies at disposal of Company Commanders for cleaning up etc. after coming out ofthe line. In view of G.O.C's inspection shortly, one hour devoted to arms drill. Awards:- MILITARY CROSS. 2/Lieut W.E.Stokes. " E.G.Andrews. MILITARY MEDAL. 43437 Pte S.Maskell. 24679 " D.Cady. 7963 Cpl C.Swansbury. 69663 Pte F.Nicholl.	Sheet 56A.
	2nd		Battalion bathed at LE RONS. Rest of day occupied in inspection of rifles by Armourer, Clothing of Companies, etc.	
	3rd		Commanding Officer's Parade. Practice Brigade ceremonial parade. Weather very fine.	
	4th		Brigade Ceremonial. Inspection by Genl. Sir Herbert Plumer, Comdg II Army. Presentations of ribbons to recipients of recent awards. G.O.C., II Army highly satisfied with steadiness of drill and movement of troops. 2/Lieut C.E.Adams joined battalion from 1st Devonshire Regt and posted to W Coy. Football and games played by Companies every afternoon.	
	5th		Very interesting morning. March to Quarry at F.11.c.7.0 to hear lecture by Colonel Campbell, P.T. & B.F. Specialist, followed by exhibitions of boxing, wrestling, etc. by champions, and address by "Woodbine Willie" C.F. Capt J.F.H.Templar joined, also Lieut M.F.Nicholls. Both posted to X Coy. Draft of 51 Other Ranks arrived from Base.	
	6th		Company training during morning. Semi-final of Brigade Cup during afternoon. 2/R.F. v. 1/L.F. on L.F. ground. 2/R.F. won by 3 goals to 1.	
	7th		Church Service at 11 a.m. Afternoon devoted to Battalion Sports, held on Field Ambulance Ground at QUIESTEDE. Weather propitious. A very enjoyable meeting.	

D. D. & L., London, E.C.
(10340) Wt W5300/P713 750,000 3/18 E 2688 Forms/C2118/16.

Army Form C. 2118.

WAR DIARY
or
INTELLIGENCE SUMMARY.
(Erase heading not required.)

Instructions regarding War Diaries and Intelligence Summaries are contained in F. S. Regs., Part II. and the Staff Manual respectively. Title pages will be prepared in manuscript.

JULY 1918.

Place	Date	Hour	Summary of Events and Information	Remarks and references to Appendices
LA SABLONNIERE.	8th		Continuance of Company Training. Miniature ranges at A.16.b. and A.23.b.9.3. at disposal of the battalion, and also the 200 yards range at A.24.a.5.5. by arrangement. 8 Scouts per Company now billeted with H.Q. Coy and training under Scout Officer. Training area N. of HEURINGHEM. Excellent open country.	Sheet 36A.
	9th		Baths and delousing at LE RONS. Draft of 56 Other ranks arrived. Divisional Horse Show at DIJPIL during afternoon. Some rain. 86th Brigade won the Section Jumping, 3 animals of 2/Royal Fusiliers in team.	
	10th		Morning occupied in training under Company arrangements. Lewis Gun drill, Arms drill, etc. Brigade Sports in afternoon, followed by concert by »Diamond» Troupe. Battalion won 100 yards (L/c Elwood). Heavy thunderstorm just after the Sports. 2/Lieut R.W.Kirke, to England on leave. »Diamond» Troupe at QUIESTEDE during the evening.	
	11th		Training on training area. Open order drill, practice of advancing under all available cover with scouts well out in front as a screen. Following officers joined battalion.- Capt H.S.Smiley to Y Coy, 2/Lieut A.H.Shields to X Coy, 2/Lieut W.H.Frith (from hospital) and 2/Lt S.V.Sparey to W Coy. Latest draft inspected by the Commanding Officer in the afternoon. Accomodation for Officers very limited. New officers in tents. Weather very good. Y and Z Companies had a joint Concert during the evening.	
	12th		Battalion Scheme abandoned owing to rain. Training under Coy arrangements in billets. Lectures, Lewis Gun drill, etc. Draft of 10 Signallers from Base - fill much needed want.	
	13th		Tactical exercise for battalion. W. X & Z Coys attacking, Y Coy defending. Use of Scouts for information, sniping and outflanking with L.G's fully illustrated. Dinners on ground, and march back afterwards. W & X Coys had a joint concert during the evening.	

D. D. & L., London, E.C.
(10340) Wt W5300/P713 750,000 3/18 E 2688 Forms/C2118/16.

Instructions regarding War Diaries and Intelligence Summaries are contained in F. S. Regs., Part II. and the Staff Manual respectively. Title pages will be prepared in manuscript.

WAR DIARY
or
INTELLIGENCE SUMMARY.
(Erase heading not required.)

Army Form C. 2118.

JULY 1918.

Place	Date	Hour	Summary of Events and Information	Remarks and references to Appendices
LA SABLONNIERE.	14th		Voluntary Church Service. Heavy showers during the afternoon. "RUFFLES" gave a concert in the evening. 2/Lt L.J.Brown joined the battalion from the East Surrey Regiment and was posted to W Coy.	MPO Sheet 36A.
	15th		W. Y and Z Coys on Battalion Training Area. X Coy on Miniature Range. W and Y Coys attacked Z Coy, practicing advancing through woods. Football in the afternoon. Final for the Brigade Cup, 2/R.F. v. 1/R.D.F. Result 1-1. To be replayed. Brigade Boxing Competition at 2-30 p.m.	MPO
	16th		Companies at the disposal of Company Commanders on account of rain. In the afternoon Final for the Brigade Cup. Won by 2/R.F. 3 - 1. Brigade Boxing won by 1/R.D.F. 2/Lt J.Fraser, M.C. rejoined the battalion and was posted to Y Coy.	MPO
	17th		Companies at the disposal of Company Commanders. Z Coy on Miniature Range. Officers' Staff ride in the afternoon to reconnoitre the ground for following day. 2/Lt E.T.Allen and 7 other ranks sent to the II Army Rest Camp.	MPO
	18th		Brigade Tactical exercise. 1/R.D.F., 1/L.F., and 2/R.F. (imaginary), attacked the enemy (2/R.F.). The Divisional General was greatly pleased with the vigour of the attack. Cookers were brought up to the training area, the men marching back to their billets after Dinner. 2/Lt C.E.Adams, granted leave to the United Kingdom.	MPO
	19th		W. X and Z Coys carried out attack over Training area. Special attention paid to sending messages by Shutter. Y Coy on Miniature Range. A/Capt W.J.Ware rejoined from Hospital.	MPO
	20th		W.Y and Z Coys Outpost scheme on Training area. X Coy on Miniature range. Scouts marched 6 km to range at LA CAMPAGNE. To train signallers, all scores were sent back to Bn H.Q. by Shutters and one Lucas Lamp.	MPO

D. D. & L., London, E.C.
(10340) Wt W5300/P713 750,000 3/18 E 2688 Forms/C2118/16.

Army Form C. 2118.

WAR DIARY
or
INTELLIGENCE SUMMARY.
(Erase heading not required.)

Instructions regarding War Diaries and Intelligence Summaries are contained in F. S. Regs., Part II. and the Staff Manual respectively. Title pages will be prepared in manuscript.

JULY 1918.

Place	Date	Hour	Summary of Events and Information	Remarks and references to Appendices
LA SABLONNIERE.	21st		Voluntary Church Parade. Commanding Officer lectured to Officers and N.C.Os on Outposts. W Coy's Sports in the afternoon. At 10-30 p.m. order came through that Battalion was to be ready to move at 8 a.m. next morning, to join Xth Corps.	Sheet 36A.
NOORDPEENE.	22nd		Battalion passed starting point at 8-30 a.m., marched 20 kilos and reached NOORDPEENE at 3-30 p.m. Six men fell out on march, 4 fainting and 2from foot trouble. Billets at NOORDPEENE good.	Sheet 27.
	23rd		No training. Men resting and cleaning up after the march. A/Capt W.J.Ware resumed duties of A/Adjutant, and A/Capt F.H.Smith returned to his Company as 2/Lieut.	
	24th		Companies at the disposal of Company Commanders for training. Men went to Baths at NOORDPEENE. Commanding Officer went up to reconnoitre the Army Front line.	
	25th		Companies at the disposal of Company Commanders. Commanding Officer inspected Z Coy in full marching order. Remainder of Battalion went to the baths at NOORDPEENE. Two Officers per Company went up to reconnoitre Army line.	
	26th		Commanding Officer inspected W Coy in full marching order. Heavy showers all day. Two Officers per Coy reconnoitring Army line. Rugger was played in the afternoon to pick a team to represent the battalion. The Brigadier lectured all Officers at 5-30 p.m. "RUFFLES" gave a concert at night.	
	27th		Commanding Officer inspected Y Coy in full marching order. W. X and Z Coys at the disposal of Company Commanders. Capt P.T.O.Boult, M.C. rejoined the battalion. In the evening the 5th Army Concert Party with Lieut Leslie Henson gave a performance in NOORDPEENE.	
	28th		Voluntary Church service in the morning. Rugger Match in the afternoon.	

D. D. & L., London, E.C.
(10340) Wt W5300/P713 750,000 3/18 E 2688 Forms/C2118/16.

Army Form C. 2118.

Instructions regarding War Diaries and Intelligence Summaries are contained in F. S. Regs., Part II. and the Staff Manual respectively. Title pages will be prepared in manuscript.

WAR DIARY
or
INTELLIGENCE SUMMARY.
(Erase heading not required.)

JULY 1918.

Place	Date	Hour	Summary of Events and Information	Remarks and references to Appendices
NOORDPEENE.	29th		Coys under Company Commanders for Training. In the afternoon a practice game of RUGGER was played to select a team. The Commanding Officer was handed a wire stating that 500,000 prisoners and 600 guns had been captured by the French. Nobody knew from where the wire had come, but the news was announced to the troops at a concert which the »RUFFLES» gave in the evening. Later it proved that the wire was a test message sent by the signallers.	Sheet 27. MPB
	30th		Companies training under Company arrangements. Rugger match in the afternoon, 2/R.F. v. 86th Bde H.Q. 2/R.F. won 3-0 Ruffles concert in the evening. News came through that the battalion is rejoining the XV Corps in a few days.	MPB
	31st		Companies training under Company arrangements. Photographs of the battalion taken in the afternoon.	MPB

E.W. Baker Lieut-Colonel.
Commanding 2nd Battn. Royal Fusiliers.

(10340) Wt W5300/P713 750,000 3/18 E 688 Forms/C2118/10. D. D. & L., London, E.C.

28031 W3125/M2250 1000m 6/17 M.R.Co.,Ltd. (1367) Forms W3091.

Army Form W. 3091.

Cover for Documents.

CONFIDENTIAL.

Natures of Enclosures.

2nd Battalion. Royal Fusiliers.

WAR DIARY - AUGUST. 1918.

VOLUME 42.

Notes, or Letters written.

Army Form C. 2118.

Instructions regarding War Diaries and Intelligence Summaries are contained in F. S. Regs., Part II. and the Staff Manual respectively. Title pages will be prepared in manuscript.

WAR DIARY
or
INTELLIGENCE SUMMARY.
(Erase heading not required.)

AUGUST.1918.

Place	Date	Hour	Summary of Events and Information	Remarks and references to Appendices
	1st		Marched from LE MENEGAT to LA KREULE. Moved 7.45 p.m. arrived 11.30 p.m. Capt. G.C. Pearson rejoined as Adjutant.	
	2nd		Relieved 1st Leinster Regt. in B and C Lines. Column passed V 15 d [illegible] 4 at 7.30 p.m.	
	3rd		Moved in evening to billets V 24 C and D. Brigade Reserve, under orders of 121 Brigade.	
	4th		Remainder of Brigade moved into area now under orders of 36th Brigade. 2/Lt W.J. BARRY took over Int. Officer. 2/Lt Chilcott to Officers Rest Camp. Coys at disposal of Coy Cmds for training.	
	5th		Coys training in vicinity of billets.	
	6th		2/Lts E.T.ALLEN and C E.ADAMS rejoined from Transport Lines. Coy training.	
	7th		Coy training.	
	8th		Capt. H.S.POWELL took over command of Brigade nucleus Coy from Major Templar. Major TEMPLAR rejoined Battalion. Demonstration platoon under Major TEMPLAR. All Officers attended.	
	9th		Working parties on the Z Line and wiring in forward area taken over from 1/Lanc.Fusiliers.	
	10th		Relieved 1/Lanc. Fusiliers in support. Battalion area moved between 8 and 9 p.m. H.Q. at Curfew House. Working parties as above.	
	11th		Curfew House shelled. 2/Lt R.I.SAUL appointed Bn. Gas Officer. Working parties as before.	

D. D. & L., London, E.C.
(10340) Wt W5300/P713 750,000 3/18 E 2688 Forms/C2118/16.

Army Form C. 2118.

WAR DIARY
or
INTELLIGENCE SUMMARY.
(Erase heading not required.)

Instructions regarding War Diaries and Intelligence Summaries are contained in F. S. Regs., Part II. and the Staff Manual respectively. Title pages will be prepared in manuscript.

AUGUST.1918.

Place	Date	Hour	Summary of Events and Information	Remarks and references to Appendices
	12th		Y Coy relieved one company of 4/Worcestershire Regt. (New inter-Brigade Boundary). Z Coy inspection of Box Respirators. Working parties as before.	
	13th		Capt. J. PEARSON rejoined from neucleus Coy, and assumed command of X Coy vice Capt. W.J.WARE. left Battn to join 40th Division as Adjt of 12th N.Staffs. Z Coy to Transport Lines for baths. etc. returned in evening. Y Coy inspection of box respirators.	
	14th		Y Coy to Transport Lines for baths. etc, returned same day. W Coy inspection of box respirators. Working parties.	
	15th		W. Coy to Transport Lines for baths. etc, returned same day. X Coy inspection of box respirators. Working parties.	
	16th		X Coy to Transport Lines for baths. etc, returned same day. Relieved by 1/R. Dublin Fusiliers evening. Moved forward to relieve 1/ Lanc.Fusiliers. Y and Z in front line and local support. X Coy in the Strazeele Station Defences. W Coy in the reserve line.	
	17th		Battalion holding line. Fairly quiet day. No casualties. Patrols at night encountered opposition from the trucks and LYNDE FARM.	
	18th		9th Division and 87th Brigade attacked and captured the OUTTERSTEENE RIDGE under a barrage, at 11 a.m. We sent out patrols in conjunction with them to endeavour to get the line of trucks and LYNDE FARM by peaceful penetration. This was unsuccessful owing to M.G.fire from the trucks and LYNDE FARM. Y Coy sent out the patril on the left, Z Coy on the right. Casualties. Killed. 2/Lt J.W.Quinn and 5 O.R. Wounded. 2/Lt C.W.Chilcott and 14 O.R. Narative attached. Appen. No. At night W Coy relieved Z Coy and X Coy relieved Y Coy.	

D. D. & L., London, E.C.
(10340) Wt W5300/P713 750,000 3/18 E 2688 Forms/C2118/16.

Instructions regarding War Diaries and Intelligence Summaries are contained in F. S. Regs., Part II. and the Staff Manual respectively. Title pages will be prepared in manuscript.

WAR DIARY
or
INTELLIGENCE SUMMARY.
(Erase heading not required.)

Army Form C. 2118.

AUGUST. 1918.

Place	Date	Hour	Summary of Events and Information	Remarks and references to Appendices
	19th		At 5.0 p.m. the Battalion attacked (W Coy on the right, X Coy on the left, 2 platoons of Z Coy in support on the right) under a barrage and captured the line of trucks, LYNDE ASSET and LESAGE FARMS, also assisting in the capture of LABIS FARM, which formed part of the objective of the 12th Norfolks, who attacked in conjunction with us on our right. The operation was completely successful and the line was established in front of the road running from F 13 A 7.2 – F. 6. C. 3. 6. We captured 111prisoners, including 1 Officer. 10 Machine Guns, and 2 Trench Mortars. In addition several casualties were inflicted on the enemy as he fled in confusion. No counter attack was delibered? Narrative attached. Appendix No. Our casualties were :- Killed. 2/Lt Whyte.) 2/Lt Brown.) and 16 other ranks. Wounded. 2/Lt ABams.) 2/Lt Walton) and 63 other ranks. After dusk the remaining 2 platoons of Z Coy went up into the line and CAPT. CLPRKE took over command of the right sub-sector, the inter-Company boundary being the cross-roads at F.13b.3.3.	
	20th		Patrols were pushed out to a line F.3.c.5.4 – F.14.c.3.4 in the morning in conjunction with the Battalion on the right, who established with patrols the line HULLEBERT FARM – BLEU. The above patrols remained out on this line. The enemy shelled the forward area heavily at intervals all day. W. Coy went back to the 2 Line in the afternoon and 2 platoons of Y Coy went up to the old front line.W of Colery Copse, the remainder of the Company remaining in the ATRAZEELE STATION defences. No casualties were incurred this day.	

D. D. & L., London, E.C.
(10340) Wt W5300/P713 750,000 3/18 E 2653 Forms/C2118/16.

Instructions regarding War Diaries and Intelligence Summaries are contained in F. S. Regs., Part II. and the Staff Manual respectively. Title pages will be prepared in manuscript.

WAR DIARY
or
INTELLIGENCE SUMMARY.
(Erase heading not required.)

Army Form C. 2118.

AUGUST 1918.

Place	Date	Hour	Summary of Events and Information	Remarks and references to Appendices
	21st		X and Z Companies rushed out patrols in the afternoon to a line HAUTE -MAISON - SCANDAL CROSSING in conjunction with the Battalion on the right who reached CUILET CORNER. No opposition was encountered and there were no casualties. 1 Field Gun, 1 heavy and 1 Light M.G. 300 rounds of 6" shell, and 150 gas shells were discovered. The forward area was again heavily shelled all day at intervals, although we sustained no casualties. The Battalion was relieved at night by the 1/Royal Dublin Fusiliers, who took over the line F.8.c.5.4. as their main line of resistance, leaving outposts on the HAUTE-MAISON line. The Battalion returned to the reserve line in relief of the 1/Lancs. Fusiliers.	
	22nd		W and Y Coys went to the Transport Lines for baths etc. Performance of Concert Party in the evening. Z Coy. cleaning up and Lewis Guns overhauled.	
	23rd		Companies under Company arrangements.	
	24th		Companies under Company Commanders for P.T. and B.F. and Lewis Gun training. Specialist training.	
	25th		Company and Specialist training.	
	27th		Inspection by Brigadier. 11.0 a.m. Company and Specialist training.	
	28th		Relieved 1st Border Regt. in right sub-sector of left Brigade. Y Coy in front line. 2 platoons W Coy in close support and two platoons in support. X and Z Coys in reserve. Active scouting and patrolling.	
			No change. Heavy rains.	
	30th		Y. Coy relieved by X Coy. 3 of our Scouts on reconnaissance patrol captured at F.3.B. 5.5. Post at F.9ccc rushed by X Coy. It was found to be unoccupied.	

Instructions regarding War Diaries and Intelligence Summaries are contained in F. S. Regs., Part II. and the Staff Manual respectively. Title pages will be prepared in manuscript.

WAR DIARY
or
INTELLIGENCE SUMMARY.
(Erase heading not required.)

Army Form C. 2118.

AUGUST 1918.

Place	Date	Hour	Summary of Events and Information	Remarks and references to Appendices
	30th	4.45	Front extended to new Inter-Brigade Boundaries in front line section of 86th Infantry Brigade front. Y Coy in front line, W Coy in support, Z Coy. in Mont de Merris Defences and X Coy in Y. Line.	
	31st.		In conjunction with troops on right and left. Battn pushed forward our line from the line SCANDAL CROSSING - KISMET HOUSE to a line F.11.d 2.1 - F 11 d.40.95. Advance was opposed only by a few snipers who retired as we moved forward and light scattered shelling from long range.	
			J.F.H. Templer Major O.C. 2nd Bn. Royal Fusiliers.	

(A9175) Wt W2353/P561 500,000 12/17 D. D. & L. Sch. 52a. Forms/C2118/15.

REPORT on MINOR OPERATIONS carried out on the 18th AUGUST.1918.

Immediately on commencement of the barrage the attacking troops began to go forward to within storming distance of the trucks and LINDE FARM. Y Coy were on the left with two platoons in front and two in support, and Z Coy were on the right with similar dispositions. The attacking platoons were preceeded by scouts who were told off in pairs to cover possible gaps, and establish liason on flanks. Working as snipers they report considerable execution as much movement occurred behind the TRUCKS and LINDE FARM. The left platoon of the left Company under 2/Lt Cheesewright moved quickly along N.side of railway to ALERT CROSSING, which was taken at about zero + 38 several Bosches being killed and eight prisoners being taken. These latter, some wounded, oassed down through the S.W.Bs. Acting under orders this Platoon Commander pushed forward from ALERT CROSSING to a line of low trees at approx F.7.d.1.7. When his scouts reached here however they were enfiladed by machine guns from ASSET and LESAGE FARMS, and suffering casualties withdrew to ALERT CROSSING, as per previous instructions. The right platoon of left Coy (2/Lt FRASER) (2/Lt QUINN having been killed) had meanwhile reached the western edge of CELERY COPSE, and commenced to move through same. On the right the platoons attacking were fired on by machine guns after having proceeded about 70 yards, fire coming from LINDE FARM, F.13.a.0.3. and points south of these places. They continued to push forward however and reached the prearranged assault positions, advancing under cover of the first two periods of trench mortar fire, and also mutual supporting fire of L.Gs. Soon after zero + 110 the prearranged signals (two white very lights) for the taking of LYNDE FARM went up from that vicinity. At the same time a blue smoke signal was put up from ALERT CROSSING by the S.W.Bs. to indicate their arrival there. The latter signal was confused by the left Coy Commander with our own signal for »TRUCKS TAKEN» . Thinking therefore that the trucks had fallen and also LYNDE FARM, the right platoon of the left Coy (Lt Fraser) pushed forward through CELERY COPSE and attempted to advance frontally on the TRUCKS.
He proceeded 50 yds clear of the east edge of CELERY COPSE, when some Bosches appeared with their hands up. These were shot and the advance continued, when suddenly the M.Gs from LYNDE FARM vicinity opened up (LYNDE FARM not having fallen). At the same time fire was opened from the trucks and the party suffered casualties. Acting under previous orders this platoon then withdrew to CELERY COPSE. The right Coy had attempted to assault LYNDE FARM at zero + 110 but owing to inadequate T.M.barrage were engaged immediately by 4 or 5 M.Gs situated in LYNDE FARM and in ditches to the south of this point. The Officer commanding the assaulting platoon considered that the place could not be taken without disproportional casualties, and reported so to the Company Commander. Two attempts were made to

outflank LYNDE FARM, but M.Gs pushed forward by the enemy prevented this. The two forward Companies therefore resumed their original line, with the exception of retaining ALERT CROSSING. In all ten prisoners were made and at least 30 of the enemy killed. Two wounded prisoners passed through the R.A.P. and the rest (non wounded) went through the S.W.Bs. from ALERT CROSSING. The right Company made no prisoners but accounted for many enemy, as suitable targets were often presented.

The failure of the assault on LYNDE FARM was probably due to the barrage of Stokes mortars not being heavy enough. Forward scouts and observers report that very few rounds fell on LYNDE FARM during the period Zero + XXX 90 + 110 i.e. just prior to the assault. Several witnesses saw the "TAKEN" signal go up from LYNDE FARM, but apparently it was not fired by the attacking platoon, who were never actually in possession of the farm. The use of identical signals on the left flank for different objectives was unfortunate and undoubtedly contributed to the casualties suffered by Lt. Fraser's platoon when advancing to the trucks.

(Sgd) E.M.BAKER.
Lt.Col.

19/8/18. O.C. 2nd Royal Fusiliers.

40 B.
(8 sheets)

CONFIDENTIAL.

=*=*=*=*=*=*=*=*=*=*=*=*=*=

Vol 31

2nd BATTALION. ROYAL FUSILIERS.

=*=

WAR DIARY. FOR

=*=

SEPTEMBER. 1918.

=*=*=*=*=*=*=*=*=*=*=*=*=*=*=*=*=

CONFIDENTIAL

WAR DIARY.

VOL. 43.

Army Form C. 2118.

WAR DIARY
or
INTELLIGENCE SUMMARY.
(Erase heading not required.)

Instructions regarding War Diaries and Intelligence Summaries are contained in F. S. Regs., Part II. and the Staff Manual respectively. Title pages will be prepared in manuscript.

VOL.43.

SEPTEMBER. 1918.

Place	Date	Hour	Summary of Events and Information	Remarks and references to Appendices
NOOTE BOOM.	1st.		Battalion advanced in conjunction with troops on right and left flanks from NOOTE BOOM CEMETERY to a line running from LA BECQUE to A.4 Central. Opposition was confined to snipers and machine guns, very little hostile shelling. Relieved by 1/Border Regiment, and went backkto Z Line, STRAZEELE.	Sheet 36.N.W
	2nd		Lt.Col.Baker.D.S.O. in command of 86th Infantry Brigade. Capt.G.C.Pearson.M.C. in command of Battalion.	
OUTERSTEENE.			Battalion moved from STRAZEELE to OUTERSTEENE.	
LA CRECHE.	3rd		Battalion moved to LA CRECHE and thence to G.H.Q.Line.	
	4th		Battalion relieved 1/Royal Dublin Fusiliers and 1/Lancashire Fusiliers in front line.	
	5th		Patrols pushed forward and organised system of shell holes. 2/Lieut. SPEAKMAN (Z. Coy) killed. Other ranks, 9 killed, 29 wounded, 6 missing. Very heavy shelling. Major Templar rejoined Battalion.	
OUTERSTEENE.	6th		Relieved in morning by Royal Welsh Fusiliers and came back to bivouacs near OUTERSTEENE.	
	7/8/9th.		Resting at OUTERSTEENE.	
	9th		2/Lieut.J.Thomas joined.	
	10th		Resting at OUTERSTEENE. 2/Lieut.Burtinshaw joined.	
HAZEBROUCK.	11th		Moved to HAZEBROUCK. Marched past Army Commander near STRAZEELE.	

D. D. & L., London E.C
(10341) W1 W3300/P713 750,000 3/18 E 683 Forms/C2118/16.

Army Form C. 2118.

WAR DIARY
or
INTELLIGENCE SUMMARY.
(Erase heading not required.)

Instructions regarding War Diaries and Intelligence Summaries are contained in F. S. Regs., Part II. and the Staff Manual respectively. Title pages will be prepared in manuscript.

Place	Date	Hour	Summary of Events and Information	Remarks and references to Appendices
HAZEBROUCK.	12th		Company and Specialist training.	
	13th		ditto. 2/Lt.V.S.L.GENDERS joined.	
	14th		ditto.	
	15th		ditto.	
	16th		ditto.	
	17th		ditto.	
	18th		Tactical Scheme near STRAZEELE.	
DIRTY BUCKET CAMP.	19th		Moved to DIRTY BUCKET CAMP, near VLAMERTINGHE.	
	20th		Capt.D.A.F.NEEDHAM joined and assumed duties of 2nd in Command.	
	21/23rd		Training.	
POPERINGHE.	24th		Moved to Camp near POPERINGHE (H.Q. Y & Z.Coys) and W & X. Coys. at PESELHOEK.	
	25/26		Training.etc.	
YPRES.	27th		Moved by Train to YPRES.	
	28/30th.		Narrative attached.	

[signature]

Major.
Cmdg.2nd Bn. Royal Fusiliers.

D. D. & L., London E.C.
(10340) Wt W5300/P713 750,000 3/18 E 688 Forms/C2118/16.

Instructions regarding War Diaries and Intelligence Summaries are contained in F. S. Regs., Part II. and the Staff Manual respectively. Title pages will be prepared in manuscript.

WAR DIARY
or
INTELLIGENCE SUMMARY.

(Erase heading not required.)

OCTOBER 1918.

Army Form C. 2118.

2 RF

Place	Date	Hour	Summary of Events and Information	Remarks and references to Appendices
GHELUWE.	Oct. 1st		Battalion in bivouacs and shelters.etc. Orders to relieve 1/Lancashire Fusiliers in sector N. of GHELUWE at night. Morning fine, but heavy rain during relief. Dispositions. X and Z in front line, Y and W. in support. No line of trench existed, outpost dispositions in farms, etc. being taken up.	See narrative of operations Sept. 28th - Oct. 2nd. attached War Diary for Sept.
	2nd	05.30	The 88th Brigade advanced on right (in front of GHELUWE) under a barrage. Battalion was ordered to endeavour to advance and conform. Some support was given by Bde 3" T.Ms. Enemy was however holding a well wired line (GHELUWE SWITCH! and owing to very heavy M.G. fire, movement was very difficult. Small tactical points were seized, but the 88th Brigade being unable to hold GHELUWE, a general advance was impossible. Some twenty casualties were suffered during this operation. The Battalion was relieved at night by the 2nd S.W.Bs. and marched back to bivouacs at approx. J.23.d. (Sheet 28)	
	3rd	1100	Battalion proceeded by march route to YPRES. Tea at ECOLE. Afterwards into billets in cellars, etc, at YPRES. All ranks fairly comfortable.	
YPRES	4th		In billets. Day spent in cleaning up, reorganisation, and filling up of battle stores. etc.	
	5th		Orders received during morning to move into line E. of LEDEGHEM. Battalion entrained at Machine Gun Siding at 14.30. Detrained at MOORSLEDE. Relieved Royal Newfoundland Regt. (9th Div.) in support just N. of DADIZEELE. Relief was difficult owing to shell fire, about 1 dozen casualties being suffered moving in. Lt.Col.Baker D.S.O. to England on leave. Major D.A.F.Needham.M.C. Cmdg Battalion. Bn.H.Q.K.6.c.0.5.	Sheet 28.

D. D. & L., London E.C. (10340) Wt W5300/P713 750,000 3/18 E 688 Forms/C2118/16.

Army Form C. 2118.

Instructions regarding War Diaries and Intelligence Summaries are contained in F. S. Regs., Part II. and the Staff Manual respectively. Title pages will be prepared in manuscript.

WAR DIARY
or
INTELLIGENCE SUMMARY.
(Erase heading not required.)

Place	Date	Hour	Summary of Events and Information	Remarks and references to Appendices
North of DADIZEELE.	6th		Battalion in support. Day quiet. Men fairly comfortable.	
	7th		At night the battalion relieved the 1/Lancs Fus. in left of Brigade Sector, East of LEDEGHEM. Tracks had been laid by Battalion Scouts under the Intelligence Officer in order to avoid shelling, and the relief was carried out quietly. Dispositions X and Y Coys left and right front respectively, Z Coy in Support, W Coy in Reserve. Battn H.Q. in pill box at K.6.c.0.5. Front line was approximately LEDEGHEM STATION.	
LEDEGHEM.	8th		In Front line. Fairly quiet Sector. Enemy very alert during night, evidently expecting attack. Counter preparation fire at dusk and dawn fairly severe.	
WESTHOEK.	9th		At night the battalion was relieved by 2/Lienster Regt. Moved to pill boxes etc in WESTHOEK AREA by march route. Relief was fairly quiet.	
	10th		After breakfasts the battalion moved by road to YPRES arriving about mid-day. The Battalion occupied the same billets as before. Companies engaged in reorganisation and replacements, etc.	
YPRES.	11th		Brigade Ceremonial parade for inspection by Lt-Gen. Sir C. JACOBS, Commanding II Corps. in field South of KRUISTRAAT ASYLUM. G.O.C. expressed satisfaction with turnout.	
	12th		Still in billets. Major TUDOR (S.W.B.) joined for 6 weeks attachment. 2/Lieut J.W. COWGILL joined for duty (to W Coy). 2/Lieut W.L.MERRITT awarded M.C..	
MOORSLEDE.	13th		Moved at 2-30 p.m. by light railway to MOORSLEDE. Teas were taken here. Later Battn moved by tracks to assembly positions at LEDEGHEM STATION ready for the attack on the 14th.	
LEDEGHEM	14th	0535	Battalion attacked under cover of a creeping barrage. See narrative of operations attached.	
		1800	Moved into billets as Brigade in Support, at BARRAKEN.	
[B]ARRAKEN.	15th		In billets (farmhouses etc). All Coys comfortably situated. Battn H.Q. at L.11.[illegible].5.4. Large numbers of escaped civilians passed through.	

(10341) W1 W3300/P713 750,000 3/18 E 688 Forms/C2118/16.

Army Form C. 2118.

Instructions regarding War Diaries and Intelligence Summaries are contained in F. S. Regs., Part II. and the Staff Manual respectively. Title pages will be prepared in manuscript.

WAR DIARY
or
INTELLIGENCE SUMMARY.
(Erase heading not required.)

Place	Date	Hour	Summary of Events and Information	Remarks and references to Appendices
	Oct.			
BARRAKEN2	16th		Morning spent in refitting.etc. At 3.0 p.m. Battalion marched forward into billets in western outskirts of HEULE. Support Battalion. Brigade very comfortably situated. Civilians living in line for first time since commencement of offensive at YPRES.	
HEULE.	17th		Day spent in Company training; reorganisation and refitting. Bombs dropped at night, but no casualties suffered. Bn.H.Q. at G.16.b.95.25. (Sheet 29).	
	18th		Training.	
	19th		do.	
	20th	0545	Battalion moved by road to assembly areas N. of HEULE. At dawn the 88th Brigade (front line) attacked the enemy positions on E. bank of LYS. N. of COURTRAI. About mid-day 86th Brigade leap-frogged 88th Brigade, this Battalion moving in support to 1/R.D.Fs. By dusk a general line KAPPAART - KROTE was occupied. Bn.H.Q. FERMSFEYS.	
KROTE.	21st		Battn. assembled at dawn in position for attack. Did not materialise until 15.30 when attack was launched. X and Z. Front line. Y and W in support. The objectives were(BANHOUT BOSCH and the high ground S.E. of it) were not distant, as the object was a straightening of the line. They were reached after a little opposition from M.Gs. and all consolidated. Very few casualties were suffered during these operations. A/Capt.J.Pearson.M.C. was wounded on the 20th. Bn.H.Q. at O.10.d.0.6. Sheet 29.	See narrative attached.
KAPPAART.	22nd		87th Brigade leapfrogged at dawn and attacked. Battalion moved back in support at KAPPAART. Good billets. B.H.Q. at Farm. I.33.c.6.0.	
	23rd	1500	Battalion marched to CUERNE via STEENBRUGGE and STACEGHEM, arriving 17.45. All rsnkd in comfortable billets. Lt.Col.Baker.D.S.O.rejoined from leave and assumed Command.	
CUERNE.	24th		Day spent in cleaning up.	

D. D. & L., London E.C.
(10340) Wt W5300/P713 750,000 3/18 E 688 Forms/C2118/16.

Army Form C. 2118.

WAR DIARY
or
INTELLIGENCE SUMMARY.
(Erase heading not required.)

Instructions regarding War Diaries and Intelligence Summaries are contained in F. S. Regs., Part II. and the Staff Manual respectively. Title pages will be prepared in manuscript.

OCTOBER.1918.

Place	Date	Hour	Summary of Events and Information	Remarks and references to Appendices
CUERNE.	25th	0600	~~XXXX~~ Moved by march route to RONCQ, via COURTRAI. Battalion passed Frontier at 0940. arriving at RONCQ at 1100. Battalion in billets.	
RONCQ.	26th		By march route to BONDUES, arriving 1300. Good billets.	
BONDUES.	27th		Companies cleaning uo & reorganisinf,etc.Church Service.	
BONDUES.	28th		Working parties on Railway at LA MADELEINE.	
	29th		ditto.	
	30th		Day spent in cleaning up, reorganising platoons, and refitting. First Round of the Bde Football Cup was played off, Battalion beating 89th Field Ambulance by 1 goal to 0.	
	31st.		Coys. at disposal of Coy.Commanders for training. First performance of RUFFLES (Battalion Concert Party) during the advance.	

E.M. Baker Lt.Col.
Cmdg. 2nd Battn.Royal Fusiliers.

D. D. & L., London E.C.
(10340) Wt W5300/P713 750,000 3/18 E 688 Forms/C2118/16.

2nd Bn. Royal Fusiliers.

Narrative of Operations - 28th Sept to 2nd Oct 1918.

On the night of the 27th/28th Sept 1918 the battalion moved by train from BRANDHOEK to the vicinity of the ECOLE, YPRES, and at 4-30 a.m. moved forward into the position of assembly.

At Zero hour (5-30 a.m.) the battalion moved forward in support to the 1st Royal Dublin Fusiliers, in diamond formation of platoons, W and X Coys in the front wave, Y and Z Coys in the rear wave.

The first objective was captured by the 1st Lancashire Fusiliers at 7-8 a.m. and the battalion then passed through the 1st Lancashire Fusiliers in rear of the 1st Royal Dublin Fusiliers. Opposition was encountered from various pillboxes on the STIRLING CASTLE RIDGE, and our artillery barrage fell short for some time. Owing to this and the mistiness of the morning W and X Coys became involved in the firing line with the 1st Royal Dublin Fusiliers before reaching the CLAPHAM JUNCTIONRIDGE. A large number of prisoners and some light machine guns were mopped up by the battalion from pillboxes on STIRLING CASTLE RIDGE, X Coy taking 40 prisoners out of one keep, and killing more who refused to come out of their dugout. Some opposition was also encountered from CLAPHAM JUNCTION and fur further prisoners taken there.

The battalion passed through the 1st Royal Dublin Fusiliers on a line CLAPHAM JUNCTION - FORT Mc.LEOD. After passing through the 1st Royal Dublin Fusiliers no opposition was met with for some time until machine gun fire was encountered from the trench in J.15.c.2 8. This was dealt with by W Coy and about 15 prisoners taken. On approaching the POLDERHOEK RIDGE, W Coy encountered opposition again at pillboxesin J.15.c.9.3. and the house at J.15.d.1.4. These were rushed and 10 prisoners captured. X Coy captured an Officer, a Sergt-Major, and 46 other ranks of German artillery from pillboxes in J.15.a. About 20 prisoners were also found by W and Y Coys in pillboxes in J.15.d.1.3.

At 9-45 a.m. the battalion rushed the line POLDERHOEK RIDGE - CAMERON HOUSE without any serious opposition, mopping up a few prisoners from pillboxes on the way, andhreorganised on this line, bending back the left flank to connect with the 9th Division on the left, about BLACK WATCH CORNER, and putting out outposts well down the east slope of the ridge.

At 10-30 a.m. the 88th Brigade went through down the MENIN Road and captured GHELUVELT.

At 12 noon the battalion moved down the left hand side of the MENIN Road to GHELUVELT, in echelon, in support to the 88th Brigade, and took up a position in J.22.a & c.

At 5 p.m. the battalion moved down and took up a position on the ridge in J.23.c. as a defensive flank to the 88th Brigade, echeloned to their left rear, with the 1st Royal Dublin Fusiliers touching our left flank. These positions were held for the night 28th/29th Sept. During the whole of the attack of the 28th Sept, the battalion suffered very few casualties and about 300 prisoners were captured. Also several machine guns, a complete battery of 5-9's in X J.15.a. and a few 77 m.m. guns. Some of the machine guns captured were found mounted on top of the pill boxes.

At 6-30 a.m. on the 29th Sept the battalion continued the advance in echelon to the left rear of the 88th Brigade, the 1st Royal Dublin Fusiliers in echelon to our left. The ridge K.26.a. - K.31.a. was captured in spite of heavy machine gun fire which caused a few casualties, and a line was established along the ridge in K.25.a. & c. Trouble was caused by an enemy French Mortar in the wood east of the cemetery in K.25.c. This was silenced by a Section of the 88th Trench Mortar Battery attached to the battalion. This line was held all day and considerable execution done to the enemy by machine gun and Lewis gun fire, especially along the slope in K.26.a. Enemy machine gun and snipers' fire was very persistent all day, and the latter part of the day there was considerable hostile shelling.

The battalion was relieved by the 1st Royal Dublin Fusiliers on the night of the 29th/30th Sept, and moved back to trenches just behind GHELUVELT.

Total casualties for the 2 days operations were 2 Officers wounded. Other ranks, 10 killed, 30 wounded, 7 missing. Total 47 other ranks.

On the morning of the 30th Sept the battalion was moved forward again to shelters and huts in the vicinity of the Cross Roads, J.30.c.0.8. and remained there for the night of the 30th Sept/1st Oct.

On the evening of the 1st Oct the battalion moved forward and relieved the 1st Lancashire Fusiliers in the line, running along the road, north and south from K.29.central, to K.35.central. and thence back to K.34.central. The dispositions were as follows:- Front line, Z Coy on the right, X Coy on the left, Support line, Y Coy on the right, W Coy on the left.

Orders were received to conform to an advance to be made by the 88th Brigade, with the object of capturing GHELUWE.

At 3 a.m. the 36th Division on the left attempted to sieze the line of the road from K.29.d.3.0. - K.30.central. They did not, however, succeed.

At 7 a.m. which was Zero hour for the 88th Brigade, X Coy endeavoured to sieze BURBURY HOUSE and HARROD HOUSE, with the aid of a bombardment by Trench Mortars and covering machine gun fire. They were, however, unable to do it, owing to heavy enemy machine gun fire, and a few casualties were suffered.

The enemy held GHELUWE SWITCH fairly strongly with machine guns, which held up any further advance on our part, and the 88th Brigade on our right were unable to capture and hold GHELUWE, although some of their patrols actually got through the village. Enemy machine gun fire was persistent all day, and during the latter part of the day the shelling became very heavy.

The battalion was relieved at night by the 2nd South Wales Borderers, and marched back to shelters near the Cross Roads at J.30.

Total casualties for the four days were, 4 Officers wounded. Other ranks, 10 Killed, 1 Died of wounds, 45 wounded, 2 Gassed, 10 Missing. Total 68 Other ranks.

(Sgd) E.M.BAKER.
Lieut.Col.
Commanding 2nd Bn. Royal Fusiliers.

Narrative of Operation of 2/Royal Fusiliers on

14th October,1918.

At 0430 the Battalion was assembled for the attack in the vicinity of LEDEGHEM STATION, the Station buildings and dumps od German R.E. material being used for forming up positiona.

Dispositions for battle - Two companies in front (X.Coy left - Z Coy right) and two companies in support. (W. Coy left - Y.Coy. right).

The barrage opened at 0532 and at zero (0535) the battalion advanced with the barrage, moving forward at the rate of 100 yards per two minutes. At the commencement a few rounds fell short and several casualties resulted. This was immediately corrected however and not remarked afterwards.
A company of the 2/Lancashire Fusiliers had assembled in the station, with the Battn. for the purpose of mopping up LEDEGHEM. The Battalion therefore proceeded straight through the village. A proportion of smoke shell was used in the barrage, rendering it impossible to keep touch with flanks or in rear. The advance had to be made by compass until the smoke cleared sufficiently.
Very little opposition was encountered moving through LEDEGHEM two or three men were wounded by spare M.G.bullets.
Small posts of 3 or 4 men were encountered at isolated points, but the smoke did not allow them to offer any resistance and they were quickly rushed and taken prisoner.
No.9 platoon of Y.Coy. came on a battery of field guns still in action, and quickly mopped them up. They were surprised from a flank and offered little resistance.
The objective of the Battn was the ridge running from G.1.d.0.0. to G.7.b.0.0. that being the limit of the field artillery barrage. It was reached by elements of all Coys.by about 0800 hours and the line consolidated. Advanced posts were pushed forward to within 100 yds of the village of DRIE MASTEN, but not having sufficient support and being under heavy M.G.fire were obliged to withdraw to the ridge, here they were fired on by field guns over open sights, but held on until supports in the shape of the R.D.F. and other elements of the Battn. arrived and supported them.
A good number of bridges (24) were carried forward with the assaulting platoons, by parties of the Monmouthshire Regt. These were placed across the WULFDAMBEEK to enable troops to cross. Some of these parties lost direction in the smoke, with the result that whilst troops on the right were able to cross, troops on the left flank were somewhat late in crossing. This did not materially affect the operation.
The R.D.F. subsequently moved forward from the ridge. followed by the Lancashire Fusiliers.
It is estimated that about 150 prisoners, 20 machine guns, and 10 field guns were taken. A battery of guns were found at POODLE FARM.

(Sgd) D.A.F.Needham. Major.
Cmdg.2nd Bn.Royal Fusiliers.

15th Oct.1918.

SECRET. 2/Royal Fusiliers. No.5/27.

Report on Operations by 2/Royal Fusiliers on
20th,21st & 22nd October.1918.

Order of Battale.	1. Battalion Commander.	Major D.A.F.Needham. M.C.
	W. Company.	Capt. J.T.Smith.
	X. "	Capt.J.Pearson.M.C.
	Y. "	Capt.J.F.H.Templar.
	Z. "	Capt.H.Clark.M.C.

Objectives. 2. Assembly positions, objectives and boundaries are shewn on attached map "A" the battalion being in support to the 1/Royal Dublin Fusiliers.

Preliminary arrangements. 3. No difficulty was encountered on the march to 2nd Assembly position, where the battalion was still in support to the 1/Royal Dublin Fusiliers.

Plan. 4. The advance on the 20th inst was to be carried out on a front of about 1500 yards. The plan was to attack with the 1/Royal Dublin Fusiliers leading, and the 2nd Royal Fusiliers moving in close support. On the objective (red line) being gained by the 1/R.D.F. the 2/R.F. were to pass through and exploit the success as far forward as possible. On the 21st inst, the advance was to be continued.

Narrative. On the morning of the 20th, the Battalion, after having breakfast at 5.0 a.m. marched out of billets at HEULE at 5.40 a.m. and passed the Brigade Starting point (G.17.d.8.1.) at 6.0 a.m. Arriving at the first assembly position at 6.20 a.m. Companies took up positions as shewn on attached map A. On arrival at 1st Assembly position, and while waiting for the order to advance, the area received a certain amount of shelling and the Battalion had a few casualties - 2 men and 2 horses. At 9.31 a.m. the battalion moved forward in column of route to 2nd assembly position (see attached map A) arriving there at 10.15 p.m when it took up a position as shewn on Map A.
At about mid-day the battalion moved forward in column of route behind the 1/R.D.F. (route shewn in purple on attached map A.) On reaching cross roads at I.32.b.3.7. the battalion deployed into diamond formation of platoons and moved forward towards the red line in order from R. to L. - Z. X. Y. W. Very shortly after this Z and X Coys. found that the right flank was open, and they thereupon filled the gap from the Canal bank to the right flank of the 1/R.D.F. East of Lock No.6. Herewith the battalion passed through the outpost line of the 88th Bde.
Some opposition was encountered, chiefly M.G. and rifle fire from farms on the western slopes of BANHOUT BOSCH (in O.10. a & c.)
At about 5.0 p.m. a line was taken up by Z and X. Coyd. covering KAPPARRT and KROTE. Y.Coy. then formed a protective left flank for A. Coy. 1/R.D.F. which had reached WOLFSBERG, taking up a position in O.4.d. facing S.S.W. W. Coy. remained in support to the 1/R.D.F. in the vicinity of ST.LOUIS. (I.34.c.)
Bn.H.Q. was established at FERME FEYS. (O.3.b.7.7.)
The Battn. remained in this position during the night, 20/21st. At dawn on the 21st, inst, the Battn. moved to assembly position (shewn in green on attached map 2) in the neighbourhood of KAPPAART and KROTE. (O.3.d & O.4.c

At 1530 the barrage fell and was closely followed by the leading companies. On reaching a line from 0.10.a.6.0 approximately half way through BANHOUT BOSCH the leading Companies were held up by heavy machine gun fire from farm in front. A M.G. was located firing from upper window of farm at 0.17.a.7.6. The platoons in Banhout Bosch were unable to move owing to hostile fire. A platoon under 2/Lt.A.H.Shields accordingly worked forward into houses at 0.17.a.1.9 and opened fire on the M.G. with 3 Lewis Guns. Under cover of this fire platoons were worked forward up hedges and ditches and the house was rushed. A M.G. position was found and cartidge cases still hot, but the enemy had managed to crawl away under cover of hedges.etc. This done, the platoons on the left (in wood) were able to come forward without loss. The line was subsequently established in 0.11.d. and 0.17.a.1.c. as shewn in green on map A. and touch with the Division on right obtained on road at 0.16.b.8.6.
After consolidation W.Coy and one platoon of X.Coy. moved back to support positions. Bn.H.Q. was established in farm at 0.10.d.'.6.
Whilst advancing under enemy fire Lewis Guns. etc. were fired from the hip with very good resulst.
At dusk, after some difficulty, liaison was obtained with the 1/L.F. in left, at 0.11.b.3.3.

<u>Reliefs.</u> 6. On the morning of Oct.22nd. the 1st Border Regt.of the 87th Brigade passed through the line and contined the attack, assisted by covering fire provided by M.Gs.attached to this Battn. and also the Lewis Guns of the Battn. At 10.0 a.m. the Battalion withdrew to billets in the KAPPAART area.

General Remarks. 7.(a) <u>Artillery.</u> The field artillery barrage on the afternoon of the 21st.inst, was good.
(b) <u>Machine Guns.</u> M.Gs. of A.Coy. 29th Bn.Machine Gun Corps. attached to the Battn. rendered good service in the front line. They were used with good result in consolidating the position on the night of the 21st inst, and relievi g the work of our Lewis gunners.
(c) <u>Trench Mortars.</u> These were used on the afternoon of the 20th, against enemy machine guns on the right flank. Unfortunately they were subjected to severe shelling, the officer in charge and one man being wounded.

(d) <u>Casualties.</u>
Officers. Wounded.1.
O.R. Killed.3. Died of wounds.1. Wounded.34.

[signature]
.Major.
Octber 23/18. Cmdg. 2/Royal Fusiliers.

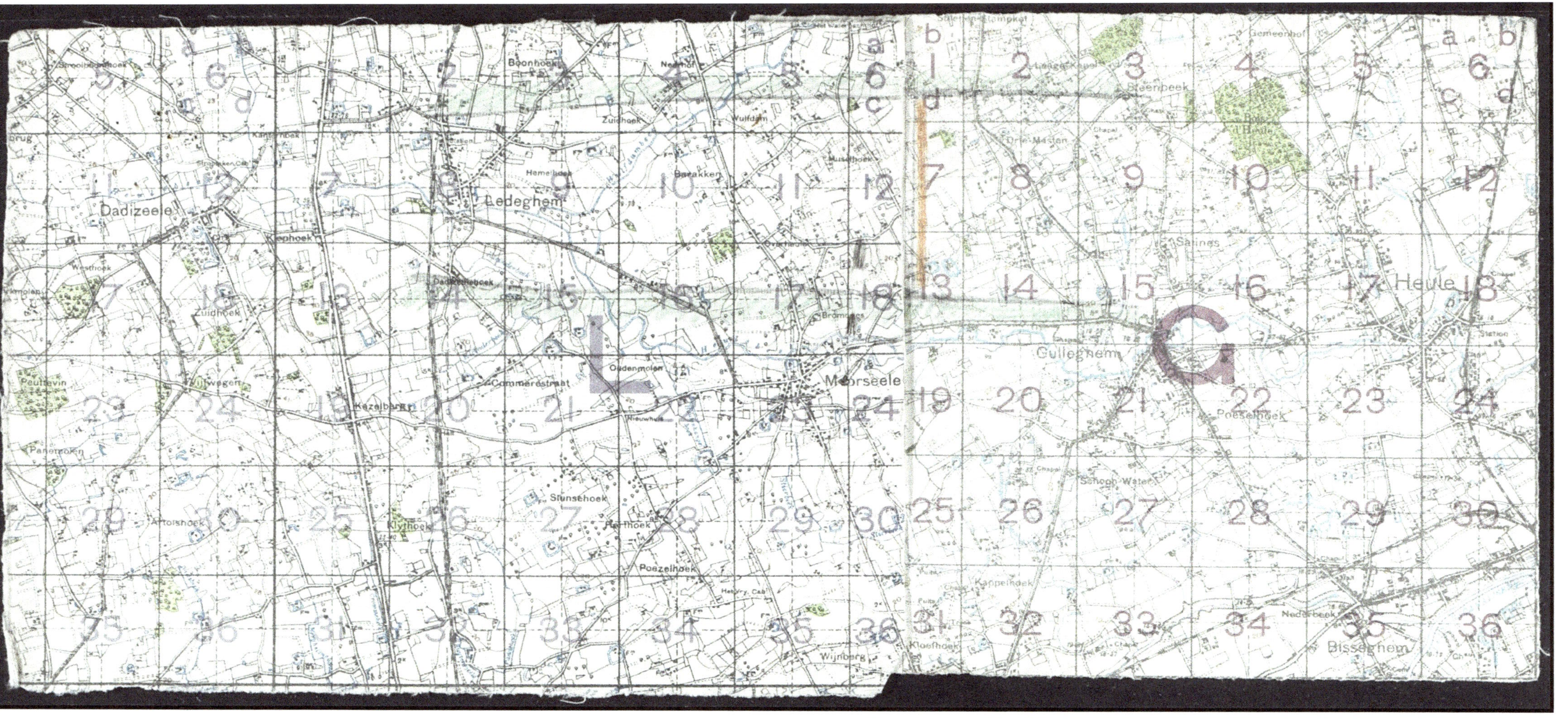

Dadizeele
Ledeghem
Boonhoek
Zuidhoek
Wulfdam
Barakken
Hamelhoek
Moorseele
Oudenmolen
Commerestraat
Kezelberg
Stunsehoek
Poezelhoek
Wijnberg
Artoishoek
Klythoek
Panemolen
Steenbeek
Drie Masten
Salines
Gulleghem
Heule
Poeselhoek
Schoon Water
Kappelhoek
Neerbeek
Bisseghem
Gemeenhof
L
G

FIRST ASSEMBLY POSITION
2nd ASSEMBLY POSITION
H
I
N
O
Harlebeke
Deerlyck
Staphoek
Beigiek
Knock
Vichte
Ooteghem
Steenbrugge
Staceghem
COURTRAI
Station
Blokken
Esschen
St Louis
Krotel
Wolfsberg
Sweveghem
Pottelberg
Walle
't Hooghe
Winkel hoek
Bree-Menisch
Kappelle Millens
Evangelie Boom
Kreupel
Kwaadestraat
Kattestraat
Ste Anne
Watermolen
Cuerne

WAR DIARY

OF

2nd BATTALION ROYALFFUSILIERS.

FOR MONTH OF NOVEMBER. 1918.

Army Form C. 2118.

WAR DIARY
or
INTELLIGENCE SUMMARY.
(Erase heading not required.)

Instructions regarding War Diaries and Intelligence Summaries are contained in F. S. Regs., Part II. and the Staff Manual respectively. Title pages will be prepared in manuscript.

NOVEMBER 1918.

Place	Date	Hour	Summary of Events and Information	Remarks and references to Appendices
BONDUES	1st		Brigade practice ceremonial.	Ref Map.
	2nd		Specialist Training.	TOURNAI 5.
	3rd		Church Parade Service at 10.00. Semi-final for the Brigade Football Cup v. 1/R.D.F. won 3 - 0. 2/Lt P.St.L.Lloyd joined the Battalion.	
	4th		Brigade ceremonial parade. Lieut-Genl de Lisle expressed satisfaction with the turnout. The RUFFLES gave a concert to the civilians of BONDUES. The jeunes filles de BONDUES presented a bouquet to the Colonel. Col BAKER made a suitable reply.	
	5th		Raining all day. Companies at disposal of Company Commanders for lectures etc.	
	6th		Two Companies at Musketry on ranges at BONDUES FORT in moat. Remaining two Coys Specialist training.	
	7th		Two Companies musketry on range. Other two Coys Specialist Training. Gas Respirator inspection by Divisional Gas Officer.	
LUINGNE.	8th		Moved to LUINGNE by march route, leaving BONDUES at 10.00. Crossed Belgian frontier at MOUSCRON at 12.22. Good billets.	
	9th		Companies at disposal of Company Commanders. In Divisional Reserve (X Corps).	
PETIT TOURCOING.	10th		Moved to PETIT TOURCOING by march route at 14.30 into billets (Farms etc). News of abdication of Kaiser and Crown Prince.	
SAINT GENOIS.	11th		Moved by march route to billets on N. outskirts of SAINT GENOIS starting at 09.00. Rather scattered and crowded. Cessation of hostilities at 11.00.	
LE QUESNOY.	12th		March continued to LE QUESNOY (POTTES). Moved by march route starting at 09.00. Full marching order carrying one blanket. Weather good for marching. Crossed SCHELDT at 10.12.	

Instructions regarding War Diaries and Intelligence Summaries are contained in F. S. Regs., Part II. and the Staff Manual respectively. Title pages will be prepared in manuscript.

WAR DIARY
or
INTELLIGENCE SUMMARY.
(Erase heading not required.)

Army Form C. 2118.

NOVEMBER 1918.

Place	Date	Hour	Summary of Events and Information	Remarks and references to Appendices
ARC AINIERES	13th		Moved by march route to ARC AINEERES starting at 09.20. Battalion rather crowded in billets. Lieut B. LIGHT rejoined Battalion.	Ref Maps. TOURNAI 5.
WODECQ	14th		Moved to WODECQ (LA PIERRE). Good billets, rather scattered. Weather fine but frosty. Headquarter Scouts reduced to 6. Lieut F.G.HAMILTON rejoined from England, and assumed duties as Transport Officer.	BRUSSELS 6. LIEGE 7.
	15/17th		Companies at disposal of Company Commanders for cleaning up etc.	MARCHE 9.
BASSILLY.	18th		Moved by march route to BASSILLY.	
	19/20th		Battalion resting at BASSILLY.	
STEENKERQUE.	21st.		Moved to STEENKERQUE. Very crowded in billets. MILITARY CROSS awarded to 2/Lieuts R.I.SAUL and R.J.LANCASTER. DISTINGUISHED CONDUCT MEDAL awarded to CSM C. O'Connor, CSM G.T.Ruddell, and Sgt Hooke.	
	22nd.		Resting at STEENKERQUE. Capt H.CLARK, M.C. and 20 Other ranks marched past the King of the Belgians on the occasion of His Majesty's entry into BRUSSELS.	
HAUT ITTRE.	23rd		Moved to HAUT ITTRE by march route.	
BOUSVAL	24th		Moved to BOUSVAL by march route. Bar to MILITARY CROSS awarded to Capt CLARK,MC. and Capt J.PEARSON, M.C.	
NIL ST VINCENT.	25th		Moved by march route to NIL ST VINCENT.	
	26th		Resting at NIL ST VINCENT.	
NOVILLE SUR MEHAIGNE.	27th		Moved to NOVILLE SUR MEHAIGNE.	
HUY.	28th		Moved to HUY (STATTE) WANZE. Weather very bad. Raining all the time.	
OUFFET.	29th.		Moved by march route to OUFFET, crossing the River MEUSE.	

(A9175) Wt W2358/P36 600,000 12/17 D. D. & L. Sch. 52a. Forms/C2118/15.

Army Form C. 2118.

WAR DIARY
or
INTELLIGENCE SUMMARY.
(Erase heading not required.)

Instructions regarding War Diaries and Intelligence Summaries are contained in F. S. Regs., Part II. and the Staff Manual respectively. Title pages will be prepared in manuscript.

NOVEMBER 1918.

Place	Date	Hour	Summary of Events and Information	Remarks and references to Appendices
AYWAILLE.			Moved by march route to AYWAILLE. Enthusiastic reception.	

E. M. Baker Lieut-Colonel.
Commanding 2nd Battn. Royal Fusiliers.

(A9175) Wt W2358/P862 600,000 12/17 D. D. & L. Sch. 52a. Forms/C2118/15.

(6414) Wt. W3906/P1607 2,500,000 7/18 McA & W Ltd (E 3591) Forms W3091/4. Army Form W.3091.

1/RL 34

Cover for Documents.

Nature of Enclosures.

2nd Battn Royal Fusiliers

War Diary

For

December 1918.

Notes, or Letters written.

Army Form C. 2118.

WAR DIARY
or
~~INTELLIGENCE SUMMARY~~.
(Erase heading not required.)

Instructions regarding War Diaries and Intelligence Summaries are contained in F. S. Regs., Part II. and the Staff Manual respectively. Title pages will be prepared in manuscript.

December. 1918.

Place	Date	Hour	Summary of Events and Information	Remarks and references to Appendices
LA REID.	1st.		Leaving AYWAILLE at 11.30. The Battalion moved along valley and up to "Four Farms" Near LA REID by march, arriving at 13.30, ~~route~~ Billets were scattered, crowded and poor. Weather dull and stormy.	
	2/3rd.		Battalion resting at LA REID (Four Farms). The move having been ~~cancelled~~ postponed.	very cold
	3rd.		Lieut.E.H.Marsh joined from England.	
			Battalion still resting. Capt.H.S.Smiley to Field Ambulance (sick)	
MALMEDY.	4th.	09.30	Moved by march route covered by Advanced Guard to MALMEDY, arriving there in the dark at 16.30. Crossed the frontier at 14.34. Good billets. Huns very tame and obliging. Weather dull and very wet.	
			2/Lieut.F.H.Cheesewright to Field Ambulance (sick).	
ELSENBORN	5th.	09.30	Moved by march route covered by Advanced Guard to ELSENBORN arriving at 14.30. Billets rather scattered but fairly good. Weather dull.	
EIDERSHEID.	6th.	09.45.	Moved by march via KALTER and MONT JOIE and INSENBROUGH to EIDERSCHEID, arriving there at 15.15. The scenery en route was very picturesque but roads very hilly especially near MONT JOIE. Billets fair. Weather dull.	
WOLLERSHEIM.	7th.	9.00.	Moved by march via NIDEGGEN (up a very steep hill) to WOLLERSHEIM arriving at 16.45.	

Wt W2351/P560 600,000 12/17 D. D. & L. Sch 52a. Forms/C2118/15.

Instructions regarding War Diaries and Intelligence Summaries are contained in F. S. Regs., Part II. and the Staff Manual respectively. Title pages will be prepared in manuscript.

WAR DIARY

or

~~INTELLIGENCE SUMMARY.~~

(Erase heading not required.)

Army Form C. 2118.

Place	Date	Hour	Summary of Events and Information	Remarks and references to Appendices
WOLLERSHEIM.	7th.	[illegible].	Billets good. Weather moderate.	
AHREM.	8th	08.25.	Moved by march route to AHREM . A halt was made en route for dinner at 12.15. AHREM was reached at 14.30. Good billets. Weather fine.	
SULZ.	9th.	08.30.	Moved by march to SULZ (S.W.outskirts of COLOGNE). Billets good. (in a large school) arrived 14.30.	
	10th.		Capt.H.S.Smiley rejoined from Hospital.	
			2/Lieut.F.H.Cheesewright rejoined from Hospital.	
	10/12th.		Companies at disposal of Company Commanders.	
			Cleaning up for march through COLOGNE, ~~and~~ Address by Commanding Officer to Battalion.	
	12th.		Capt.Heath.R.W.K.Regt. attached as interpreter.	

(A9175) Wt W2352/P 60 600,000 12/17 D. D. & L. Sch 52a. Forms/C2118/15

Army Form C. 2118.

Instructions regarding War Diaries and Intelligence Summaries are contained in F. S. Regs., Part II. and the Staff Manual respectively. Title pages will be prepared in manuscript.

WAR DIARY
or
~~INTELLIGENCE SUMMARY~~.
(Erase heading not required.)

December 1918.

Place	Date	Hour	Summary of Events and Information	Remarks and references to Appendices
BENSBERG.	13th.	8.45	Covered by an Advanced Guard under the command of Major.D.A.F.Needham.M.C, the Battalion marched through COLOGNE via the Cathedral and past General Plumer, Commanding 2nd Army who took the salute at the Western entrance to the Hohenzollern Bridge, over the Rhine at 09.32. Long march and very wet day. Very good billets, in Cadet School. Arrived at BENSBERG 13.10.	
	14/20th.		Capt.P.G.Barton to Field Ambulance (sick). 2/Lieut.E.Wilkinson rejoined from leave.	
	14th.		Companies at disposal of Company Commanders for training, cleaning up etc.	
	16th.		Colour Party to England.(Lt.R.I.Saul.M.C.2/Lt.C.W.Chillcot.M.M.) C.S.M.Russel, SgtBousey, L/Sgt Davison. Inspection of the Battalion by the Commander in Chief, F.M.Sir Douglas Haig at 10.00.	
			2/Lt.M.S.Ekins to Field Ambulance (sick)	
			2/Lt.S.V.Sparey proceeded on leave.	
	18th.		Lieut.F.W.Tibballs.M.C. proceeded to ROUEN (Course of Hindustani.)	
	19th.		Lieut.E.H.Marsh proceeded on leave to England.	
			2/Lt.A.H.Shields proceeded on leave to England.	
	20th.		2/Lt.G.S.B.Metheringham and 150 Other ranks joined.	

(A9175) Wt W2358/P.60 600,000 12/17 D. D. & L. Sch 52a. Forms/C2118/13.

Army Form C. 2118.

WAR DIARY
or
~~INTELLIGENCE SUMMARY~~.
(Erase heading not required.)

Instructions regarding War Diaries and Intelligence Summaries are contained in F. S. Regs., Part II, and the Staff Manual respectively. Title pages will be prepared in manuscript.

Place	Date	Hour	Summary of Events and Information	Remarks and references to Appendices
BERG GLADBACH.	21st.	10.	Moved to BERG GLADBACH arriving at 11.00, Very good billets - in „Zanders" Paper Mills. Battalion Dining Room and Sergeants Mess started.	
			Capt.P.G.Barton rejoined from Hospital.	
	22nd.		Capt.E.Harding.M.C. rejoined from leave.	
	22nd.		Training under Company arrangements. ~~Sports a very enjoyable Xmas~~.	
	23rd.		Lieut.R.J.Maingot rejoined from BERLIN - SPA train Guard.	
	24th.		Preparation for Xmas. Canteen taking £152.	
	25th.		Xmas: all the Battalion dined in large Hall starting at 1.0 p.m. Colonel and Regtl. Staff all present. Played R.F.A. and lost 1 - 4.	
			Battn. concert in dining hall with music and dancing after tea. Snow on ground.	
	26th.		Very quiet day. Ruffles gave first concert in Germany in MARIENSAAL at 6.0	
	27th.		Company Training. Dull day.	
	28th.		do.	
	29th.		do 120 Other ranks joined Battalion mostly composed of A.S.C.	
	30th.		do General Cayley and A.D.C. came to dinner and Ruffles.	
	31st.		New Years eve. This was celebrated in the usual good humoured manner.	E.M. Baker Lt Col. Cmdg 2/Royal Fusiliers

(A9175) Wt W2353/P 60 600,000 12/17 D. D. & L. Sch 52a. Forms C2118/15.

SOUTHERN (LATE 29TH) DIVN

86TH INFY BDE

2ND BN ROYAL FUSILIERS

JAN - MAR 1919

43.B.
(general)

(6414) Wt. W3906/P1607 2,500,000 7/18 McA & W Ltd (E 3591) Forms W3091/4.

Army Form W.3091.

WO 95

Cover for Documents.

Nature of Enclosures.

2nd Battalion Royal Fusiliers. War Diary.

For

January. 1919.

-*-*-*-*-*-*-*-*-*-*-*-*-*-*-*-

VOL 47

Jan - Mar
1919

29

Notes, or Letters written.

Army Form C. 2118.

Instructions regarding War Diaries and Intelligence Summaries are contained in F. S. Regs., Part II. and the Staff Manual respectively. Title pages will be prepared in manuscript.

WAR DIARY
or
INTELLIGENCE SUMMARY.

JANUARY 1918.

(Erase heading not required.)

Place	Date	Hour	Summary of Events and Information	Remarks and references to Appendices
GLADBACH.	1st.		Company training. Lieut.F.O.Parry rejoined from leave.	
	2nd.		2/Lt.W.J.Cowgill rejoined Battalion. 2/Lt.W.Sinclair. to R.O.D.for attachment. Companies at disposal of Company Commanders.	
	3rd.		Companies at disposal of Company Commanders.	
	4th.		G.S.O.1.visited the Battalion and inspected Barracks. 2/Lt.F.H.Cheesewright and 8 Other ranks to ROTTERDAM Boat guard for conducting Prisoners of War.	
	5th.		Major D.A.F.Needham.M.C. went on leave. Church Parade under command of Capt.P.G.Barton MC	
	6th		Y and Z Company on Range. W and X practice ceremonial.	
	7th.		X.Company beat W.Company in the Brigade inter company soccer league, by 1-0.	

D. D. & L., London, E.C. (A7883) Wt. W809/M1672 350,000 4/17 Sch. 52a Forms/C/2118/14

Instructions regarding War Diaries and Intelligence Summaries are contained in F. S. Regs., Part II. and the Staff Manual respectively. Title pages will be prepared in manuscript.

WAR DIARY
or
INTELLIGENCE SUMMARY.
(Erase heading not required.)

Army Form C. 2118.

Place	Date	Hour	Summary of Events and Information	Remarks and references to Appendices
GLADBACH.	8th.		Battalion practice Ceremonial parade. 6 Other ranks from Base.	
	9th		W and X Coy on Range. Y and Z practice ceremonial.	
			Final of Brigade Soccer Cup versus the 1st Lancs.Fusiliers - a very hard game in which resulted in a draw of 2 all, although the Royal Fusiliers were 2 up on the first half.	
	10th.		Colour Party rejoined from England. 20 Other ranks for demobilization.	
			Companies at disposal of Company Commanders.	
	11th.		Ceremonial Parade - Presentation of medals by Divisional Commander.	
			2/Lt.L.J.Burtinshaw to England conducting demobilization details - 11 men from Battalion for demobilization.	
	12th.		Baths for Battalion. In the Brigade inter Company Soccer League Z.CoyRoyal Fusiliers was beaten by A.Coy.1st Lancs.Fusiliers by 2-0. 7 Other ranks for demobilization.	

D. D. & L., London, E.C.
(A7883) Wt. W803/M1672 350,000 4/17 Sch. 52a Forms/C/2118/14

Instructions regarding War Diaries and Intelligence Summaries are contained in F. S. Regs., Part II. and the Staff Manual respectively. Title pages will be prepared in manuscript.

WAR DIARY
or
INTELLIGENCE SUMMARY.
(Erase heading not required.)

Army Form C. 2118.

Place	Date	Hour	Summary of Events and Information	Remarks and references to Appendices
BERG GLADBACH.	13th.		Capt.G.C.Pearson.M.C. proceeded on leave to U.K. 38 Other ranks for demobilization. The Regtl. team was defeated by 1st Lancs.Fusiliers by 4-0 after a hard game in the final of the Brigade Soccer Cup, which was previously held by the Royal Fusiliers.	
FORWARD ZONE.	14th.		Moved to Outpost Zone of Brigade Sector in relief of the 1st Royal Dublin Fusiliers. Companies very scattered - Z at BECHEN, Y at WIPPERFELD, X at JUNKERMUHLE and W at DELLING, with Battn.Hd.Qtrs. and H.Q.Coy at KURTEN. (spelt CÜRTEN by the natives). 45 Other ranks of Band and Drums from Hounslow including 23 boys arrived under Bandmaster VICKERS. X.Coy Royal Fusiliers beat No.2.Coy A.S.C.by 2-0 in the Brigade inter Company league. Lieut.E.T.Allen proceeded on course Sketch attached.	
	15th.		Commanding Officer visited all companies in outpost line.	
			Lieut.Col.E.M.Baker.D.S.O. temporarily to Command of 87th Brigade and Capt.P.G.Barton. assumed command of Battalion. Lieut.F.O.Parry took over command of W.Company.	

D. D. & L., London, E.C.
(A7883) Wt. W809/M1672 350,000 4/17 Sch. 52a Forms/C/2118/14

Instructions regarding War Diaries and Intelligence Summaries are contained in F. S. Regs., Part II, and the Staff Manual respectively. Title pages will be prepared in manuscript.

WAR DIARY
or
INTELLIGENCE SUMMARY.
(Erase heading not required.)

Army Form C. 2118.

Place	Date	Hour	Summary of Events and Information	Remarks and references to Appendices
	27th.		Lieut. R.I.Saul.M.C. to Battalion H.Q. to understudy demobilization	
FORWARD ZONE	18th.		Rev.E.V.Robinson joined Battalion from 1st Battn.S.W.Bdrs. 27 Other ranks for demobilization.	
			" The Army Commander now directs that demobilization is not to continue in the case of any Battalion, whose ration strength falls below 500 Other ranks"	
	19th.		2/Lt.W.R.Webb conducting details to England.	
	20th.		Very cold and snowed.	
	21st.			
	22nd.		G.O.C.Brigade visited Battalion.	

D. D. & L., London, E.C.
(A7883) Wt. W809/M1672 350,000 4/17 Sch. 52a Forms C/2118/14

Army Form C. 2118.

WAR DIARY
or
INTELLIGENCE SUMMARY.
(Erase heading not required.)

Instructions regarding War Diaries and Intelligence Summaries are contained in F. S. Regs., Part II. and the Staff Manual respectively. Title pages will be prepared in manuscript.

Place	Date	Hour	Summary of Events and Information	Remarks and references to Appendices
FORWARD ZONE.	23rd		X.Coy Royal Fusiliers beat W.Coy.1st Royal Dublin Fus. by 2-1 in the Brigade inter Coy league. W.Coy Royal Fusiliers lost to Brigade H.Q. by 2-0.	
	24th.		Major Slingsby.M.C. (1st Lancs.Fusiliers) took over temporarily command ~~ed~~ of Battn	
	25th.		Lt.Col.E.M.Baker.D.S.O. rejoined Battn. from 87th Brigade - Major Slingsby returning to his Battn. 10 Other ranks for demobilization, conducted by 2/Lt. R.E.Martin.M.C.	
	26th.		2/Lt.V.S.L.Genders to England to report to War Office. 2/Lt.M.S.Ekins rejoined from Hospital. Regt.Band gave performance at MARIENSAAL,BERG GLADBACH. 86th Bgde. beat X.Coy Royal Fus. by 2-1 in the semi-final of Bgde. inter Company Soccer League.	
	27th.		All horses classified ready for demobilization. Major.D.A.F.Needham.M.C. rejoined from leave.	

Army Form C. 2118.

Instructions regarding War Diaries and Intelligence Summaries are contained in F. S. Regs., Part II. and the Staff Manual respectively. Title pages will be prepared in manuscript.

WAR DIARY
or
INTELLIGENCE SUMMARY.
(Erase heading not required.)

Place	Date	Hour	Summary of Events and Information	Remarks and references to Appendices
FORWARD ZONE.	28th.		Commanding Officer visited all companies to attest men for re-enlistment.	
			Snowed heavily.	
	29th.		Capt.Templar went on leave. Very Cold.	
	30th.		G.O.C.Division and A/Brigadier visited outpost line.	
	31st.		Capt.P.T.O.Boult.M.C. proceeded on leave.	

Eric Baker Lt Col
2/ Royal Fusiliers
1/2/19-

(A9173) Wt W2358/P.160 600,000 12/17 D. D. & L. Sch. 52a. Forms/C2118/15.

VOL. 48 2 R Fus Vol 36

Army Form C. 2118.

Instructions regarding War Diaries and Intelligence Summaries are contained in F. S. Regs., Part II. and the Staff Manual respectively. Title pages will be prepared in manuscript.

WAR DIARY
or
~~INTELLIGENCE SUMMARY.~~
(Erase heading not required.)

February 1919.

Place	Date	Hour	Summary of Events and Information	Remarks and references to Appendices
Forward Zone.	1st.		2/Lt.W.J.COWGILL proceeded to ENGLAND for course at OXFORD. 28 O.R. leave to U.K. Quarterly Audit of Accounts for Quarter ending 31/12/18, Major D.A.F.NEEDHAM.M.C. president. Capt HARDING.M.C. and Lieut.F.G.HAMILTON.M.C. attended a commemorative dinner of 29th Division at BERG GLADBACH.	RH
	2nd		Major D.A.F.NEEDHAM.M.C. as Second in Command proceeded to BERG GLADBACH to take over billets from 1st LANCASHIRE FUSILIERS. Major.SLINGSBY 1st LANCASHIRE FUSILIERS arrived to take over relief of Battalion. Chaplain visited all companies and conducted Divine Service.	RH
	3rd.		Relieved by 1st LANCASHIRE FUSILIERS. Moved to BERG GLADBACH, Rendezvous SPITZ 11.30 am. Band met Battalion at HERRENSTRUNDEN, arrived BERG GLADBACH 13.00. Capt.J.F.H.TEMPLAR admitted to Hospital BOULOGNE en route to U.K. on leave.	RH
GLADBACH.	4th.		Baths allotted to Battalion. 34 men to U.K. on leave. Commanding Officers conference all Coy.Commanders 2.30 p.m.H.Q.Mess. Snowing all day.	RH
	5th.		2/Lt.P.S.CUBLEY, 3 N.C.Os and 24 men mounted Railhead Guard. 2/Lt.L.J.BURTINSHAW rejoined from ENGLAND. Capt.E.HARDING.M.C.proceeded to U.K. for two months leave to report Regtl.Depôt on expiration of same. 2/Lt.E.WILKINSON with concert party	RH

D. D. & L., London, E.C.
(A10266) Wt W5300/P713 750,000 2/18 Sch. 52 Forms/C2118/16

Army Form C. 2118.

Instructions regarding War Diaries and Intelligence Summaries are contained in F. S. Regs., Part II. and the Staff Manual respectively. Title pages will be prepared in manuscript.

WAR DIARY
or
INTELLIGENCE SUMMARY.
(Erase heading not required.)

Place	Date	Hour	Summary of Events and Information	Remarks and references to Appendices
			rejoined from COLOGNE. 2/Lt.C.W.CHILLCOT.M.M. took over duties of Actg.Quarter Mstr.	RH
	6th.		Capt.G.C.PEARSON.M.C.(Adjutant) rejoined from leave in U.K.	RH
			Lieut.B.LIGHT conducting demobilization details to ENGLAND and for dispersal.	
	7th.		Very cold. Guard left at HUY on the march to GERMANY rejoined.	RH
			Band played selections to the Battalion in the Dining Hall 4 - 6 p.m.	
	8th.		Commanding Officer lectured the Battalion on Demobilization and Extension of Service.	RH
			Lieut.F.L.THOMERSON struck off strength pending Demobilizatoon.	
	9th.		Church Parade Cinema BERG GLADBACH 10.a.m. News of Capt.J.F.H.TEMPLAR'S death received. Orchestra played to the Battalion in Dining Hall. In the evening. ~~the Band~~	
			The Band gave a concert in MARIENSAAL HALL 2 to 4 p.m.	
	10th.		Companies at the disposal of Company Commanders.	
	11th		X.Company allotted Rifle Range. Lieut.E.H.MARSH rejoined from leave.	RH
			Band played selections in Dining Hall 3.30 to 5 p.m.	
	13th.		2/Lt.W.R.WEBB.M.C. returned from conducting Demobilization details to U.K.	RH
			2/Lt.W.E.STOKES.M.C. and 2/Lt.P.S.CUBLEY proceeded to ENGLAND on leave.	
	14th.		Lt.Col.E.M.BAKER.D.S.O. to Bde.Hdqtrs. MAJOR NEEDHAM.M.C. assumed Command of Battn.	

D. D. & L., London, E.C.
(A10266) Wt W5300/P713 750,000 2/15 Sch. 52 Forms/C2118/16

Army Form C. 2118.

WAR DIARY
or
INTELLIGENCE SUMMARY.
(Erase heading not required.)

Instructions regarding War Diaries and Intelligence Summaries are contained in F. S. Regs., Part II. and the Staff Manual respectively. Title pages will be prepared in manuscript.

Place	Date	Hour	Summary of Events and Information	Remarks and references to Appendices
GLADBACH.	15th.		Thaw set in, raining slightly all day. 2/Lt.S.V.SPAREY struck off strength pending Demobilization.	
	16th.		Church Parade Lutheran Church under command of Capt.N.S.POWELL.	
			Band played selections in MARIENSAAL at 2.p.m.	
	18th.		Very mild. Band played selections in Dining Hall 4 to 5 p.m.	
			Whist Drive open to the Battalion in Dining Hall 5.30 p.m.	
	19th.		Capt.H.CLARK.M.C. proceeded on leave to U.K.	
	20th.		Capt.P.G.BARTON.M.C. proceeded on 2 months leave to report to Depôt on expiration.	
	21st.		Companies at disposal of Company Commanders.	
			Trial Football Match to select team for Divisional Knockout Tournament.	
	22nd.		Lt.Col.E.M.BAKER.D.S.O. proceeded on 14 days leave to U.K.	
			Battalion Officers Mess started, Band played at Dinner.	
	23rd.		Church parade 11.15 a.m. in Lutheran Church. Second Round Divisional Knockout Tournament versus 29th Divisional Train result lost 2-1.	
	24th		Companies at disposal of Company Commanders.	
			Y.Company on Range.	
			Lecture to All Officers by O.C.89th Field Ambulance.	

D. D. & L., London, E.C.
(A10266) Wt W5300/P713 750,000 2/18 Sch. 52 Forms/C2118/16

Army Form C. 2118.

Instructions regarding War Diaries and Intelligence Summaries are contained in F. S. Regs., Part II. and the Staff Manual respectively. Title pages will be prepared in manuscript.

WAR DIARY
or
INTELLIGENCE SUMMARY.
(Erase heading not required.)

Place	Date	Hour	Summary of Events and Information	Remarks and references to Appendices
GLADBACH.	25th.		Conference of Commanding Officers of the Brigade 10.30 a.m.	
			Band played to troops in Battalion Dining Hall.	
	26th.		Army Commander at Divisional H.Q. Commanding Officer attended.	
			Concert to the Battalion by " TUI PIERROTS " (NEW ZEALAND DIVISION)	
	27th.		Football Match versus Divisional H.Q, result won 8-1.	
			X.Company on R nge.	
	28th.		Route March 9.30 a.m.	

[signature] Major.
Commanding.2nd Bn. Royal Fusiliers.

D. D. & L., London, E.C.
(A10266) Wt W5300/P713 750,000 2/15 Sch. 52 Forms/C2118/16

Army Form C. 2118.

WAR DIARY
or
~~INTELLIGENCE SUMMARY.~~
(Erase heading not required.)

Instructions regarding War Diaries and Intelligence Summaries are contained in F. S. Regs., Part II. and the Staff Manual respectively. Title pages will be prepared in manuscript.

Place	Date	Hour	Summary of Events and Information	Remarks and references to Appendices
OUTPOST ZONE.	11/3/19.		Four Germans apprehended by „X„ Company and one German by „Z„ Company attempting to cross the perimeter with foodstuffs. handed over to A.P.M.	
„	12/3/19.		2/Lieut.W.E.Stokes.M.C. rejoined from leave in United Kingdom.	
„	15/3/19.		Sharp Frost. Corps and Brigade Commander visited Outpost line.	
„	16/3/19.		Captain. P.T.O.Boult.M.C. rejoined from leave in United Kingdom.	
„	18/3/19		Relieved in Outpost Zone by 1st Battn.Lancashire Fusiliers. Companies marched to BERG GLADBACH independently. Whole Battalion billeted in Paper Factory. Lieut. F.O.Parry rejoined from Hospital.	
GLADBACH.	19/3/19.		Capt.N.S.Powell, A/Capts.P.T.O.Boult.M.C.and J.T.Smith,Lieuts R.I.Saul.M.C. E.T.Allen, F.O.Parry and 2/Lieuts W.R.Webb.M.C. G.S.B.Metheringham, E.Wilkinson and P.st L.Lloyd, ~~XXXXXX~~ also 128 Other ranks posted and proceeded to join 17th Battlion Royal Fusiliers, 2nd Division. Remainder of Battalion moved by march route to MULHEIM billeted in School. Lieuts F.G.Hamilton.M.C.,E.H.Marsh and 81 Other ranks proceeded to Concentration Camp COLOGNE for demobilization.	
MULHEIM.	21/3/19.		2/Lieut.W.E.Stokes M.C.and 166 Other ranks proceeded to Concentration Camp COLOGNE for demobilization.	
„	22/3/19.		All Leave and Demobilization postponed on account of strikes in England.	
„	25/3/19.		Capt.H.Clark.M.C. rejoined from leave in United Kingdom. 16 Other ranks to Concentration Camp for demobilization.	
„	26/3/19.		Seven Other ranks to Concentration Camp for demobilization.	

D. D. & L., London E.C.
(10341) Wt W5300/P713 750,000 3/18 E 688 Forms/C2118/16.

Army Form C. 2118.

WAR DIARY
or
~~INTELLIGENCE SUMMARY.~~
(Erase heading not required.)

Instructions regarding War Diaries and Intelligence Summaries are contained in F. S. Regs., Part II. and the Staff Manual respectively. Title pages will be prepared in manuscript.

Place	Date	Hour	Summary of Events and Information	Remarks and references to Appendices
GLADBACH.	1/3/19.		Alarm Test at 09.00 hours. Battalion Cross Country Run at 11.00 hours. Summer Time came into force, clocks put forward one hour at 23 hours	
"	2/3/19.		Divine Service at the LUTHERAN CHURCH, BERG GLADBACH at 11.30 hours. Capt. G.C.Pearson.M.C., 2/Lieuts. G.S.B.Metheringham and S.R.Gresham admitted to Hospital.	
"	3/3/19.		Lecture by Mr.M.SMITH in Cinema Hall at 11.00 hours.	
"	4/3/19.		Raining all day. Advance Party of One Officer and one platoon per Company left for Outpost Zone, to take over Billets and Outposts. Band played to Battalion in the Dining Hall at 16.00 hours. 2/Lieut. F.O.Parry admitted to Hospital, sick. Lieut. E.T.Allen rejoined from Course at Second Army College, COLOGNE. Lieut. F.W.Tibballs rejoined from Hindustani Course at ROUEN.	
"	5/3/19.		Battalion moved to Outpost Zone in relief of 1st Bn.Royal Dublin Fusiliers., paraded at 08.00 hours, raining during whole of the march. Companies distributed as follows:- "W" Coy. FORSTEN. "X" Coy. WIPPERFELD. "Y" Coy. LAUDENBERG. "Z" Company JÜNKERMUHLE. Battalion Headquarters at KURTEN. 2/Lieut. P.S.Cubley rejoined from leave in the United Kingdom.	
OUTPOST ZONE.	6/3/19.		Raining all day. Commanding Officer visited all companies in the Outpost Line.	
"	10/3/19.		Brigade Commander visited Battalion and went round Outpost line with C.O. Battalion Concert Party "Ruffles" rejoined Battalion.	
	11/3/19.		Band proceeded to KALK to give series of concerts to 9th Division.	

D. D. & L., London E.C.
(103ac) Wt W5300/P713 750,000 3/18 E 688 Forms/C2118/16.

Army Form C. 2118.

Instructions regarding War Diaries and Intelligence Summaries are contained in F. S. Regs., Part II. and the Staff Manual respectively. Title pages will be prepared in manuscript.

WAR DIARY

or

~~INTELLIGENCE SUMMARY.~~

(Erase heading not required.)

Place	Date	Hour	Summary of Events and Information	Remarks and references to Appendices
MULHEIM.	28/3/19.		The Cadre (Major.D.A.F.Needham.M.C.,Lieuts.F.W.Tibballs.M.C.,R.J.Maingot., 2/Lieuts.M.S.Ekins.,P.S.Cubley.,C.W.Chilcott.M.M.,R.W.Kirke.M.C.,M.M.,and 105 Other ranks including 43 Band) proceeded by train to DUNKERQUE leaving COLOGNE at 9.30.a.m.	DN
DUNKERQUE.	30/3/19.		Arrived DUNKERQUE at 2.30.a.m. detrained at 9.a.m.and proceeded to „Hospice Camp A". Bathed and proceeded to No.2.Embarkation Camp.ST.POL.	DN
„	31/3/19.		Paraded for embarkation at 11.30.a.m. Embarkation cancelled,returned to Camp.	DN
„	1/4/19.		Embarked at 8.30.a.m. S.S.„CAESEREA„,set sail at 9.20.a.m. and arrived at DOVER 12.noon. Entrained at DOVER for Victoria Station at 2.15.p.m.arrived at Victoria.5.p.m. Entrained for HOUNSLOW by Special Train at 7.30.a.m. arriving at HOUNSLOW 8.15.p.m. Marched to Barracks with Band.	DN

D.A.F. Needham

Major.

Commanding 2nd Battalion Royal Fusiliers.

(10340) Wt W5300/P713 750,000 3/18 E 2683 Forms/C2118/16.
D. D. & L., London, E.C.

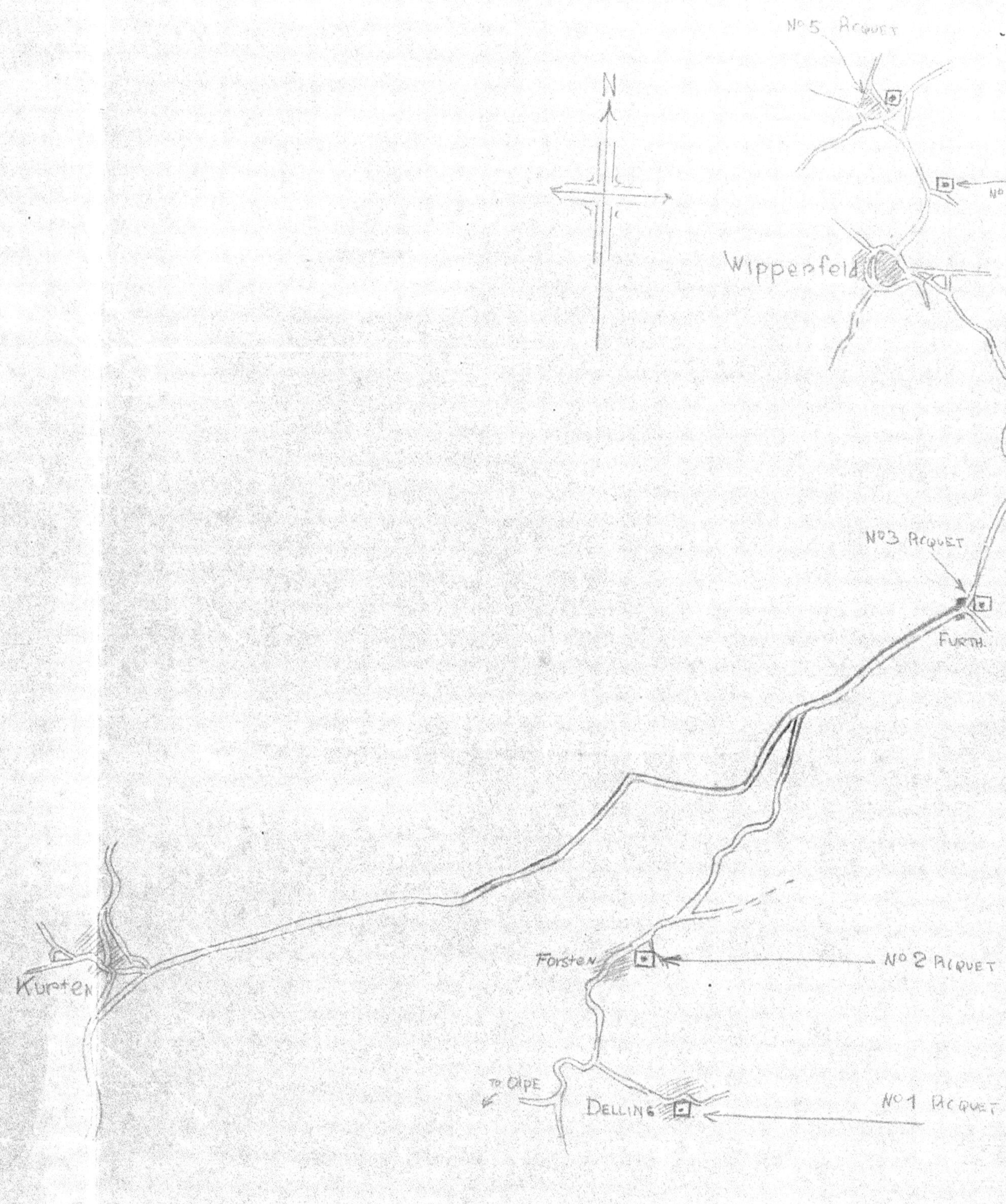

Nº5 PICQUET

N

Nº4

Wipperfeld

Nº3 PICQUET

FURTH.

Forsten

Nº2 PICQUET

Kurten

TO OLPE

DELLING

Nº1 PICQUET

www.ingramcontent.com/pod-product-compliance
Lightning Source LLC
Chambersburg PA
CBHW080840010526
44114CB00017B/2345

* 9 7 8 1 4 7 4 5 1 4 7 6 7 *